Days Past

THE DESERTED VILLAGE

Sweet Auburn! loveliest
    village of the plain;
Where health and plenty cheered
    the labouring swain,
Where smiling spring its
    earliest visit paid,
And parting summer's lingering
    blooms delayed;
Dear lovely bowers of innocence
    and ease,
Seats of my youth, when every
    sport could please,
How often have I loitered
    o'er thy green,
Where humble happiness endeared
    each scene!
How often have I paused on
    every charm,
The sheltered cot, the cultivated
    farm,
The never-failing brook, the
    busy mill,
The decent church that topt
    the neighboring hill,
The hawthorn bush, with seats
    beneath the shade,
For talking age and whispering
    lovers made!

How often have I blessed the
    coming day,
When toil remitting lent its
    turn to play,
And all the village train, from
    labour free,
Led up their sports beneath the
    spreading tree,
While many a pastime circled
    in the shade,
The young contending as
    the old surveyed;

And many a gambol frolicked
    o'er the ground,
And sleights of art and feats
    of strength went round.
And still, as each repeated
    pleasure tired,
Succeeding sports the mirthful
    band inspired;
. . . With sweet succession,
    taught e'en toil to please:
These round thy bowers their
    cheerful influence shed:
These were thy charms—but all
    these charms are fled.

Sweet smiling village,
    loveliest of the lawn,
Thy sports are fled, and all
    thy charms withdrawn;
Amidst thy bowers the tyrant's
    hand is seen,
And desolation saddens all
    thy green:
One only master grasps the
    whole domain,
And half a tillage stints
    thy smiling plain.
No more thy glassy brook
    reflects the day,
But, choked with sedges,
    works its weedy way;
Along thy glades, a solitary
    guest,
The hollow-sounding bittern
    guards its nest;
Amidst thy desert walks the
    lapwing flies,
And tires their echoes with
    unvaried cries;
Sunk are thy bowers in
    shapeless ruin all,
And the long grass o'ertops
    the mouldering wall;

And, trembling, shrinking
 from the spoiler's hand,
Far, far away thy children
 leave the land.

Ill fares the land, to hastening ills a prey,
Where wealth accumulates, and
 men decay:
Princes and lords may flourish,
 or may fade;
A breath can make them, as a
 breath has made:
But a bold peasantry, their
 country's pride,
When once destroyed, can never
 be supplied.
Oliver Goldsmith

REMEMBRANCE OF THINGS PAST

When to the sessions of sweet silent
 thought
I summon up remembrance of
 things past,
I sigh the lack of many a
 thing I sought,
And with old woes' new wail my
 dear time's waste:
Then can I drown an eye, unused
 to flow,
For precious friends hid in
 death's dateless night,
And weep afresh love's long
 since cancell'd woe,
And moan the expense of many a
 vanish'd sight:
Then can I grieve at grievances
 foregone,
And heavily from woe to woe
 tell o'er
The sad account of fore-bemoaned
 moan,
Which I new pay as if not paid
 before,
But if the while I think on
 thee, dear friend,
All losses are restored and
 sorrows end.
William Shakespeare

THOSE OLD SONGS

There was once an emotional outlet my people always had when they had the blues. That was singing. I'd listen, fascinated by the stories told in the songs. Later, when I sang those same old songs, both folk songs and popular numbers, on the stage or on the radio, they gained na-tion-wide attention. In 1949, when I appeared on the Tex and Jinx program, I sang some of those songs, humming the parts where I didn't remember the lines. I got letters from all over the country from people who sent me the words I'd forgotten. They'd remembered the old songs all those years and kept them in their minds like treasures.

My whole family could sing. Vi had a sweet soft voice, Ching's was bell-like and resonant, Louise's rich and warm. One of the first pieces I remember Vi singing was "I Don't Want to Play in Your Yard." Ching's favorites were "There'll Come a Time" and "Volunteer Organist."

But in the beginning it was always the story told in the song that enchanted me. I'd ask one of them, "Tell me a story," when I was little, and they'd sing it.

My family and the other families who lived in those alley homes harmonized without any instruments to accompany them. There were musicians in the neighborhood, fellows who played the banjo, mandolin, guitar, and the bells (sometimes one man would play all of them). But they played at parties and sometimes on street corners. And we never had the money for a party. There were always people in the house, but that wasn't for any party.

Then, of course, there was the hurdy-gurdy man. We kids would dance to the music he made and sing the words of the songs that came out of his tired, battered street organ.
Ethel Waters

THE HEART REMEMBERS

The heart remembers everything
Although the mind forgets—
The raptures and the agonies,
The hopes and the regrets.
The heart remembers April
When the snows of winter fall—
Hearing on the bitter wind
The sweetest song of all.

When Youth has had its shining
     hour
And Love its golden day,
Time may fade the colors
And the glory turn to gray;
But something of the magic
     lingers,
Never to depart,
Deep down in the secret places
     of the quiet heart.
                    Patience Strong

IN SCHOOL-DAYS

Still sits the school-house
     by the road,
A ragged beggar sleeping;
Around it still the sumachs
     grow,
And blackberry vines are creep-
     ing.

Within, the master's desk is
     seen,
Deep scarred by raps official;
The warping floor, the battered
     seats,
The jack-knife's carved initial;

The charcoal frescos on its
     wall;
Its door's worn sill, betraying
The feet that, creeping slow
     to school,
Went storming out to playing!

Long years ago a winter sun
Shone over it at setting;
Lit up its western window
     panes,
And low eaves' icy fretting.

It touched the tangled golden
     curls,
And brown eyes full of
     grieving,
Of one who still her steps de-
     layed
When all the school were leaving.

For near her stood the little
     boy
Her childish favor singled:
His cap pulled low upon a face
Where pride and shame were
     mingled.

Pushing with restless feet
     the snow
To right and left, he lingered;
As restlessly her tiny hands
The blue checked apron fingered.

He saw her lift her eyes; he
     felt
The soft hand's light caressing,
And heard the tremble of her
     voice,
As if a fault confessing.

"I'm sorry that I spelt the
     word:
I hate to go above you,
Because," the brown eyes lower
     fell,
"Because, you see, I love you!"

Still memory to a gray-haired
     man
That sweet child-face is showing.
Dear girl! the grasses on her
     grave
Have forty years been growing!

He lives to learn, in life's
     hard school,
How few who pass above him
Lament their triumph and his
     loss,
Like her,—because they love
     him.
                    John Greenleaf Whittier

Appreciation

THE NIGHTINGALE AND GLOW-WORM

A nightingale, that all day
   long
Had cheered the village with
   his song,
Nor yet at eve his note sus-
   pended,
Nor yet when eventide was ended,
Began to feel—as well he might—
The keen demands of appetite;
When, looking eagerly around,
He spied, far off, upon the
   ground
A something shining in the
   dark,
And knew the glow-worm by his
   spark;
So, stooping down from hawthorn
   top,
He thought to put him in his
   crop.

The worm, aware of his intent,
Harangued him thus, quite
   eloquent,
"Did you admire my lamp,"
   quoth he,
"As much as I your minstrelsy,
You would abhor to do me wrong,
As much as I to spoil your
   song;
For 'twas the self-same Power
   divine
Taught you to sing, and me to
   shine;
That you with music, I with
   light,
Might beautify and cheer the
   night."
The songster heard his short
   oration,
And, warbling out his ap-
   probation,

Released him, as my story tells,
And found a supper somewhere
   else.
                    Author Unknown

To me every hour of the day and night is an
unspeakably perfect miracle.
                    Walt Whitman

HERE THERE ARE ROSES

One of the most tragic things I know about
human nature is that all of us tend to put off
living. We dream of some magical rose garden
over the horizon—instead of enjoying the roses
that are blooming outside our window today.
                    Dale Carnegie

EARTH IS ENOUGH

We men of Earth have here the
   stuff
Of Paradise—we have enough!
We need no other stones to build
The Temple of the Unfulfilled—
No other ivory for the doors—
No other marble for the floors—
No other cedar for the beam
And dome of man's immortal
   dream.

Here on the paths of every-day—
Here on the common human way
Is all the stuff the gods would
   take
To build a Heaven, to mold and
   make
New Edens. Ours the stuff sub-
   lime
To build Eternity in time!
                    Edwin Markham

FILL YOUR HEART WITH THANKSGIVING

Take nothing for granted,
    for whenever you do
The "joy of enjoying"
    is lessened for you—
For we rob our own lives
    much more than we know
When we fail to respond
    or in any way show
Our thanks for the blessings
    that daily are ours . . .
The warmth of the sun,
    the fragrance of flowers,
The beauty of twilight,
    the freshness of dawn,
The coolness of dew
    on a green velvet lawn,
The kind little deeds
    so thoughtfully done,
The favors of friends
    and the love that someone
Unselfishly gives us
    in a myriad of ways,
Expecting no payment
    and no words of praise—
Oh, great is our loss
    when we no longer find
A thankful response
    to things of this kind,
For the joy of enjoying
    and the fullness of living
Are found in the heart
    that is filled with thanks-
        giving.
                Helen Steiner Rice

AUGURIES OF INNOCENCE

To see a World in a grain of
    sand,
And a Heaven in a wild flower,
Hold Infinity in the palm of
    your hand,
And Eternity in an hour.
                William Blake

There is beauty in homely things which many people have never seen. For instance, do you know

Sunlight through a jar of
    beach-plum jelly;
A rainbow in soapsuds in
    dishwater;
An egg yolk in a blue bowl;
White ruffled curtains sifting
    moonlight;
The color of cranberry glass;
A little cottage with blue
    shutters;
Crimson roses in an old stone
    crock;
The smell of newly baked bread;
Candlelight on old brass;
The soft brown of a cocker's
    eyes?
                Peter Marshall

I WILL NOT HURRY

I will not hurry through this
    day!
Lord, I will listen by the way,
To humming bees and singing
    birds,
To speaking trees and friendly
    words;
And for the moments in between
Seek glimpses of Thy great
    Unseen.

I will not hurry through this
    day;
I will take time to think and
    pray;
I will look up into the sky,
Where fleecy clouds and
    swallows fly;
And somewhere in the day, maybe
I will catch whispers, Lord,
    from Thee!
                Ralph Spaulding Cushman

THIS IS MY FATHER'S WORLD

This is my Father's world;
And to my listening ears,
All nature sings, and round me
    rings
The music of the spheres.
This is my Father's world;
I rest me in the thought
Of rocks and trees, of skies
    and seas,
His hand the wonders wrought.
Maltbie D. Babcock

PRAYER

Oh, Lord, I thank you for the privilege and
gift of living in a world filled with beauty and
excitement and variety. I thank you for the gift
of loving and being loved, for the friendliness
and understanding and beauty of the animals
on the farm and in the forest and marshes, for
the green of the trees, the sound of a waterfall,
the darting beauty of the trout in the brook.
I thank you for the delights of music and children, of other men's thoughts and conversation
and their books to read by the fireside or in
bed with the rain falling on the roof or the snow
blowing past outside the window.
Louis Bromfield

A HEART TO PRAISE THEE

Thou hast given so much to me,
Give one thing more—a grate-
    ful heart:
Not thankful when it pleaseth
    me,
As if thy blessings had spare
    days,
But such a heart whose Pulse
    may be Thy Praise.
George Herbert

A PURPLE FINCH

A little girl has just brought me a purple finch
or American linnet. These birds are now moving
south. It reminds me of the pine and spruce,
and the juniper and cedar on whose berries it
feeds. It has the crimson hues of the October
evenings, and its plumage still shines as if it
had caught and preserved some of their tints
(beams?) We know it chiefly as a traveller. It
reminds me of many things I had forgotten.
Many a serene evening lies snugly packed under
its wing.
Henry David Thoreau

WE THANK THEE

For flowers that bloom about
    our feet,
Father, we thank Thee.
For tender grass so fresh,
    so sweet,
Father, we thank Thee.
For the song of bird and hum
    of bee,
For all things fair we hear
    or see,
Father in heaven, we thank Thee.

For blue of stream and blue of
    sky,
Father, we thank Thee.
For pleasant shade of branches
    high,
Father, we thank Thee.
For fragrant air and cooling
    breeze,
For beauty of the blooming
    trees,
Father in heaven, we thank Thee.

For this new morning with its
    light,
Father, we thank Thee.
For rest and shelter of the
    night,
Father, we thank Thee
For health and food, for love
    and friends,
For everything Thy goodness
    sends,
Father in heaven, we thank Thee.
Ralph Waldo Emerson

Loneliness

SOLITUDE

When you have tidied all things
   for the night,
And while your thoughts are
   fading to their sleep,
You'll pause a moment in the
   late night,
Too sorrowful to weep.

The large and gentle furniture
   has stood
In sympathetic silence all the
   day
With that old kindness of
   domestic wood;
Nevertheless the haunted room
   will say:
"Someone must be away."

The little dog rolls over half
   awake,
Stretches his paws, yawns,
   looking up at you,
Wags his tail very slightly
   for your sake,
That you may feel he is unhappy
   too.

A distant engine whistles, or
   the floor
Creaks, or the wandering night-
   wind bangs a door.

Silence is scattered like a
   broken glass.
The minutes prick their ears and
   run about,
Then one by one subside again
   and pass
Sedately in, monotonously out.

You bend your head and wipe
   away a tear
Solitude walks one heavy
   step more near.

Harold Monro

OFT, IN THE STILLY NIGHT

I feel like one who treads alone
Some banquet-hall deserted,
Whose lights are fled, whose
   garlands dead,
And all but he departed!

Thomas Moore

BRING US TOGETHER

Oh, God, we go through life so lonely, needing what other people can give us, yet ashamed to show that need.

And other people go through life so lonely, hungering for what it would be such a joy for us to give.

Dear God, please bring us together, the people who need each other, who can help each other, and would so enjoy each other.

Marjorie Holmes

When you have closed your doors and darkened your room, remember never to say that you are alone, for you are not alone; God is within, and your genius is within—and what need have they of light to see what you are doing?

Epictetus

TO BE ALONE

I have seen a wealthy and open-handed sheik of Damascus, pitching his tents in the wilderness of the Arabian desert, and by the sides of the mountains. In the evening he sent his slaves out to waylay travelers and bring them to his tents to be sheltered and entertained. But the rough roads were deserted, and the servants brought him no guests.

And I pondered the plight of the lonely sheik, and my heart spoke to me, saying: "Surely it is better for him to be a straggler, with a staff in

his hand and an empty bucket hanging from his arm, sharing at noontide the bread of friendship with his companions by the refuse heaps at the edge of the city."

Kahlil Gibran

The devils enter uninvited when the house stands empty. For other kinds of guests, you have first to open the door.

Dag Hammarskjöld

We are most of us very lonely in this world, you who have any who love you, cling to them and thank God.

William Makepeace Thackeray

IT'S HOME

He loitered along the road. The sun was strong. The winter was over. He thought hazily that it must now be April. Spring had taken over the scrub, and the birds were mating and singing in the bushes. Only he, in all the world, was homeless. He had been out in the world, and the world was a troubled dream, fluid and desolate, flanked by swamps and cypresses. He stopped to rest in mid-morning at the intersection of the main road and the north road. The low vegetation here was open to the heat of the sun. His head began to ache and he got to his feet and headed north toward Silver Glen. He told himself that he did not mean to go home. He would only go to the spring, and go down between the cool dark banks, and lie a little while in the running water. The north road dipped and rose and dipped again. The sand was scalding under his bare feet. The sweat ran down the grime of his face. At the top of a rise, he could look down and see Lake George far below him to the east. It was pitilessly blue. Thin white lines were the implacable choppy waves that had turned him back to the unfriendly shore. He trudged on.

To the east, the vegetation became luxuriant. There was water near. He turned down the

trail to Silver Glen. The steep bank dropped to the ribbon of creek that ran south of the great spring itself, and had a kindred source. He ached in all his bones. He was so thirsty that his tongue seemed glued to the roof of his mouth. He stumbled down the bank and fell flat beside the cool shallow water and drank. The water bubbled over his lips and nose. He drank until his belly was swollen. He felt sickened and rolled over on his back and closed his eyes. The nausea passed and he was drowsy. He lay in a stupor of weariness. He hung suspended in a timeless space. He could go neither forward nor back. Something was ended. Nothing was begun.

In the late afternoon, he roused. He sat up. An early magnolia blossom was wax-white over him.

He thought, " 'Tis April."

A memory stirred him. He had come here a year ago, on a bland and tender day. He had splashed in the creek water and lain, as now, among the ferns and grasses. Something had been fine and lovely. He had built himself a flutter-mill. He rose and moved with a quickening of his pulse to the location. It seemed to him that if he found it, he would discover with it all the other things that had vanished. The flutter-mill was gone. The flood had washed it away, and all its merry turning.

He thought stubbornly, "I'll build me another."

He cut twigs for the supports, and the roller to turn across them, from the wild cherry tree. He whittled feverishly. He cut strips from a palmetto frond and made his paddles. He sunk the uprights in the stream bed and set the paddles turning. Up, over, down. Up, over, down. The flutter-mill was turning. The silver water dripped. But it was only palmetto strips brushing the water. There was no magic in the motion. The flutter-mill had lost its comfort.

He said, "Play-dolly—"

He kicked it apart with one foot. The broken bits floated down the creek. He threw himself on the ground and sobbed bitterly. There was no comfort anywhere.

There was Penny. A wave of homesickness washed over him so that it was suddenly intolerable not to see him. The sound of his

father's voice was a necessity. He longed for the sight of his stooped shoulders as he had never, in the sharpest of his hunger, longed for food. He clambered to his feet and up the bank and began to run down the road to the clearing, crying as he ran. His father might not be there. He might be dead. With the crops ruined, and his son gone, he might have packed up in despair and moved away and he would never find him.

He sobbed, "Pa—Wait for me."

The sun was setting. He was in a panic that he would not reach the clearing before dark. He exhausted himself, and was obliged to slow down to a walk. His flesh quivered. His heart pounded. He had to stop entirely and rest. Darkness overtook him half a mile from home. Even in the dusk, landmarks were familiar. The tall pines of the clearing were recognizable, blacker than the creeping night. He came to the slat fence. He felt his way along it. He opened the gate and went into the yard. He passed around the side of the house to the kitchen stoop and stepped up on it. He crept to the window on bare silent feet and peered in.

A fire burned low on the hearth. Penny sat hunched beside it, wrapped in quilts. One hand covered his eyes. Jody went to the door and unlatched it and stepped inside. Penny lifted his head.

"Ory?"

"Hit's me."

He thought his father had not heard him.

"Hit's Jody."

Penny turned his head and looked at him wonderingly, as though the gaunt ragged boy with sweat and tear-streaks down the grime, with hollow eyes under matted hair, were some stranger of whom he expected that he state his business.

He said, "Jody."

Jody dropped his eyes.

"Come close."

He went to his father and stood beside him. Penny reached out for his hand and took it and turned it over and rubbed it slowly between his own. Jody felt drops on his hand like a warm rain.

"Boy—I near about give you out."

Penny felt along his arm. He looked up at him.

"You all right?"

He nodded.

"You all right—You ain't dead nor gone. You all right." A light filled his face. "Glory be."

It was unbelievable, Jody thought. He was wanted.

He said, "I had to come home."

"Why, shore you did."

"I ain't meant what I said. Hatin' you—"

The light broke into the familiar smile.

"Why, shore you ain't. 'When I was a child, I spake as a child.' "

Penny stirred in his chair.

"They's rations in the safe. In the kittle there. You hungry?"

"I ain't et but oncet. Last night."

"Not but oncet? Then now you know. Ol' Starvation—" His eyes shone in the firelight as Jody had pictured them. "Ol' Starvation—he's got a face meaner'n ol' Slewfoot, ain't he?"

"Hit's fearful."

"There's biscuits there. Open the honey. There's due to be milk in the gourd."

Jody fumbled among the dishes. He ate standing, wolfing down the food. He dipped into a dish of cooked cow-peas with his fingers, scooping them into his mouth. Penny stared at him.

He said, "I'm sorry you had to learn it that-a-way."

"Where's Ma?"

"She's drove the wagon to the Forresters to trade for seedcorn. She figgered she'd try to plant a part of a crop again. She carried the chickens, to trade. It hurted her pride turrible, but she was obliged to go."

Jody closed the door of the cabinet.

He said, "I should of washed. I'm awful dirty."

"There's warm water on the hearth."

Jody poured water in the basin and scrubbed his face and arms and hands. The water was too dark even for his feet. He threw it out of the door and poured more, and sat on the floor and washed his feet.

Penny said, "I'd be proud to know where you been."

"I been on the river. I aimed to go to Boston."

"I see."

He looked small and shrunken inside the quilts.

Jody said, "How you makin' it, Pa? You better?"

Penny looked a long time into the embers on the hearth.

He said, "You jest as good to know the truth. I ain't scarcely wuth shootin'."

Jody said, "When I git the work done, you got to leave me go fetch ol' Doc to you."

Penny studied him.

He said, "You've done come back different. You've takened a punishment. You ain't a yearlin' no longer. Jody—"

"Yes, sir."

"I'm goin' to talk to you, man to man. You figgered I went back on you. Now there's a thing ever' man has got to know. Mebbe you know it. 'Twa'n't only me. 'Twa'n't only your yearlin' deer havin' to be destroyed. Boy, life goes back on you."

Jody looked at his father. He nodded.

Penny said, "You've seed how things goes in the world o' men. You've known men to be low-down and mean. You've seed ol' Death at his tricks. You've messed around with ol' Starvation. Ever' man wants life to be a fine thing, and a easy. 'Tis fine, boy, powerful fine, but 'tain't easy. Life knocks a man down and he gits up and knocks him down again. I've been uneasy all my life."

His hands worked at the folds of the quilt.

"I've wanted life to be easy for you. Easier'n 'twas for me. A man's heart aches, seein' his young uns face the world. Knowin' they got to get their guts torn out, the way his was tore. I wanted to spare you, long as I could. I wanted you to frolic with your yearlin'. I knowed the lonesomeness he eased for you. But ever' man's lonesome. What's he to do then? What's he to do when he gits knocked down? Why, take it for his share and go on."

Jody said, "I'm 'shamed I runned off."

Penny sat upright.

He said, "You're near enough growed to do your choosin'. Could be you'd crave to go to sea, like Oliver. There's men seems made for the land, and men seems made for the sea. But

I'd be proud did you choose to live here and farm the clearin'. I'd be proud to see the day when you got a well dug, so's no woman here'd be obliged to do her washin' on a seepage hillside. You willin'?"

"I'm willin'."

"Shake hands."

He closed his eyes. The fire on the hearth had burned to embers. Jody banked them with the ashes, to assure live coals in the morning.

Penny said, "Now I'll need some he'p, gittin' to the bed.

Looks like your Ma's spending the night."

Jody put his shoulder under him and Penny leaned heavily on it. He hobbled to his bed. Jody drew the quilt over him.

"Hit's food and drink to have you home, boy. Git to bed and git your rest. 'Night."

The words warmed him through.

" 'Night, Pa."

He went to his room and closed the door. He took off his tattered shirt and breeches and climbed in under the warm quilts. His bed was soft and yielding. He lay luxuriously, stretching his legs. He must be up early in the morning to milk the cow and bring in wood and work the crops. When he worked them, Flag would not be there to play about with him. His father would no longer take the heavy part of the burden. It did not matter. He could manage alone.

He found himself listening for something. It was the sound of the yearling for which he listened, running around the house or stirring on his moss pallet in the corner of the bedroom. He would never hear him again. He wondered if his mother had thrown dirt over Flag's carcass, or if the buzzards had cleaned it. Flag—He did not believe he should ever again love anything, man or woman or his own child, as he had loved the yearling. He would be lonely all his life. But a man took it for his share and went on.

In the beginning of his sleep, he cried out, "Flag!"

It was not his own voice that called. It was a boy's voice. Somewhere beyond the sink-hole, past the magnolia, under the live oaks, a boy and a yearling ran side by side, and were gone forever.

(From *The Yearling*)
Marjorie Kinnan Rawlings

LONELY

They're all away
And the house is still,
And the dust lies thick
On the window sill,
And the stairway creaks
In a solemn tone
This taunting phrase:
"You are all alone."

They've gone away
And the rooms are bare;
I miss his cap
From a parlor chair,
And I miss the toys
In the lonely hall,
But most of any
I miss his call.

I miss the shouts
And the laughter gay
Which greeted me
At the close of day,
And there isn't a thing
In the house we own
But sobbingly says:
"You are all alone."

It's only a house
That is mine to know,
An empty house
That is cold with woe;
Like a prison grim
With its bars of black,
And it won't be home
Till they all come back.

Edgar Guest

SOLITUDE

To be alone I find it necessary to escape the present—I avoid myself. How could I be alone in the Roman emperor's chamber of mirrors? I seek a garret. The spiders must not be disturbed, nor the floor swept, nor the lumber arranged.

Henry David Thoreau

Silence is the element in which great things fashion themselves.

Thomas Carlyle

DAFFODILS

I wandered lonely as a cloud
That floats on high o'er vales
    and hills,
When all at once I saw a crowd,
A host, of golden daffodils;
Beside the lake, beneath the
    trees,
Fluttering and dancing in the
    breeze.

Continuous as the stars that
    shine
And twinkle on the milky way,
They stretched in never-ending
    line
Along the margin of a bay:
Ten thousand at a glance,
Tossing their heads in sprightly
    dance.

The waves beside them danced;
    but they
Out-did the sparkling waves in
    glee:
A poet could not but be gay,
In such a jocund company:
I gazed—and gazed—but
    little thought
What wealth the show to me had
    brought:

For oft, when on my couch I lie
In vacant or in pensive mood,
They flash upon that inward
    eye
Which is the bliss of solitude;
And then my heart with pleasure
    fills,
And dances with the daffodils.

William Wordsworth

I'VE GOT TO TALK
TO SOMEBODY, GOD

I've got to talk to somebody, God.

I'm worried, I'm unhappy. I feel inadequate so often, hopeless, defeated, afraid.

Or again I'm so filled with delight I want to run into the streets proclaiming, "Stop, the world, listen! Hear this wonderful thing."

But nobody pauses to listen, out there or here —here in the very house where I live. Even those closest to me are so busy, so absorbed in their own concerns.

They nod and murmur and make an effort to share it, but they can't; I know they can't before I begin.

There are all these walls between us—husband and wife, parent and child, neighbor and neighbor, friend and friend.

Walls of self. Walls of silence. Even walls of words.

For even when we try to talk to each other new walls begin to rise. We camouflage, we hold back, we make ourselves sound better than we really are. Or we are shocked and hurt by what is revealed. Or we sit privately in judgment, criticizing even when we pretend to agree.

But with you, Lord, there are no walls. You, who made me, know my deepest emotions, my most secret thoughts. You know the good of me and the bad of me; you already understand.

Why, then, do I turn to you?

Because as I talk to you my disappointments are eased, my joys are enhanced. I find solutions to my problems, or the strength to endure what I must.

From your perfect understanding I receive understanding for my own life's needs.

Thank you that I can always turn to you. I've got to talk to somebody, God.

Marjorie Holmes

Friendship

TWO AT A FIRESIDE

I built a chimney for a comrade
  old;
I did the service not for hope
  or hire:
And then I traveled on in
  winter's cold,
Yet all the day I glowed before
  the fire.

Edwin Markham

Friendship cheers like a sunbeam; charms like a good story; inspires like a brave leader; binds like a golden chain; guides like a heavenly vision.

Newell D. Hillis

TO MY FRIEND

I love you not only for what
  you are, but for what I am
    when I am with you.

I love you not only for what
  you have made of yourself,
    but for what you are making
      of me.

I love you because you have
  done more than any creed
    could have done to make me
good, and more than any
    fate could have done to make
      me happy.

You have done it without a
  touch, without a word,
    without a sign.

You have done it by being yourself. Perhaps that is what
    being a friend means, after all.

Anonymous

FAMILIARITY

As old wood is best to burn, old horses to ride, old books to read, and old wine to drink, so are old friends always most trusty to use.

Leonard Wright

TO YOU

I turn to you,
Who have known pain and fear
And failure and despair,
And in your eyes I read
Companionship;
And though your cloak be
Threadbare, half of it is mine.
You are my friend.

Lilla Cabot Perry

CONDUCT OF LIFE

He who has a thousand friends
has not a friend to spare,
And he who has one enemy shall
meet him everywhere.

Ralph Waldo Emerson

Friendship hath the skill and observation of the best physician, the diligence and vigilance of the best nurse, and the tenderness and patience of the best mother.

Edward Clarendon

A friend is a person with whom I may be sincere. Before him, I may think aloud.

Ralph Waldo Emerson

OLD FRIENDS

I do not say new friends are
   not considerate and true,
Or that their smiles ain't
   genuine,
But still I'm tellin' you
That when a feller's heart
   is crushed and achin'
   with the pain,
And teardrops come a-splashin'
   down his cheeks like summer
   rain,
Becoz his grief an' loneliness
   are more than he can bear,
Somehow it's only old friends,
   then, that really seem to
   care.
The friends who've stuck through
   thick an' thin, who've known
   you, good an' bad,
Your faults an' virtues, an'
   have seen the struggles
   you have had,
When they come to you gentle-
   like an' take your hand an'
   say:
"Cheer up! We're with you still,"
   it counts,
   for that's the old friends' way.

The new friends may be fond of
   you for what you are to-day;
They've only known you rich,
   perhaps, an' only seen you
   gay;
You can't tell what's attracted
   them; your station may appeal;
Perhaps they smile on you
   because you're doin' something real;
But old friends who have seen
   you fail, an' also seen you win,
Who've loved you either up or
   down, stuck to you,
   thick or thin,
Who knew you as a budding youth,
   an' watched you start to climb,
Through weal an' woe, still
   friends of yours an' constant
   all the time,
When troubles comes an' things
   go wrong,
I don't care what you say,

They are the friends you'll
   turn to, for you want the
   old friends' way.

The new friends may be richer,
   an' more stylish, too,
   but when
Your heart is achin' an' you
   think your sun won't shine
   again,
It's not the riches of new
   friends you want, it's not
   their style,
It's not the air of grandeur
   then, it's just the old
   friend's smile,
The old hand that has helped
   before, stretched out once
   more to you,
The old words ringin' in your
   ears, so sweet an',
   oh, so true!
The tenderness of folks who know
   just what your sorrow means,
These are the things on which,
   somehow, your spirit always
   leans.
When grief is poundin' at
   your breast—the new friends
   disappear
An' to the old ones tried an'
   true, you turn for aid an'
   cheer.

Edgar Guest

As gold more splendid from the fire appears;
Thus friendship brightens by the length of
   years.

Thomas Carlyle

A TIME TO TALK

When a friend calls to me from
   the road
And slows his horse to a
   meaning walk,
I don't stand still and look
   around

On all the hills I haven't hoed
And shout from where I am,
  'What is it?'
No, not as there is a time to
  talk.
I thrust my hoe in the mellow
  ground,
Blade-end up and five feet tall,
And plod: I go up to the stone
  wall
For a friendly visit.
        Robert Frost

So long as we love, we serve. So long as we
are loved by others, I would almost say we
are indispensable; and no man is useless while
he has a friend.
        Robert Louis Stevenson

A friend may well be reckoned the masterpiece
of nature.
        Ralph Waldo Emerson

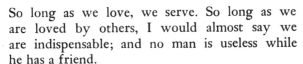

LINKED LIVES

In all your thoughts, and in all your acts, in
every hope and in every fear, when you soar
to the skies and when you fall to the ground,
always you are holding the other person's hand.
        A. A. Milne

A TRIBUTE

By friendship you mean the greatest love, the
greatest usefulness, the most open communica-
tion, the noblest sufferings, the severest truth,
the heartiest counsel, and the greatest union of
minds of which brave men and women are
capable.

        Jeremy Taylor

THERE IS NO FRIEND
LIKE AN OLD FRIEND

There is no friend like an old
  friend
Who has shared our morning
  days.
No greeting like his welcome,
No homage like his praise.
        Oliver Wendell Holmes

If we build on a sure foundation in friendship,
we must love our friends for their sakes rather
than for our own.

        Charlotte Brontë

THE GESTURE OF LOVE

Oh, the comfort, the inexpressible comfort of
feeling safe with a person; having neither to
weigh thoughts nor measure words, but to pour
them all out, just as they are, chaff and grain
together, knowing that a faithful hand will take
and sift them, keep what is worth keeping, and
then, with the breath of kindness, blow the rest
away.

        George Eliot

MY FRIEND

To me you are the happiness
That fills a June time day,
You've laughter that can fill
  my heart
In such a special way,
You're all the many little
  things
That make each day sublime,
The many dreams that may come
  true
That bless this life of mine.

To me you are a hope and faith
That seems to know no end,
Tomorrow's plans I cherish so
An understanding friend,
You're everything that I could
  wish
The sun that fills the sky,

The rainbow when the storm is
    through
The cloud that's drifting by.

You seem to be the helping hand
When troubles come my way,
The stars that light a darkened
    sky
The dawn at break of day,
You always wear a special smile
So much a joy indeed,
You lend a courage real and sure
In every hour of need.

To me you are the dearest
    friend
That I have ever known,
No matter what tomorrow sends
I never feel alone,
As faithful as the rising sun
With peace and joy to lend,
I thank God in my every prayer
For giving me my friend.

Garnett Ann Schultz

OUTWITTED

He drew a circle that shut me
    out,
Heretic, rebel, a thing to
    flout.
But love and I had the wit to
    win;
We drew a circle that took him in.

Edwin Markham

HEREDITY

True friendship is of royal lineage. It is of the
same kith and breeding as loyalty and self-
forgetting devotion and proceeds upon a higher
principle even than they. For loyalty may be
blind, and friendship must not be; devotion may
sacrifice principles of right choice which friendship must guard with an excellent and watchful
care. . . . The object of love is to serve, not to
win.

Woodrow Wilson

Greater love hath no man than this, that a man
lay down his life for his friends.

John 15:13,
King James Version

A TREASURE

People who have warm friends are healthier and
happier than those who have none. A single
real friend is a treasure worth more than gold
or precious stones. Money can buy many things,
good and evil. All the wealth of the world could
not buy you a friend or pay you for the loss
of one.

C. D. Prentice

God never loved me in so sweet a way before.
'Tis He alone who can such blessings send. And
when His love would new expressions find, He
brought thee to me and He said—"Behold a
friend."

Anonymous

And Ruth said, Intreat me not to leave thee, or
to return from following after thee: for whither
thou goest, I will go; and where thou lodgest,
I will lodge: thy people shall be my people,
and thy God my God:
    Where thou diest, will I die, and there will
I be buried: the Lord do so to me, and more also.

Ruth 1:16–17,
King James Version

To me, fair friend, you never
    can be old,
For as you were when first your
    eye I ey'd,
Such seems your beauty still.
        William Shakespeare

Go often to the house of thy friend, for weeds
choke the unused path.

Ralph Waldo Emerson

CONVERSATION

It happened on a solemn even-
    tide,
Soon after He who was our
    Surety died;
Two bosom friends, each
    pensively inclined,
The scene of all those
    sorrows left behind;
Sought their own village,
    busied as they went,
In musings worthy of the
    great event:
They spake of Him they loved,
    of Him whose life
Tho' blameless had incurred
    perpetual strife:
They thought Him, and they
    justly thought Him One
Sent to do more than He ap-
    peared to have done;
To exalt their nation and to
    lift them high
Above all else, and wondered He
    should die.
Ere yet they brought their
    journey to its end
A Stranger joined them, courte-
    ous as a friend,
And asked them, with a kind,
    engaging air,
What their affliction was, and
    begged a share.
Informed, He gathered up the
    broken thread,
And, truth and wisdom gracing
    all He said,
Explained, illustrated, and
    searched so well
The tender theme on which they
    chose to dwell,

That, reaching home, they said,
    "The night is near,
We must not now be parted,
    sojourn here."
The humble Stranger soon became
    their Guest,
And, made so welcome at their
    simple feast,
He blest the bread, but van-
    ished at the word,
And left them both exclaiming,
    "Twas the Lord!
Did not our hearts feel all He
    deigned to say!
Did not they burn within us by
    the way?"

William Cowper

One of the most beautiful qualities of true
friendship is to understand and to be understood.

Seneca

Friendship is the marriage of the soul.

Voltaire

I didn't find my friends; the good **God** gave
them to me.

Ralph Waldo Emerson

Character

TEST OF CHARACTER

There is no more searching test of the human spirit than the way it behaves when fortune is adverse and it has to pass through a prolonged period of disappointing failures. Then comes the real proof of the man. Achievement, if a man has the ability, is a joy; but to take hard knocks and come up smiling, to have your mainsail blown away and then rig a sheet on the bowsprit and sail on—this is perhaps the deepest test of character.

Harry Emerson Fosdick

Character is like a tree and reputation like its shadow. The shadow is what we think of it; the tree is the real thing.

Abraham Lincoln

SPLENDID GIFT

Live your life while you have it. Life is a splendid gift. There is nothing small in it. For the greatest things grow by God's Law out of the smallest. But to live your life you must discipline it. You must not fritter it away in "fair purpose, erring act, inconstant will" but make your thoughts, your acts, all work to the same end and that end, not self but God.

That is what we call character.

Florence Nightingale

Character is what you are in the dark.

Dwight L. Moody

Good habits are not made on birthdays, nor Christian character at the new year. The workshop of character is everyday life. The uneventful and commonplace hour is where the battle is lost or won.

Maltbie D. Babcock

No one can be wrong with man and right with God.

Harry Emerson Fosdick

The nearest way to glory is to strive to be what you wish to be thought to be.

Socrates

I AM NOT BOUND TO WIN

I am not bound to win, but I am bound to be true, I am not bound to succeed, but I am bound to live up to what light I have. I must stand with anybody that stands right; stand with him while he is right, and part with him when he goes wrong.

Abraham Lincoln

Who steals my purse steals
   trash; 'tis something,
   nothing;
'Twas mine, 'tis his, and has
   been slave to thousands;
But he that filches from me
   my good name
Robs me of that which not
   enriches him,
And makes me poor indeed.
    William Shakespeare

What you are, so is your world.

James Allen

For what is a man profited, if he shall gain the whole world, and lose his own soul?

Matthew 16:26,
King James Version

THIS ABOVE ALL

This above all: to thine own
self be true,
And it must follow, as the
night the day,
Thou canst not then be false
to any man.
William Shakespeare

If I take care of my character, my reputation will take care of itself.

Dwight L. Moody

Practice yourself what you preach.

Plautus

IF

If you can keep your head when
all about you
Are losing theirs and blaming
it on you;
If you can trust yourself when
all men doubt you,
And make allowance for their
doubting, too;

If you can wait and not be
tired of waiting,
Or, being lied about, don't
deal in lies;
Or, being hated, don't give way
to hating;
And yet don't look too good, nor
talk too wise;

If you can dream, and not make
dreams your master;
If you can think, and not make
thoughts your aim;
If you can meet with Triumph
and Disaster,
And treat those two imposters
just the same;

If you can bear the truth
you've spoken
Twisted by knaves to make a
trap for fools,
Or watch the things you gave
your life to, broken,
And stoop, and build them up
with worn-out tools;

If you can make one heap of
all your winnings
And risk it on one turn of
pitch-and-toss,
And lose, and start again at
your beginnings
And never breathe a word about
your loss;

If you can force your heart
and nerve and sinew
To serve your turn long after
they are gone,
And so hold on when there is
nothing in you
Except the Will which says to
them: "Hold on!"

If you can walk with crowds
and keep your virtue,
Or walk with Kings—nor lose
the common touch—
If foes nor loving friends can
hurt you,
If all men count on you—but
none too much;

If you can fill the unforgiv-
ing minute
With sixty seconds' worth of
distance run,
Yours is the Earth and everything that's in it,
And—which is more—you'll be
a Man, my son!
Rudyard Kipling

Men do not attract that which they want, but that which they are.

James Allen

THE WAY OF WISDOM

A good name is better than precious ointment; and the day of death than the day of one's birth.

It is better to go to the house of mourning, than to go to the house of feasting: for that is the end of all men; and the living will lay it to his heart.

Sorrow is better than laughter: for by the sadness of the countenance the heart is made better.

The heart of the wise is in the house of mourning; but the heart of fools is in the house of mirth.

It is better to hear the rebuke of the wise, than for a man to hear the song of fools.

Ecclesiastes 7:1–5,
King James Version

Labor to keep alive in your heart that little spark of celestial fire called conscience.

George Washington

ON DOING RIGHT

I do the very best I know how—the very best I can; and I mean to keep doing so until the end. If the end brings me out all right, what is said against me won't amount to anything. If the end brings me out wrong, ten angels swearing I was right would make no difference.

Abraham Lincoln

DO WHAT THY MANHOOD BIDS THEE DO

Do what thy manhood bids thee
    do,
from none but self expect ap-
    plause;
He noblest lives and noblest
    dies
who makes and keeps his self-
    made laws.

All other living is living
    death,
a world where none but phantoms
    dwell,
A breath, a wind, a sound, a
    voice, a tinkling of the
    camel bell.

Richard Burton

Only he deserves power who every day justifies it.

Dag Hammarskjöld

The entire object of true education is to make people not merely to do the right things, but enjoy them; not merely industrious, but to love industry; not merely learned, but to love knowledge; not merely pure, but to love purity; not merely just, but to hunger and thirst after justice.

John Ruskin

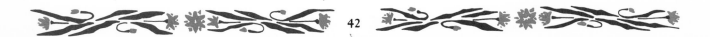

Generosity

THE TIDES OF PROVIDENCE

It's not what you gather but
   what you sow
That gives the heart a warming
   glow.
It's not what you get but what
   you give
Decides the kind of life you
   live.

It's not what you hoard but
   what you spare.
It's not what you take but
   what you share—
That pays the greater dividend
And makes you richer in the end.

It's not what you spend upon
   yourself
Or hide away upon a shelf,
That brings a blessing for
   the day.
It's what you scatter by the
   way.

A wasted effort it may seem,
But what you cast upon the
   stream,
Comes back to you in recom-
   pense
Upon the tides of Providence.
           Patience Strong

It is more blessed to give than to receive.
           Acts 20:25,
       King James Version

Instead of a gem or a flower, cast the gift of a
lovely thought into the heart of a friend.
           George Macdonald

If you have knowledge, let others light their
candles at it.
           Thomas Fuller

BEYOND OUR ASKING

More than our hearts can imagine
Or minds comprehend,
God's bountiful gifts
Are ours without end—
We ask for a cupful
When the vast sea is ours,
We pick a small rosebud
From a garden of flowers,
We reach for a sunbeam
But the sun still abides,
We draw one short breath
But there's air on all sides—
Whatever we ask for
Falls short of God's giving
For His greatness exceeds
Every facet of living,
And always God's ready
And eager and willing
To pour out His mercy
Completely fulfilling
All of man's needs
For peace, joy and rest
For God gives His children
Whatever is best
Just give Him a chance
To open His treasures
And He'll fill your life
With unfathomable pleasures,
Pleasures that never
Grow worn out and faded
And leave us depleted,
Disillusioned and jaded—
For God has a "storehouse"
Just filled to the brim
With all that man needs
If we only ask Him.
           Helen Steiner Rice

PARADOX

It is in loving—not in being
    loved,—The heart is blest;
It is in giving—not in seeking
    gifts,—We find our quest.

If thou art hungry, lacking
    heavenly food,—Give hope and
    cheer.
If thou art sad and wouldst be
    comforted,—Stay sorrow's tear.

Whatever be thy longing and thy
    need,—That do thou give;
So shall thy soul be fed, and
    thou indeed, shalt truly live.
              Author Unknown

Cast thy bread upon the waters: for thou shalt
find it after many days.

              Ecclesiastes 11:1,
              King James Version

It is another's fault if he be ungrateful, but it is
mine if I do not give.

              Seneca

What I kept I lost,
What I spent I had,
What I gave I have.
    Persian Proverb

GOOD KING WENCESLAS

Good King Wenceslas looked out,
On the feast of Stephen,
When the snow lay round about,
Deep, and crisp, and even:
Brightly shone the moon that
    night,
Though the frost was cruel,
When a poor man came in sight,
Gathering winter fuel.

"Hither, page, and stand by me,
If thou know'st it, telling,

Yonder peasant, who is he?
Where and what his dwelling?"
"Sire, he lives a good league
    hence,
Underneath the mountain;
Right against the forest
    fence,
By Saint Agnes' fountain."

"Bring me flesh and bring me
    wine,
Bring me pine logs hither;
Thou and I will see him dine,
When we bear them thither."
Page and monarch forth they
    went,
Forth they went together;
Through the rude wind's wild
    lament,
And the bitter weather.

"Sire, the night is darker now,
And the wind blows stronger;
Fails my heart, I know not how,
I can go no longer."
"Mark my footsteps, good my page
Tread thou in them boldly;
Thou shalt find the winter's
    rage
Freeze thy blood less coldly."

In his master's steps he trod,
Where the snow lay dinted;
Heat was in the very sod
Which the saint had printed.
Therefore, Christian men, be
    sure,
Wealth or rank possessing,
Ye who now will bless the
    poor,
Shall yourselves find blessing.
              John Mason Neale

MYSELF

Behold, I do not give lectures
    or a little charity,
When I give I give myself.
              Walt Whitman

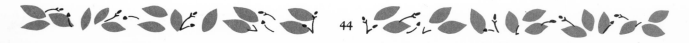

Faith

FAITH

I will not doubt, though all
   my ships at sea
Come drifting home with broken
   masts and sails;
I shall believe the Hand which
   never fails,
From seeming evil worketh good
   to me;
And, though I weep because
   those sails are battered,
Still will I cry, while my
   best hopes lie shattered,
"I trust in Thee."

I will not doubt, though all
   my prayers return
Unanswered from the still,
   white realm above;
I shall believe it is an all-
   wise Love
Which has refused those things
   for which I yearn;
And though, at times, I cannot
   keep from grieving,
Yet the pure odor of my fixed
   believing undimmed shall burn.

I will not doubt, though sorrows
   fall like rain,
And troubles swarm like bees
   about a hive;
I shall believe the heights for
   which I strive,
Are only reached by anguish
   and by pain;
And, though I groan and
   tremble with my crosses,
I yet shall see, through my
   severest losses,
The greater gain.

I will not doubt, well anchored
   in the faith,
Like some stanch ship, my
   soul braves every gale,

So strong its courage that it
   will not fail
To breast the mighty, unknown
   sea of death.
Oh, may I cry when body parts
   with spirit,
"I do not doubt," so listening
   worlds may hear it
With my last breath.
       Ella Wheeler Wilcox

THE WAY

Not for one single day
Can I discern my way,
   But this I surely know—
Who gives the day
Will show the way,
So I securely go.
       John Oxenham

ROAD TO CHRIST

Just as from every village in Britain there is a road which, linking on to other roads, brings you to London at last, so from every text in the Bible, even the remotest and least likely, there is a road to Christ.
       James S. Stewart

Have courage for the great sorrows of life and patience for the small ones; and when you have laboriously accomplished your daily task, go to sleep in peace. God is awake.
       Victor Hugo

CREDO

Not what, but Whom, I do
    believe,
That, in my darkest hour of
    need,
Hath comfort that no mortal
    creed
To mortal man may give;
Not what, but Whom!
For Christ is more than all
    the creeds,
And His full life of gentle
    deeds
Shall all the creeds outlive.
Not what I do believe, but
    Whom!
Who walks beside me in the
    gloom?
Who shares the burden wear-
    isome?
Who all the dim way doth
    illume,
And bids me look beyond the
    tomb
The larger life to live?
But whom!
Not what,
But Whom!

John Oxenham

Faith is not belief without proof, but trust without reservations.

Elton Trueblood

Depend upon it, God's work done in God's way
will never lack God's supplies.

J. Hudson Taylor

FAITH AND DOUBT

Doubt sees the obstacles,
    Faith sees the way;
Doubt sees the blackest night,
    Faith sees the day;
Doubt dreads to take a step,
    Faith soars on high;
Doubt questions, "Who believes?"
    Faith answers, "I!"

Author Unknown

WHO HAS SEEN THE WIND?

Who has seen the wind?
    Neither I nor you:
But when the leaves hang
    trembling,
The wind is passing through.

Who has seen the wind?
    Neither you nor I:
But when the trees bow down
    their heads,
The wind is passing by.

Christina Rossetti

As a plant upon the earth, so man rests upon
the bosom of God; he is nourished by unfailing
fountains, and draws at his need inexhaustible
power.

Ralph Waldo Emerson

THE GOLDEN CENSER

Eternal Love, we have no
    good to bring Thee,
No single good of all our
    hands have wrought,
No worthy music have we
    found to sing Thee,
No jeweled word, no quick
    upsoaring thought.

And yet we come; and when
    our faith would falter,
Show us, O Love, the quiet
    place of prayer;
The golden censer and the
    golden altar,
And the great angel waiting
    for us there.

Amy Carmichael

BEYOND DOUBT

The sun, with all those planets moving around
it, can ripen the smallest bunch of grapes as if
it had nothing else to do. Why then should I
doubt His power?

Galileo

FAITH

God knows, not I, the reason
  why
His winds of storm drive through
  my door;
I am content to live or die
Just knowing this, nor knowing
  more.
My Father's hand appointing me
My days and ways, so I am free.
Margaret Sangster

Faith lifts up shining arms and points to a happier world where our loved ones await us.
Helen Keller

Hope is wishing for a thing to come true; faith is believing that it will come true.
Norman Vincent Peale

What things soever ye desire, when ye pray, believe that ye receive them, and ye shall have them.

Mark 11:24,
King James Version

Who brought me hither
Will bring me hence;
  no other guide I seek.
John Milton

Every one that asketh receiveth;
  and he that seeketh findeth.

Matthew 7:8,
King James Version

They never sought in vain that sought the Lord aright!

Robert Burns

THE WORLD'S BIBLE

Christ has no hands but our
  hands
To do His work today;
He has no feet but our feet
  To lead men in His way;
He has no tongues but our
  tongues
To tell men how He died;
He has no help but our help
  To bring them to His side.

We are the only Bible
The careless world will read;
We are the sinner's gospel,
We are the scoffer's creed;
We are the Lord's last message
Given in deed and word—
What if the line is crooked?
What if the type is blurred?

What if our hands are busy
With other work than His?
What if our feet are walking
Where sin's allurement is?
What if our tongues are
  speaking
Of things His lips would spurn?
How can we hope to help Him
Unless from Him we learn?
Annie Johnson Flint

THE GATE OF THE YEAR

And I said to the man who stood
  at the gate of the year:
"Give me a light, that I may
  tread safely into the unknown."
And he replied:
"Go out into the darkness and
  put your hand into the Hand
  of God.
That shall be to you better than
  light and safer than a known
  way."
So, I went forth, and finding
  the Hand of God, trod gladly
  into the night.
And he led me towards the hills
  and the breaking of the day
  in the lone East.
So, heart, be still:

What need our little life,
Our human life, to know,
If God hath comprehension?
In all the dizzy strife
Of things both high and low
God hideth His intention.
M. Louise Haskins

GATEWAY

The Gateway to Christianity is not through an intricate labyrinth of dogma, but by a simple belief in the person of Christ.
William Lyon Phelps

I CAN TRUST

Thank God that I can trust,
That tho' a thousand times I
    feel the thrust
Of Faith betrayed, I still
    have faith in man,
Believe him pure and good since
    time began,
Thy child forever, tho' he
    may forget
The perfect mold in which his
    soul was set.
Angela Morgan

I think the best way to arrive at the right decision is to first pray about it, placing it in God's hands. Then sleep on it. The next morning, when you get up, I believe that the first solution that comes to your mind will be the right one—that is, if you have complete confidence in God's guidance. "But let him ask in faith, nothing wavering. For he that wavereth is like a wave of the sea driven with the wind and tossed" (James 1:6). Ask God's help in faith, and your decision will be right. I have found it unwise to make important decisions at the end of the day, when we are weary and tired. But once we have made a decision, we must not look back, like Lot's wife. We must act then on the faith that God has given us the answer—and know that only good will come out of it.
Dale Evans Rogers

LET US HAVE FAITH THAT RIGHT MAKES MIGHT

Let us have faith that right makes might; and in that faith let us to the end dare to do our duty as we understand it.
Abraham Lincoln

FAITH

Nothing before, nothing behind,
The steps of faith
Fall on the seeming void, and
    find
The rock beneath.
John Greenleaf Whittier

Blessed are they that have not seen, and yet have believed.
John 20:29,
King James Version

ONE DAY AT A TIME

One day at a time, with its
    failures and fears,
With its hurts and mistakes,
    with its weakness and tears,
With its portion of pain and
    its burden of care;
One day at a time we must meet
    and must bear.
One day at a time—but the day
    is so long.

And the heart is not brave, and
    the soul is not strong.
O thou pitiful Christ, be Thou
    near all the way:
Give courage and patience and
    strength for the day.

Swift cometh His answer, so
    clear and so sweet;
"Yea, I will be with thee,
    thy troubles to meet;
I will not forget thee, nor
    fail thee, nor grieve;
I will not forsake thee; I will
    never leave."

One day at a time, and the day
   is His day;
He hath numbered its hours,
   though they haste or delay,
His grace is sufficient; we
   walk not alone;
As the day, so the strength
   that He giveth His own.
Annie Johnson Flint

Even if I knew that tomorrow the world would
go to pieces, I would still plant my apple tree.
Martin Luther

I know that my redeemer liveth.
Job 19:25,
King James Version

THE NEW TESTAMENT

Matthew and Mark, and Luke
   and John.
The Holy Gospels wrote,
Describing how the Saviour
   died—
His life—and all He taught;
Acts prove how God the Apostles
   owned
With signs in every place;
St. Paul, in Romans, teaches
   us
How man is saved by grace;
The Apostle, in Corinthians,
Instructs, exhorts, reproves;
Galatians shows that faith in
   Christ
Alone the Father loves.
Ephesians and Philippians tell
What Christians ought to be;
Colossians bids us live to
   God
And for eternity.
In Thessalonians we are taught
The Lord will come from Heaven;
In Timothy and Titus
A bishop's rule is given.

Philemon marks a Christian's
   love,
Which only Christians know;
Hebrews reveals the Gospel
Prefigured by the law;
James teaches without holiness
Faith is but vain and dead;
St. Peter points the narrow way
In which the saints are led;
John, in his three Epistles,
On love delights to dwell;
St. Jude gives awful warning
Of judgment, wrath, and hell;
The Revelation prophesies
   of that tremendous day
When Christ, and Christ alone,
   shall be
The trembling sinner's stay.
Thomas Russell

THE SHADOWS

My little boy, with pale,
   round cheeks,
And large, brown, dreamy eyes,
Not often, little wisehead,
   speaks,
But yet will make replies.

His sister, always glad to show
Her knowledge, for its praise,
Said yesterday: "God's here,
   you know;
He's everywhere, always.

"He's in this room." His
   large brown eyes
Went wandering round for God;
In vain he looks, in vain, he
   tries,
His wits are all abroad.

"He is not here, mama? No,
   no;
I do not see Him at all,
He's not the shadows, is he?"
   So
His doubtful accents fall.

Fall on my heart, like precious
   seed,
Grow up to flowers of love;

For as my child, in love and
   need,
Am I to Him above.

How oft before the vapors
   break,
And day begins to be,
In our dim-lighted rooms we take
The shadows, Lord, for Thee;

While every shadow lying there,
Slow remnant of the light,
Is but an aching, longing prayer,
For Thee, O Lord, the light.
George Macdonald

Now faith is the substance of things hoped for,
the evidence of things not seen.
Hebrews 11:1,
King James Version

I NEVER SAW A MOOR

I never saw a moor,
I never saw the sea;
Yet know I how the heather looks,
And what a wave must be.

I never spoke with God
Nor visited in Heaven;
Yet certain am I of the spot
As if the chart were given.
Emily Dickinson

HE SUFFICES

Let nothing disturb thee;
Let nothing afright thee;
All things are passing;
God never changes.

Patience gains all things;
Who has God wants nothing;
God alone suffices.
St. Theresa of Ávila

The reason why birds can fly and we can't is
simply that they have perfect faith, for to have
faith is to have wings.
James M. Barrie

In the breast of a bulb
Is the promise of spring;

In the little blue egg
Is a bird that will sing;

In the soul of a seed
Is the hope of the sod;

In the heart of a child
Is the Kingdom of God.
William L. Stidger

SILENCE

I need not shout my faith.
   Thrice eloquent
Are quiet trees and the green
   listening sod;
Hushed are the stars, whose
   power is never spent;
The hills are mute: yet how
   they speak of God!
Charles Hanson Towne

THE BOOK

We search the world for truth;
   we cull
The good, the true, the
   beautiful,
From graven stone and written
   scroll,
And all old flower-fields of
   the soul;
And, weary seekers of the best,
We come back laden from our
   quest,
To find that all the sages
   said
Is in the Book our mothers
   read.
John Greenleaf Whittier

All I have seen teaches me to trust the Creator for all I have not seen.

Ralph Waldo Emerson

THE INNER LIFE

You say you are chained by circumstances; you cry out for better opportunities, for a wider scope, for improved physical conditions, and perhaps you inwardly curse the fate that binds you hand and foot. It is for you that I write; it is to you that I speak. Listen, and let my words burn themselves into your heart, for that which I say to you is truth:—You may bring about that improved condition in your outward life which you desire, if you will unswervingly resolve to improve your inner life. . . .

There is no room for a complainer in a universe of law, and worry is soul-suicide. By your very attitude of mind you are strengthening the chains which bind you, and are drawing about you the darkness by which you are enveloped. Alter your outlook upon life, and your outward life will alter. Build yourself up in the faith and knowledge, and make yourself worthy of better surroundings and wider opportunities. Be sure, first of all, that you are making the best of what you have. Do not delude yourself into supposing that you can step into greater advantages whilst overlooking smaller ones, for if you could, the advantage would be impermanent and you would quickly fall back again in order to learn the lesson which you had neglected. As the child at school must master one standard before passing on to the next, so, before you can have that greater good which you so desire, must you faithfully employ that which you already possess. . . . "If you have faith, and doubt not, ye shall not only do this, . . . but if ye shall say unto this mountain, be thou removed and be thou cast into the sea, it shall be done."

James Allen

I know the Bible is inspired because it inspires me.

Dwight L. Moody

THERE IS NO UNBELIEF

There is no unbelief;
Whoever plants a seed beneath
    the sod
And waits to see it push away
    the clod,
He trusts in God.

There is no unbelief;
Whoever says, when clouds are
    in the sky,
"Be patient, heart; light
    breaketh by and by."
Trusts the Most High.

There is no unbelief;
Whoever sees 'neath winter's
    field of snow,
The silent harvest of the
    future grow—
God's power must know.

There is no unbelief;
Whoever lies down on his couch
    to sleep,
Content to lock each sense in
    slumber deep,
Knows God will keep.

There is no unbelief;
Whoever says, "to-morrow,"
    "The unknown,"
"The future," trusts that
    power alone
He dares disown.

There is no unbelief;
The heart that looks on when
    dear eyelids close,
And dares to live when life
    has only woes,
God's comfort knows.

There is no unbelief;
For thus by day and night unconsciously
The heart lives by the faith the
    lips deny.
God knoweth why.

Lizzie York Case

MY BED IS A BOAT

My bed is like a little boat;
Nurse helps me when I embark;
She girds me in my sailor's coat
And starts me in the dark.

At night, I go on board and say
Good-night to all my friends
   on shore;
I shut my eyes and sail away
And see and hear no more.

And sometimes things to bed
   I take,
As prudent sailors have to
   do;
Perhaps a slice of wedding cake,
Perhaps a toy or two.
            Robert Louis Stevenson

Every day is a birthday, for every day we are born anew.
            Ellen Browning Scripps

ALL THROUGH THE NIGHT

Sleep, my love, and peace attend
   thee,
All through the night;
Guardian angels God will lend
   thee,
All through the night;
Soft the drowsy hours are
   creeping,
Hill and dale in slumber
   steeping,
Love alone his watch is keeping—
All through the night.
            Anonymous

HOPE

Hope is the thing with feathers
That perches in the soul,
And sings the tune without
   the words,
And never stops at all,

And sweetest in the gale is
   heard;
And sore must be the storm
That could abash the little
   bird
That kept so many warm.

I've heard it in the chillest
   land,
And on the strangest sea;
Yet, never, in extremity,
It asked a crumb of me.
            Emily Dickinson

The steadfast love of the Lord
   never ceases,
   his mercies never come to an end;
They are new every morning;
   great is thy faithfulness.
"The Lord is my portion," says
   my soul,
   "therefore I will hope in Him."
The Lord is good to those who
   wait for him, to the soul
   that seeks him.
            Lamentations 3:22–25,
            Revised Standard Version

IN EARTHEN VESSELS

The dear Lord's best interpreters
Are humble human souls;
The gospel of a life like His
Is more than books or scrolls.

From scheme and creed the
   light goes out,
The saintly fact survives;
The blessed Master none can
   doubt,
Revealed in holy lives.
            John Greenleaf Whittier

"Do not be worried and upset," Jesus told them. "Believe in God, and believe also in me. There are many rooms in my Father's house, and I am going to prepare a place for you. I would not tell you this if it were not so. And after I go and prepare a place for you, I will come back and take you to myself, so that you will be where I am. You know how to get to the place where I am going." Thomas said to him, "Lord, we do not know where you are going; how can we know the way to get there?" Jesus answered him: "I am the way, I am the truth, I am the life; no one goes to the Father but by me. Now that you have known me," he said to them, "you will know my Father also; and from now on you do know him, and you have seen him."

Philip said to him, "Lord, show us the Father; that is all we need." Jesus answered: "For a long time I have been with you all; yet you do not know me, Philip? Whoever has seen me has seen the Father. Why, then, do you say, 'Show us the Father'? Do you not believe, Philip, that I am in the Father and the Father is in me? The words that I have spoken to you," Jesus said to his disciples, "do not come from me. The Father, who remains in me, does his own works. Believe me that I am in the Father and the Father in me. If not, believe because of these works. I tell you the truth: whoever believes in me will do the works I do—yes, he will do even greater ones, for I am going to the Father. And I will do whatever you ask for in my name, so that the Father's glory will be shown through the Son. If you ask me for anything in my name, I will do it."

John 14:1–14,
The New Testament
in Today's English

Seasons

SUMMER

Some time in June's first week I waken and am up before five. A whole chorus of birdsong is in progress. A whippoorwill is reiterating his calls, for some mysterious reason, but he only makes the songsters sound more musical. As nearly as I can sort them out, there are robins, Baltimore orioles, scarlet tanagers, possibly a rose-breasted grosbeak, a couple of brown thrashers, and several I can't identify.

I have a cup of coffee, pull on a windbreaker and go out to feel the morning, see it, hear it. This is the time of year when every sense a man possesses gets a workout. You don't merely see this world; you participate in it.

I go down to the riverbank, see that the river is faintly steaming, the thin mist eddying in the air currents and lying only a few feet above the water. The grass is dripping with dew, the trunks of the maples black with moisture. Somewhere out on the water a fish leaps and splashes, probably a rock bass, maybe a yellow perch, maybe a German carp.

I walk down the road a way, to the middle pasture, and by now the light is bright enough that I can see the individual trees on the mountainside, though the top of the hill is still misted in. Out in the pasture I hear a snort and turn to look and see three deer, all does, standing only fifty yards away, watching me. I stop and they turn, flaunt their white flag-tails at me and lope off a little way, then pause and look at me again. They are cautious, but not really alarmed. I stand beside the fence and they watch me warily for a few minutes; then, deciding it is time to go, they float over the far fence and vanish into the brush on the hillside. Two of them were heavy with fawn, probably will drop their fawns within another two weeks.

I start on down the road, and a redwinged blackbird sees me, makes quite a fuss from a roadside tree. Probably his mate—or one of his mates, since redwings are polygamous—has a nest in the reeds on the riverbank nearby. Then a bluejay, the loudmouth of birddom, announces

to the world that A Man is in sight. It doesn't seem to matter to the robins and orioles, who go right on singing.

Hal Borland

RAIN IN SUMMER

How beautiful is the rain!
After the dust and heat,
In the broad and fiery street,
In the narrow lane,
How beautiful is the rain!

How it clatters along the
   roofs,
Like the tramp of hoofs!
How it gushes and struggles
   out
From the throat of the overflowing spout!

Across the windowpane
It pours and pours;
And swift and wide,
With a muddy tide,
Like a river down the
   gutter roars
The rain, the welcome rain!
Henry Wadsworth Longfellow

TO AUTUMN

Season of mists and mellow
   fruitfulness,
Close bosom-friend of the
   maturing sun;
Conspiring with him how to
   load and bless
With fruit the vines that
   round the thatch-eaves run;
To bend with apples the moss'd
   cottage-trees,
And fill all fruit with ripeness to the core;

To swell the gourd, and plump
the hazel shells
With a sweet kernel; to set
budding more,
And still more, later flowers
for the bees,
Until they think warm days
will never cease,
For Summer has o'er-brimmed
their clammy cells.

Where are the songs of Spring?
Ay, where are they?
Think not of them, thou hast
thy music too,—
While barred clouds bloom the
soft-dying day,
And touch the stubble-plains
with rosy hue;
Then in a wailful choir the
small gnats mourn
Among the river sallows,
borne aloft
Or sinking as the light wind
lives or dies;
And full-grown lambs loud bleat
from hilly bourn;
Hedge crickets sing; and now
with treble soft
The redbreast whistles from a
garden croft;
And gathering swallows twitter
in the skies.

John Keats

The shadows, lengthening, stretch
at noon;
The fields are stripped, the
groves are dumb;
The frost-flowers greet the icy
moon,—
Then blooms the bright
Chrysanthemum.

Oliver Wendell Holmes

AUTUMN LANDSCAPE

Autumn creeps in on moccasins silent as the glow of the Harvest Moon. Now the nights will have the touch and the smell of the frosty air. Days will have the crisp-leaf rustle of fall as the reds and golds, browns and purples signal another year come to ripeness and to maturity. That is autumn's dominant note: maturity. Autumn brings a summing up of sweetness in the apple, of ripeness in the golden corn, of tartness in the wild grape. Spring was all eager reaching for the April sunlight. Summer was growth, and blossom, and August fruiting. Now comes ripeness, toward which bud and leaf and blossom all were aimed. The color creeps through the woodland. Cricket and katydid scratch frantically at the dark. The hoarding squirrel is busy in the oak. The drowsy woodchuck fattens for his long sleep. The barred owl's questions echo in the starry night. Autumn comes over the hills and down the valleys, in the smoky mists of Indian Summer, in the frost-crisp dawns of October. It is the power and the glory, to see and hear and taste and touch, to celebrate.

Hal Borland

THE GOLDEN FLOWER

When spring is but a spend-
thrift's dream,
And summer's wealth a wasted
dower,
No dews nor sunshine may re-
deem,—
Then autumn coins his Golden
Flower.

AUTUMN

When Autumn flings her banners
wide upon October air,
All nature seems to thank its
God for making life so fair.
The hills go robed in amethyst,
the trees are dressed in fire,
The very air seems thrilling
with a passionless desire.

One somehow feels that God on
   high must love this season best,
He holds it as a mother holds
   her baby close to her breast.
The pressure of his hand is
   on all nature like a prayer—
When Autumn flings her banners
   wide upon October air.
            Margaret Sangster

THE AUTUMN FOREST

The autumn forest's like a
   blanket.
So stuffed with silence, shade
   and sleep.
No squirrel, owl or woodpecker
Will wake it from its slumber
   deep.

Along those autumn paths, the
   sun,
When it adventures in at close
   of day,
Will move in fearfulness alert
Lest it may fall into a snare.

Inside are swamps and stumps
   and aspens,
And alder thickets, spreading
   moss;
And somewhere past the forest
   fens,
The village-cocks are crowing
   hoarse.

A cock will raise a raucous
   shout;
Then silence dominates again
As if, immersed in deepest
   thought,
He puzzles the meaning of his
   strain.

But somewhere else and more
   remote
A neighboring cock bawls out
   reply;
And like a watchman on his
   beat,
Our cock will answer his cry.

Like certain echo, he'll
   respond;
And all the cocks with little
   rest
Will hoarsely mark, as with a
   bond,
Both North and South, and East
   and West.

Upon this clamoring exchange,
The forest opens wide its
   ranks
And spies the unaccustomed
   range
Of fields, horizons and blue
   skies.
            Boris Pasternak

SNOW CAME LAST NIGHT

Snow came last night.
I woke to find on iron
   fence and gate a kind of joy,
   a feathery, wild thing that
   will take wing.

O magical, enchanting snow!
From other winters long ago,
Come traveling the starry way
Horses and sleigh.

And children wearing sweaters
   bright
And bells that jingle in the
   night
And whiteness settling everywhere like angel's hair.
            Helen F. Dougher

WOODS IN WINTER

With solemn feet I tread the
   hill,
And through the hawthorn blows
   the gale;

With solemn feet I tread the
   hill,
That overbrows the lonely
   vale.

O'er the bare upland, and away
Through the long reach of desert
   woods,
The embracing sunbeams chastely
   play
And gladden these deep
   solitudes.

Where, twisted round the
   barren oak
The summer vine in beauty
   clung
And summer winds the stillness
   broke,
The crystal icicle is hung.

Where, from their frozen urns,
   mute springs
Pour out the river's gradual
   tide,
Shrilly the skater's iron
   rings
And voices fill the woodland
   side.

Alas! how changed from the
   fair scene,
When birds sang out their
   mellow lay
And winds were soft, and woods
   were green,
And the song ceased not with
   the day!

But still wild music is abroad;
Pale, desert woods! within
   your crowd;
And gathering winds, in hoarse
   accord
Amid the vocal reeds pipe loud.

Chill airs and wintry winds!
   my ear
Has grown familiar with your
   song;
I hear it in the opening year;
I listen, and it cheers me long.
   Henry Wadsworth Longfellow

WINTER EVENING

Last night, after a day of winter's cold, still mag-
nificence, I went out into the dark of early
evening to bring an armload of fireplace wood
from the woodshed. I looked to the north and
there beneath the Pole Star the Big Dipper lay
close to the horizon, pointing the time of all time
since stars were first patterned in night sky and
man was here to wonder at them. The thin curl
of a new moon was low in the west, almost down
on the dark grove of pines on the mountain, a
ridge of rock that was old when mankind was
young. And somehow I knew that I was with the
wind and the stars and the earth itself. Winter
was all around me, simple as the glittering breath
from my lungs. I was a part of the mystery, the
wonder and the awe, part of the holiness and
the wholeness of life and the reason beyond all
my reasoning.

   Hal Borland

DIVINE POETRY

I saw God write a gorgeous poem this very
morning. With the fresh sunbeam for a pencil,
on the broad sheet of level snow, the diamond
letters were spelled out one by one, till the whole
was aflame with poetry.

   Phillips Brooks

Over the winter glaciers
I see the summer glow,
And through the wide-piled
   snowdrift
The warm rosebuds below.
   Ralph Waldo Emerson

For, lo, the winter is past, the rain is over and
gone; the flowers appear on the earth; the time
of the singing of birds is come, and the voice of
the turtle is heard in our land.

   Song of Solomon 2:11–12,
   King James Version

If Winter comes, can Spring be far behind?
Percy Bysshe Shelley

ODE ON THE SPRING

Still is the toiling hand of
 Care;
The panting herds repose;
Yet hark, how through the
 peopled air
The busy murmur glows!

The insect youth are on the
 wing,
Eager to taste the honied
 spring,
And float amid the liquid
 noon;
Some lightly o'er the current
 skim,
Some show their gaily-gilded
 trim
Quick-glancing to the sun.
Thomas Gray

Close to my heart I fold each
 lovely thing
The sweet day yields; and, not
 disconsolate,
With the calm patience of the
 woods I wait
For leaf and blossom when God
 gives us Spring!
John Greenleaf Whittier

ALL'S RIGHT

The year's at the spring,
 And day's at the morn;
Morning's at seven;
The hill-side's dew-pearled,
The lark's on the wing;
The snail's on the thorn:
God's in his heaven—
All's right with the world!
Robert Browning

ROBIN

The robin is the one
That interrupts the morn
With hurried, few, express
 reports
When March is scarcely on.

The robin is the one
That overflows the noon
With her cherubic quantity,
An April but begun.

The robin is the one
That speechless from her nest
Submits that home and certainty
And sanctity are best.
Emily Dickinson

LOVELIEST OF TREES

Loveliest of trees, the cherry
 now
Is hung with bloom along the
 bough,
And stands about the woodland
 ride
Wearing white for Eastertide.

Now, of my threescore years
 and ten,
Twenty will not come again,
And take from seventy springs
 a score,
It only leaves me fifty more.

And since to look at things in
 bloom
Fifty springs are little room,
About the woodlands I will go
To see the cherry hung with
 snow.
A. E. Housman

Our Lord has written the promise of the Resur-
rection, not in books alone, but in every leaf in
Springtime.

Martin Luther

THE RHODORA

In May, when sea-winds
    pierced our solitudes,
I found the fresh Rhodora in
    the woods,
Spreading its leafless blooms
    in a damp nook,
To please the desert and the
    sluggish brook.
The purple petals, fallen in
    the pool,
Made the black water with
    their beauty gay;
Here might the red-bird come
    his plumes to cool,
And court the flower that
    cheapens his array.
Rhodora! if the sages ask
    thee why
This charm is wasted on the
    earth and sky,
Tell them, dear, that if eyes
    were made for seeing,
Then beauty is its own excuse
    for being:
Why thou were there, O rival
    of the rose!
I never thought to ask, I never
    knew:
But, in my simple ignorance,
    suppose
The self-same Power that
    brought me there brought you.
        Ralph Waldo Emerson

MY MIND LETS GO
A THOUSAND THINGS

My mind lets go a thousand
    things,
Like dates of wars and deaths
    of kings,
And yet recalls the very hour—
'Twas noon by yonder village
    tower,

And on the last blue noon in
    May—
The wind came briskly up this
    way,
Crisping the brook beside the
    road;
Then, pausing here, set down
    its load
Of pine scents, and shook
    listlessly
Two petals from that wild-rose
    tree.
        Thomas Bailey Aldrich

THE MYSTERY

An altered look about the hills;
A Tyrian light the village
    fills;
A wider sunrise in the dawn;
A deeper twilight on the lawn;
A print of a vermilion foot;
A purple finger on the slope;
A flippant fly upon the pane;
A spider at his trade again;
An added strut in chanticleer;
A flower expected everywhere;
An axe shrill singing in the
    woods;
Fern-odors on untravelled roads—
All this, and more I cannot
    tell,
A furtive look you know as
    well,
And Nicodemus' mystery
Receives its annual reply.
        Emily Dickinson

Beauty

SHE WALKS IN BEAUTY

She walks in beauty, like the
    night
Of cloudless climes and starry
    skies;
And all that's best of dark and
    bright
Meet in her aspect and her
    eyes:
Thus mellowed to that tender
    light
Which heaven to gaudy day denies.

One shade the more, one ray
    the less,
Had half impaired the nameless
    grace
Which waves in every raven
    tress,
Or softly lightens o'er her face;
Where thoughts serenely sweet
    express
How pure, how dear their
    dwelling place.

And so on that cheek, and o'er
    that brow,
So soft, so calm, yet eloquent,
The smiles that win, the tints
    that glow,
But tell of days in goodness spent,
A mind at peace with all below,
    A heart whose love is innocent!
        George Gordon, Lord Byron

THE MASTERPIECE

The human face is the masterpiece of God. The eyes reveal the soul, the mouth the flesh. The chin stands for purpose, the nose means will. But over and behind all is that fleeting something we call "expression."

Elbert Hubbard

Who knows her smile has known a **perfect** thing.

Edmund Rostand

Beauty is altogether in the eye of the beholder.
Lew Wallace

The perfection of outward loveliness is the soul shining through its crystalline covering.
Jane Porter

What is beautiful is good and who is good will soon also be beautiful.

Sappho

Truth, and goodness, and beauty are but different faces of the same all.

Ralph Waldo Emerson

SOURCE

Though we travel the world over to find the beautiful, we must have it in us or find it not.
Ralph Waldo Emerson

VISION

I find earth not gray but rosy,
    Heaven not grim but fair
        of hue.
    Do I stoop? I pluck a posy.
Do I stand and stare? All's
        blue.

Robert Browning

A CUP OF BLESSING

Never lose an opportunity of seeing anything that is beautiful; for beauty is God's handwriting—a wayside sacrament. Welcome it in every fair face, in every fair sky, in every fair flower, and thank God for it as a cup of blessing.

Ralph Waldo Emerson

Why should we think about things that are lovely? Because thinking determines life. It is a common mistake to blame life upon environment. Environment modifies but does not govern life. The soul is stronger than its surroundings.

William James

A THING OF BEAUTY

A thing of beauty is a joy
  forever;
Its loveliness increases; it
  will never
Pass into nothing-
  ness; but still will keep
A bower quiet for us, and a
  sleep
Full of sweet dreams, and
  health, and quiet breathing.

John Keats

HIS GIFT TO ALL

In all ranks of life the human heart yearns for the beautiful; and the beautiful things that God makes are his gift to all alike.

Harriet Beecher Stowe

Happily there exists more than one kind of beauty. There is the beauty of infancy, the beauty of youth, the beauty of maturity, and . . . the beauty of age.

George Augustus Sala

Our Creator would never have made such lovely days, and have given us the deep hearts to enjoy them, above and beyond all thought, unless we were meant to be immortal.

Nathaniel Hawthorne

OPEN OUR EYES

O heavenly Father, who hast filled the world with beauty: open, we beseech Thee, our eyes to behold Thy gracious hand in all Thy works; that rejoicing in Thy whole creation, we may learn to serve Thee with gladness.

From the Book of Common Prayer

Goodness

Ye are the light of the world. A city that is set on an hill cannot be hid. Neither do men light a candle, and put it under a bushel, but on a candlestick; and it giveth light unto all that are in the house.

Let your light so shine before men, that they may see your good works, and glorify your Father which is in heaven.

Matthew 5:14–16,
King James Version

Our opportunities to do good are our talents.
Cotton Mather

ROAMING IN THOUGHT

Roaming in thought over the Universe, I saw the little that is Good steadily hastening towards immortality, And the vast all that is call'd Evil I saw hastening to merge itself and become lost and dead.

Walt Whitman

Goodness is something so simple: always to live for others, never to seek one's own advantage.
Dag Hammarskjöld

I pray thee, O God, that I may be beautiful within.

Socrates

God shall be my hope . . .
My stay, my guide and lantern
to my feet.
William Shakespeare

SERMONS WE SEE

I'd rather see a sermon than
hear one, any day;
I'd rather one would walk with
me than merely tell the way;
The eye's a better pupil and
more willing than the ear.
Fine counsel is confusing,
but example's always clear,
And the best of all the preachers
are the men who live their creeds,
For to see good put in action
is what everybody needs.

I soon can learn to do it if
you'll let me see it done;
I can watch your hands in
action, but your tongue too
fast may run.
And the lecture you deliver may
be very wise and true,
But I'd rather get my lessons
by observing what you do.
For I might misunderstand you
and the high advice you give.
But there's no misunderstanding
how you act and how you live.
Edgar Guest

'Tis only noble to be good.
Alfred, Lord Tennyson

JACQUELINE

She was good as she was fair,
None, none on earth above her!
As pure in thoughts as angels
are:
To know her was to love her.
Samuel Rogers

GOD OUR FRIEND

In this vast universe
There is but one supreme truth—
That God is our friend!
By that truth meaning is
    given
To the remote stars, the
    numberless centuries,
The long and heroic struggle
    of mankind . . .
O my Soul, dare to trust this
    truth!
Dare to rest in God's kindly
    arms,
Dare to look confidently into
    His face,
Then launch thyself into life
    unafraid!
Knowing that thou art within
    thy Father's house,
That thou art surrounded by
    His love,
Thou wilt become master of
    fear,
Lord of life, conqueror even
    of death!

Joshua Loth Liebman

Not I, but God in me.

Dag Hammarskjöld

Without the Way there is no going; without
the Truth there is no knowing; without the Life
there is no living.

Thomas à Kempis

HIS DWELLINGPLACE

All His glory and beauty come
    from within,
And there He delights to dwell.
His visits there are frequent,
His conversation sweet,
His comforts refreshing,
    and His peace passing all
    understanding.

Thomas à Kempis

LORD OF ALL

A vision wakens on my inner
    mind;
My spirit, wakened by the
    vision, sings.
The God who spread the golden
    sand of suns
Upon the measureless black
    beach of night
Has made the sand I feel
    warm in my hand.
The Lord of cosmic mystery
    and might
Is also Lord of all the little
    things.

Lon Woodrum

Behold, I stand at the door, and knock: if any
man hear my voice, and open the door, I will
come in to him, and will sup with him, and he
with me.

Revelation 3:20,
King James Version

HE LOVES YOU!

It's amazing and incredible,
But it's as true as it can be,
God loves and understands us
    all
And that means you and me—
His grace is all sufficient
For both the young and old,
For the lonely and the timid,
For the brash and for the bold—
His love knows no exceptions,
So never feel excluded,
No matter who or what you are
Your name has been included—
And no matter what your past
    has been,
Trust God to understand,
And no matter what your problem
    is
Just place it in His Hand—
For in all of our unloveliness
This great God loves us still,
He loved us since the world
    began
And what's more, He always will!

Helen Steiner Rice

LIGHT SHINING OUT OF DARKNESS

God moves in a mysterious way
His wonders to perform;
He plants his footsteps in the
sea,
And rides upon the storm.

Deep in unfathomable mines,
With never-failing skill,
He treasures up his bright
designs,
And works his sovereign will.

Ye fearful saints, fresh courage
take;
The clouds ye so much dread
Are big with mercy, and shall
break
In blessings on your head.

Judge not the Lord by feeble
sense,
But trust him for his grace;
Behind a frowning providence
He hides a smiling face.

His purposes will ripen fast,
Unfolding every hour;
The bud may have a bitter taste,
But sweet will be the flower.

Blind unbelief is sure to err,
And scan his work in vain;
God is his own interpreter,
And he will make it plain.

William Cowper

I have held many things in my hands, and I have lost them all; but whatever I have placed in God's hands, that I still possess.

Martin Luther

Lord, thou hast been our dwelling place in all generations. Before the mountains were brought forth, or ever thou hadst formed the earth and the world, even from everlasting to everlasting, thou art God. For a thousand years in thy sight are but as yesterday when it is past, and as a watch in the night.

Psalm 90:1–2,4,
King James Version

THE EXTRAVAGANCE OF GOD

More sky than man can see,
More seas than he can sail,
More sun than he can bear to
watch,
More stars than he can scale.

More breath than he can breathe,
More yield than he can sow,
More grace than he can com-
prehend,
More love than he can know.

Ralph W. Seager

REVELATION

I made a pilgrimage to find
the God:
I listened for his voice at
holy tombs,
Searched for the print of his
immortal feet
In dust of broken altars; yet
turned back
With empty heart. But on the
homeward road,
A great light came upon me,
and I heard
The God's voice singing in a
nestling lark;
Felt his sweet wonder in a
swaying rose;
Received his blessing from a
wayside well;
Looked on his beauty in a
lover's face;
Saw his bright hand send signals from the sun.

Edwin Markham

I am the light of the world.

John 8:12,
King James Version

Only God can fully satisfy the hungry heart of man.

Hugh Black

PRAYER

O Holy Spirit of God, abide
   with us;
Inspire all our thoughts;
Pervade our imaginations;
Suggest all our decisions;
Order all our doings.
Be with us in our silence and
   in our speech,
In our haste and in our leisure,
In company and in solitude,
In the freshness of the morning
   and the weariness of the
   evening;
And give us grace at all times
   humbly to rejoice in Thy
   mysterious companionship.
        John Baillie

THE SHEPHERD'S PSALM

The Lord is my shepherd;
   I shall not want.
He maketh me to lie down
   in green pastures:
he leadeth me beside the still
   waters.
He restoreth my soul:
   he leadeth me in the paths
of righteousness for his name's
   sake.
Yea, though I walk through the
   valley of the shadow of death,
I will fear no evil:
   for thou art with me;
thy rod and thy staff they
   comfort me.
Thou preparest a table before
   me in the presence of mine
   enemies:
Thou anointest my head with
   oil;
   my cup runneth over.
Surely goodness and mercy shall
   follow me
all the days of my life:
   and I will dwell in the house
   of the Lord for ever.
        Psalm 23,
        King James Version

All that is good, all that is true, all that is beautiful, all that is beneficent, be it great or small, be it perfect or fragmentary, natural as well as supernatural, moral as well as material, comes from God.

        John Henry Newman

THE UNKNOWN GOD

The Lord hath builded for
   Himself,
He needs no earthly dome;
The Universe His dwelling is,
   Eternity His home.

Yon glorious sky His temple
   stands,
So lofty, bright, and blue,
All lamped with stars, and
   curtained round
With clouds of every hue.

Earth is His altar: Nature
   there
Her daily tribute pays;
The elements upon Him wait;
The seasons roll His praise.

Where shall I see Him? How
   describe
The Dread, Eternal One?
His foot-prints are in every
   place
Himself is found in none.

He called the world, and it
   arose;
The heavens, and they ap-
   peared:
His hand poured forth the
   mighty deep;
His arm the mountains reared.

He sets His foot upon the
   hills,
And earth beneath Him quakes;
He walks upon the hurricane,
And in the thunder speaks.

I search the rounds of space and time,
Nor find His semblance there:
Grandeur has nothing so sublime,
Nor Beauty half so fair.
        Henry Francis Lyte

THE TWO ANGELS

All is of God! If he but
  wave his hand,
The mists collect, the rain
  falls thick and loud,
Till, with a smile of light
  on sea and land,
Lo! he looks back from the
  departing cloud.

Angels of Life and Death alike
  are his;
Without his leave they pass no
  threshold o'er;
Who, then, would wish or dare,
  believing this,
Against his messengers to shut
  the door?
Henry Wadsworth Longfellow

A CHILD'S THOUGHT OF GOD

They say that God lives very
  high!
But if you look above the pines
You cannot see our God. And why?

And if you dig down in the
  mines
You never see Him in the gold,
Though from Him all that's
  glory shines.

God is so good, He wears a fold
Of heaven and earth across His
  face—
Like secrets kept, for love,
  untold.

But still I feel that His embrace
Slides down by thrills, through
  all things made,
Through sight and sound of
  every place:

As if my tender mother laid
On my shut lids, her kisses'
  pressure,
Half waking me at night; and
  said,
"Who kissed you through the
  dark, dear guesser?"
Elizabeth Barrett Browning

NONE OTHER LAMB

None other Lamb, none other Name,
None other Hope in heaven or
  earth or sea,
None other Hiding place from guilt
  and shame,
None beside Thee.

My faith burns low, my hope
  burns low
Only my heart's desire cries
  out in me
By the deep thunder of its
  want and woe
Cries out to Thee.

Lord, Thou art Life tho' I
  be dead,
Love's Fire Thou art, however
  cold I be:
Nor heaven have I nor place
  to lay my head,
Nor home, but Thee.
Christina Rossetti

WHEN I CONSIDER THE HEAVENS

O Lord our Lord, how excellent is thy name in all the earth! who hast set thy glory above the heavens.

. . . When I consider thy heavens, the work of thy fingers, the moon and the stars, which thou hast ordained;

What is man, that thou art mindful of him? and the son of man, that thou visitest him?

For thou hast made him a little lower than the angels, thou hast crowned him with glory and honour.

Thou madest him to have dominion over the works of thy hands; thou hast put all things under his feet:

All sheep and oxen, yea, and the beasts of the field;

The fowl of the air, and the fish of the sea, and whatsoever passeth through the paths of the seas. O Lord our Lord, how excellent is thy name in all the earth!
Psalm 8:1,3–9,
King James Version

MY GARDEN

My garden is a lovesome thing,
  God wot!
Rose plot,
Fringed pool,
Fern'd grot—
The veriest school
Of peace; and yet the fool
Contends that God is not—
Not God! in gardens! when
  the eve is cool?
Nay, but I have a sign;
'Tis very sure God walks in
  mine.
    Thomas Edward Brown

HIM EVERMORE I BEHOLD

Him evermore I behold
Walking in Galilee,
Through the cornfield's waving
  gold,
In hamlet or grassy wold,
By the shores of the Beautiful
  Sea.
He toucheth the sightless eyes;
Before Him the demons flee;

To the dead He sayeth: Arise!
To the living: Follow me!
And that voice still soundeth
  on
From the centuries that are
  gone,
To the centuries that shall be!
    Henry Wadsworth Longfellow

HOLY, HOLY, HOLY

Holy, Holy, Holy, Lord God
  Almighty!
Early in the morning our song
  shall rise to Thee;
Holy, Holy, Holy, Merciful
  and Mighty!
God in Three Persons, blessed
  Trinity!
    Reginald Heber

Happiness

DARE TO BE HAPPY

Dare to be happy—
   don't shy away,
Reach out and capture
   the joy of Today!

Life is for living!
   Give it a try;
Open your heart to that
   sun in the sky.

Dare to be loving, and
   trusting, and true;
Treasure the hours with
   those dear to you.

Dare to be kind—it's
   more fun than you know;
Give joy to others, and
   watch your own grow.

Dare to admit all your
   blessings, and then
Every day count them
   all over again.

Dare to be happy,
   don't be afraid—
This is the day which
   the Lord hath made!
     Helen Lowrie Marshall

IT HAIN'T NO USE

It hain't no use to grumble
   and complane;
It's jest as cheap and easy to
   rejoice,—
When God sorts out the weather
   and sends rain,
W'y rain's my choice.
     James Whitcomb Riley

SOLITUDE

Happy the man, whose wish and
   care
A few paternal acres bound,
Content to breathe his native air
In his own ground.

Whose herds with milk, whose
   fields with bread,
Whose flocks supply him with
   attire;
Whose trees in summer, yield
   him shade,
In winter, fire.
     Alexander Pope

CORNERSTONE

I rejoice in my life because
   the lamp still glows;
I seek no thorny ways;
I love the small pleasures of
   life.
If the doors are too low, I
   bend;
If I can remove a stone from
   the path, I do so;
If it is too heavy, I go
   round it.
I find something in every
   day that pleases me.
The cornerstone, my belief
   in God, makes my heart glad
   and my face shining.
     Goethe's Mother

I have learned, in whatsoever state I am, therewith to be content.

     Philippians 4:11,
     King James Version

THE BEST THING IN THE WORLD

What's the best thing in the
    world?
June-rose by May-dew impearled;
Sweet south-wind, that means no
    rain;
Truth, not cruel to a friend;
Pleasure, not in haste to end;
Beauty, not self-decked and
    curled
Till its pride is over-plain;
Light, that never makes you wink;
Memory, that gives no pain;
Love, when, so, you're loved
    again.
What's the best thing in the
    world?
—Something out of it, I think.
                Elizabeth Barrett Browning

WHAT MAKES MEN HAPPY?

To watch the corn grow, or the blossoms set; to
draw hard breath over the ploughshare or
spade; to read, to think, to love, to pray, are the
things that make men happy.

                        John Ruskin

THE SHEPHERD BOY'S SONG

He that is down needs fear no
    fall,
He that is low, no pride;
He that is humble ever shall
Have God to be his guide.

I am content with that I have,
Little be it or much;
And Lord, contentment still I
    crave,
Because Thou savest such.

Fullness to such a burden is
That go on pilgrimage;
Here little, and hereafter
    bliss,
Is best from age to age.
                        John Bunyan

CHARACTER OF A HAPPY LIFE

How happy is he born and
    taught
That serveth not another's
    will;
Whose armor is his honest
    thought
And simple truth his utmost
    skill!

Whose passions not his masters
    are,
Whose soul is still prepared
    for death,
Not tied unto the world with
    care
Of public fame, or private
    breath;

Who envies none that chance doth
    raise,
Or vice; Who never understood
How deepest wounds are given
    by praise;
Nor rules of state, but rules
    of good:

Who hath his life from rumors
    freed,
Whose conscience is his strong
    retreat;
Whose state can neither
    flatterers feed,
Nor ruin make accusers great;

Who God doth late and early
    pray
More of his grace than gifts
    to lend;
And entertains the harmless
    day
With a well-chosen book or
    friend;

This man is freed from servile
    bands
Of hope to rise, or fear to fall;
Lord of himself, though not
    of lands,
And having nothing, yet hath all.
                        Sir Henry Wotton

THESE JOYS ARE MINE

The joy of a rose with its
  sweet perfume
On a lazy summer day.

The blue of the sky as the dawn
  steals through
To welcome a bright new day.

A little child with a
  laughing heart . . .
A hope and a peace supreme.

A hilltop fair with its
  whispering wind
And a valley nestled between.

A friendly smile and a hand-
  clasp warm
A gladness to call my own.

A fireside warm and a happy
  thought
Whenever I'm alone.

A quiet joy that can fill my
  mind
Each night at the long day's
  end.

A thrill complete and a rich
  content
Because I have been a friend.

These joys are mine as I walk
  life's road
Wherever the journey might
  lead.

These are the hope and the faith
  I know,
All that my heart can need.

The richest treasures, the
  brightest dreams
To last throughout all time.

My heart holds a smile and my
  soul is content.
I'm rich, for these joys are
  mine!

Garnett Ann Schultz

A SURE WAY TO A HAPPY DAY

Happiness is something
  we create in our mind,
It's not something you
  search for
And so seldom find—
It's just waking up
  And beginning the day
By counting our blessings
  and kneeling to pray—
It's giving up thoughts
  that breed discontent
And accepting what comes
  as a "gift heaven-sent"—
It's giving up wishing
  for things we have not
And making the best of
  whatever we've got—
It's knowing that life
  is determined for us,
And pursuing our tasks
  without fret, fume or fuss—
For it's by completing
  what God gives us to do
That we find real contentment
  and happiness, too.

Helen Steiner Rice

TO THOSE WHO ARE CONTENT

To those who are content
I lift my song—
To those who are at peace
Where they belong—

Who rise and question not,
Who go their way
Happily from dawn
To close of day;

Who labor and who earn
The bread they eat,
Who find their rest at night
Is deep and sweet;

Who ask no more of life
Than they can give,
Oh, beautifully fine
I think they live;

Who are content to serve,
To love and pray,
Leading their simple lives
From day to day.

Grace Noll Crowell

THE ENCHANTED SHIRT

The King was sick. His cheek
  was red,
And his eye was clear and bright;
He ate and drank with a kingly
  zest,
And peacefully snored at night.

But he said he was sick, and a
  king should know,
And doctors came by the score.
They did not cure him. He cut
  off their heads,
And sent to the schools for more.

At last two famous doctors came,
And one was as poor as a rat,
He had passed his life in
  studious toil,
And never found time to grow
  fat.

The other had never looked in
  a book;
His patients gave him no trouble:
If they recovered, they paid him
  well;
If they died, their heirs paid
  double.

Together they looked at the
  royal tongue,
As the King on his couch re-
  clined;
In succession they thumped his
  august chest,
But no trace of disease could
  find.

The old sage said, "You're as
  sound as a nut."
"Hang him up," roared the King
  in a gale—
In a ten-knot gale of royal
  rage;
The other leech grew a shade
  pale;

But he pensively rubbed his
  sagacious nose,
And thus his prescription ran—
The King will be well, if he
  sleeps one night
In the shirt of a Happy Man.

Wide o'er the realm the
  couriers rode,
And fast their horses ran,
And many they saw, and to many
  they spoke,
But they found no Happy Man.

They found poor men who would
  fain be rich,
And rich who thought they
  were poor;
And men who twisted their
  waist in stays,
And women that shorthose wore.

They saw two men by the road-
  side sit,
And both bemoaned their lot;
For one had buried his wife,
  he said,
And the other one had not.

At last they came to a village gate,
A beggar lay whistling there;
He whistled, and sang, and
  laughed, and rolled
On the grass in the soft June air.

The weary couriers paused and
  looked
At the scamp so blithe and gay;
And one of them said, "Heaven
  save you, friend!
You seem to be happy to-day."

"Oh, yes, fair sirs," the
  rascal laughed,
And his voice rang free and
  glad;
"An idle man has so much to do
That he never has time to be
  sad."

"This is our man," the courier
  said;
"Our luck has led us aright.
I will give you a hundred ducats,
  friend,
For the loan of your shirt tonight."

The merry blackguard lay back
  on the grass,
And laughed till his face was
  black;

"I would do it, God wot," and he
   roared with the fun,
"But I haven't a shirt to my
   back."

Each day to the King the reports
   came in
Of his unsuccessful spies,
And the sad panorama of human
   woes
Passed daily under his eyes.

And he grew ashamed of his useless
   life,
And his maladies hatched in
   gloom;
He opened his windows and let
   the air
Of the free heaven into his
   room.

And out he went in the world, and
   toiled
In his own appointed way;
And the people blessed him,
   the land was glad,
And the King was well and gay.
              John Hay

If I have faltered more or
   less
In my great task of happiness;
If I have moved among my race
And shown no glorious morning
   face;
If beams from happy human eyes
Have moved me not; if morning
   skies,
Books, and my food, and summer
   rain
Knocked on my sullen heart in
   vain—
Lord, Thy most pointed pleasure
   take
And stab my spirit broad awake;
Or, Lord, if too obdurate I,
Choose Thou, before that spirit
   die,
A piercing pain, a killing sin,
And to my dead heart run them
   in!
        Robert Louis Stevenson

YOUR PLACE

Is your place a small place?
Tend it with care;
He set you there.

Is your place a large place?
Guard it with care!
He set you there.

Whate'er your place, it is
Not yours alone, but his
Who set you there.
        John Oxenham

HELP YOURSELF TO HAPPINESS

Everybody, everywhere
   seeks happiness, it's true.
But finding it and keeping it
   seems difficult to do,
Difficult because we think
   that happiness is found
Only in the places where
   wealth and fame abound
And so we go on searching
   in "palaces of pleasure"
Seeking recognition
   and monetary treasure,
Unaware that happiness
   is just a "state of mind"
Within the reach of everyone
   who takes time to be kind
For in making Others Happy
   we will be happy, too,
For the happiness you give away
Returns to "shine on you."

        Helen Steiner Rice

THE PRAYER PERFECT

Dear Lord! Kind Lord!
Gracious Lord! I pray
Thou wilt look on all I love,
Tenderly today!

Weed their hearts of weariness;
Scatter every care
Down a wake of angel-wings
Winnowing the air.

Bring unto the sorrowing
All release from pain;
Let the lips of laughter
Overflow again;
And with all the needy
O divide, I pray,
This vast measure of content
That is mine today!

James Whitcomb Riley

GO THY WAY

Go thy way, eat thy bread with joy, and drink thy wine with a merry heart; for God now accepteth thy works.

Let thy garments be always white; and let thy head lack no ointment.

Live joyfully with the wife whom thou lovest all the days of the life of thy vanity, which he hath given thee under the sun, all the days of thy vanity: for that is thy portion in this life, and in thy labour which thou takest under the sun.

Ecclesiastes 9:7–9,
King James Version

Be happy with that you have and are, be generous with both, and you won't have to hurt for happiness.

William Gladstone

GOD'S MEDICINE

Mirth is God's medicine. Everybody ought to bathe in it. Grim care, moroseness, anxiety—all this rust of life ought to be scoured off by the oil of mirth. It is better than emery. Every man ought to rub himself with it. A man without mirth is like a wagon without springs, in which everyone is caused disagreeably to jolt by every pebble over which it runs.

Henry Ward Beecher

THE COMPLEAT ANGLER

Oh, the gallant fisher's life!
It is the best of any;
'Tis full of pleasure, void of
strife,
And 'tis beloved by many.

Izaak Walton

Cheerfulness and content are great beautifiers and are famous preservers of youthful looks.

Charles Dickens

It is not fitting, when one is in God's service, to have a gloomy face or a chilling look.

St. Francis of Assisi

People are always good company when they are doing what they really enjoy.

Samuel Butler

Work

THE SOLITARY REAPER

Behold her, single in the
    field,
Yon solitary Highland Lass!
Reaping and singing by herself;
Stop here, or gently pass!
Alone she cuts and binds the
    grain,
And sings a melancholy strain;
O listen! for the Vale pro-
    found
Is overflowing with the sound.

Will no one tell me what she
    sings?
Perhaps the plaintive numbers
    flow
For old, unhappy, far-off
    things,
And battles long ago:
Or is it some more humble
    lay,
Familiar matter of to-day?
Some natural sorrow, loss, or
    pain,
That has been, and may be again?

Whate'er the theme, the Maiden
    sang
As if her song could have no
    ending;
I saw her singing at her work,
And o'er the sickle bending:—
I listened, motionless and
    still;
And, as I mounted up the hill,
The music in my heart I bore,
Long after it was heard no
    more.

          William Wordsworth

Work is love made visible.

          Kahlil Gibran

TOM SAWYER AT WORK

Tom appeared on the sidewalk with a bucket of whitewash and a long-handled brush. He surveyed the fence, and all gladness left him and a deep melancholy settled down on his spirit. Thirty yards of broad fence nine feet high. Life to him seemed hollow, and existence but a burden. Sighing he dipped his brush and passed it along the topmost plank; repeated the operation; did it again; compared the insignificant whitewashed streak with the far-reaching continent of unwhitewashed fence, and sat down on a tree-box discouraged. Jim came skipping out at the gate with a tin pail, and singing "Buffalo Gals." Bringing water from the town pump had always been hateful work in Tom's eyes, before, but now it did not strike him so. He remembered that there was company at the pump. White, mulatto, and Negro boys and girls were always there waiting their turns, resting, trading playthings, quarreling, fighting, skylarking. And he remembered that although the pump was only a hundred and fifty yards off, Jim never got back with a bucket of water under an hour—and even then somebody generally had to go after him.

. . . Tom's energy did not last. He began to think of the fun he had planned for this day, and his sorrows multiplied. Soon the free boys would come tripping along on all sorts of delicious expeditions, and they would make a world of fun of him for having to work—the very thought of it burnt him like fire. He got out his worldly wealth and examined it—bits of toys, marbles, and trash; enough to buy an exchange of *work*, maybe, but not half enough to buy so much as half an hour of pure freedom. So he returned his straitened means to his pocket, and gave up the idea of trying to buy the boys. At this dark and hopeless moment an inspiration burst upon him! Nothing less than a great, magnificent inspiration.

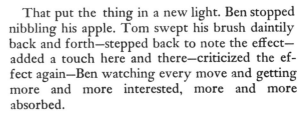

He took up his brush and went tranquilly to work. Ben Rogers hove in sight presently—the very boy, of all boys, whose ridicule he had been dreading. Ben's gait was the hop-skip and jump—proof enough that his heart was light and his anticipations high. He was eating an apple, and giving a long, melodious whoop, at intervals, followed by a deep-toned ding-dong-dong, ding, dong—dong, for he was personating a steamboat. As he drew near, he slackened speed, took the middle of the street, leaned far over to the starboard and rounded to ponderously and with laborious pomp and circumstance—for he was personating the *Big Missouri*, and considered himself to be drawing nine feet of water. He was boat and captain and engine bells combined, so he had to imagine himself standing on his own hurricane deck giving the orders and executing them:

. . . Tom went on whitewashing—paid no attention to the steamboat. Ben stared a moment and then said:

"Hi-yi! You're up a stump, ain't you!"

No answer. Tom surveyed his last touch with the eye of an artist, then he gave his brush another gentle sweep and surveyed the result, as before. Ben ranged up alongside of him. Tom's mouth watered for the apple, but he stuck to his work. Ben said:

"Hello, old chap, you got to work, hey?"

Tom wheeled suddenly and said:

"Why it's you, Ben! I warn't noticing."

"Say—I'm going in a-swimming, I am. Don't you wish you could? But of course you'd druther *work*—wouldn't you? Course you would!"

Tom contemplated the boy a bit, and said:

"What do you call work?"

"Why ain't *that* work?"

Tom resumed his whitewashing, and answered carelessly:

"Well, maybe it is, and maybe it ain't. All I know is, it suits Tom Sawyer."

"Oh come, now, you don't mean to let on that you *like* it?"

The brush continued to move.

"Like it? Well, I don't see why I oughtn't to like it. Does a boy get a chance to whitewash a fence every day?"

That put the thing in a new light. Ben stopped nibbling his apple. Tom swept his brush daintily back and forth—stepped back to note the effect—added a touch here and there—criticized the effect again—Ben watching every move and getting more and more interested, more and more absorbed.

Presently he said:

"Say, Tom, let *me* whitewash a little."

Tom considered, was about to consent; but he altered his mind:

"No—no—I reckon it wouldn't hardly do, Ben. You see, Aunt Polly's awful particular about this fence—right here on the street, you know—but if it was the back fence I wouldn't mind and *she* wouldn't. Yes, she's awful particular about this fence; it's got to be done very careful; I reckon there ain't one boy in a thousand, maybe two thousand, that can do it the way it's got to be done."

"No—is that so? Oh come, now—lemme just try. Only just a little—I'd let *you*, if you was me, Tom."

"Ben, I'd like to, honest injun; but Aunt Polly—well, Jim wanted to do it, but she wouldn't let him; Sid wanted to do it, and she wouldn't let Sid. Now don't you see how I'm fixed? If you was to tackle this fence and anything was to happen to it—"

"Oh shucks, I'll be just as careful. Now let me try. Say—I'll give you the core of my apple."

"Well, here—No, Ben, now don't. I'm afeard—"

"I'll give you *all* of it!"

Tom gave up the brush with reluctance in his face, but alacrity in his heart. And while the late steamer *Big Missouri* worked and sweated in the sun, the retired artist sat on a barrel in the shade close by, dangled his legs, munched his apple, and planned the slaughter of more innocents. There was no lack of material; boys happened along every little while; they came to jeer, but remained to whitewash. By the time Ben was fagged out, Tom had traded the next chance to Billy Fisher for a kite, in good repair; and when *he* played out, Johnny Miller bought in for a dead rat and a string to swing it with—and so on, and so on, hour after hour. And when the middle of the afternoon came, from being a poor poverty-stricken boy in the morning, Tom was literally rolling in wealth. He had be-

sides the things before mentioned, twelve marbles, part of a jew's harp, a piece of blue bottle glass to look through, a spool cannon, a key that wouldn't unlock anything, a fragment of chalk, a glass stopper of a decanter, a tin soldier, a couple of tadpoles, six firecrackers, a kitten with only one eye, a brass doorknob, a dog collar—but no dog—the handle of a knife, four pieces of orange peel, and a dilapidated old window sash.

He had a nice, good, idle time all the while—plenty of company—and the fence had three coats of whitewash on it! If he hadn't run out of whitewash he would have bankrupted every boy in the village.

Tom said to himself that it was not such a hollow world, after all. He had discovered a great law of human action, without knowing it—namely, that in order to make a man or a boy covet a thing, it is only necessary to make the thing difficult to attain. If he had been a great and wise philosopher, . . . he would now have comprehended that Work consists of whatever a body is *obliged* to do and that Play consists of whatever a body is not obliged to do.

(From *Tom Sawyer*)
Mark Twain

RESULTS AND ROSES

The man who wants a garden fair,
  Or small or very big,
With flowers growing here and
  there,
Must bend his back and dig.

The things are mighty few on
  earth
That wishes can attain.
Whate'er we want of any worth
  We've got to work to gain.

It matters not what goal you
  seek
Its secret here reposes:
You've got to dig from week to
  week
To get Results or Roses.
        Edgar Guest

Rest

I NEEDED THE QUIET

I needed the quiet so He drew
   me aside.
Into the shadows where we
   could confide.
Away from the bustle where all
   the day long
I hurried and worried when
   active and strong.

I needed the quiet tho at
   first I rebelled
But gently, so gently, my cross
   He upheld
And whispered so sweetly of
   spiritual things
Tho weakened in body, my
   spirit took wings
To heights never dreamed of
   when active and gay.
He loved me so greatly He drew
   me away.

I needed the quiet. No prison
   my bed,
But a beautiful valley of
   blessings instead—
A place to grow richer in
   Jesus to hide.
I needed the quiet so He
   drew me aside.
      Alice Hansche Mortenson

Every now and then go away, have a little
relaxation, for when you come back to your
work your judgment will be surer; since to re-
main constantly at work will cause you to lose
power of judgment.
      Leonardo Da Vinci

TRUE REST

Rest is not quitting
The busy career;
Rest is the fitting
Of self to one's sphere.

'Tis the brook's motion
Clear without strife,
Fleeting to ocean,
After this life.

'Tis loving and serving,
The highest and best;
'Tis onward, unswerving,
And this is true rest.
      Johann Wolfgang von Goethe

Something attempted, something done, has earned
a night's repose.
      Henry Wadsworth Longfellow

PRAYER

Calm soul of all things! make
   it mine
To feel, amid the city's jar,
That there abides a peace of
   thine,
Man did not make, and cannot
   mar!

The will to neither strive nor
   cry,
The power to feel with others
   give!
Calm, calm me more! nor let me
   die
Before I have begun to live.
      Matthew Arnold

TO MY SISTER

It is the first mild day of
    March:
Each minute sweeter than before
The redbreast sings from the
    tall larch
That stands beside our door.

There is a blessing in the air,
Which seems a sense of joy to
    yield
To the bare trees, and mountains
    bare,
And grass in the green field.

My sister! ('tis a wish of mine)
Now that our morning meal is
    done,
Make haste, your morning task
    resign;
Come forth and feel the sun.

Edward will come with you;—
    and, pray,
Put on with speed your woodland
    dress;
And bring no book: for this
    one day
We'll give to idleness.

No joyless forms shall regulate
Our living calendar:
We from to-day, my Friend,
    will date
The opening of the year.

Love, now a universal birth,
From heart to heart is
    stealing,
From earth to man, from man
    to earth:
—It is the hour of feeling.

One moment now may give us
    more
Than years of toiling reason:
Our minds shall drink at every
    pore
The spirit of the season.

Some silent laws our hearts
    will make,
Which they shall long obey:

We for the year to come may
    take
Our temper from to-day.

And from the blessed power
    that rolls
About, below, above,
We'll frame the measure of our
    souls:
They shall be tuned to love.

Then come, my Sister! come,
    I pray,
With speed put on your wood-
    land dress;
And bring no book: for this
    one day
We'll give to idleness.
                William Wordsworth

THE WISE REST

Nature never makes haste; her systems revolve
at an even pace. The bud swells impercepti-
bly, without hurry or confusion, as though the
short spring days were an eternity. All her op-
erations seem separately, for the time, the single
object for which all things tarry. Why, then,
should man hasten as if anything less than eternity were allotted for the least deed. Let him
consume ever so many eons, so that he go about
the meanest task well, though it be but the par-
ing of his nails. If the setting sun seems to hurry
him to improve the day while it lasts, the chant
of the crickets fails not to reassure him, even-
measured as of old, teaching him to take his own
time henceforth forever. This wise man is rest-
ful, never restless or impatient. He each moment abides there where he is, as some walk-
ers actually rest the whole body at each step,
while others never relax the muscles of the leg
till the accumulated fatigue obliges them to stop
short.

As the wise is not anxious that time wait for
him, neither does he wait for it.
                Henry David Thoreau

Brotherhood

ELEMENTS OF MAN

My soul preached to me and showed me that I am neither more than the pygmy, nor less than the giant.

Ere my soul preached to me, I looked upon humanity as two men: one weak, whom I pitied, and the other strong, whom I followed or resisted in defiance.

But now I have learned that I was as both are and made from the same elements. My origin is their origin, my conscience is their conscience, my contention is their contention, and my pilgrimage is their pilgrimage.

If they sin, I am also a sinner. If they do well, I take pride in their well-doing. If they rise, I rise with them. If they stay inert, I share their slothfulness.

Kahlil Gibran

He that hath no brother hath weak legs.
Persian Proverb

A FATHER AND HIS SONS

A very honest man happened to have a contentious brood of children. He called for a rod, and bade them try one after another, with all their force, if they could break it. They tried, and could not. Well, says he, unbind it now, and take every twig of it apart, and see what you can do that way. They did so, and with great ease, by one and one, they snapped it all to pieces. This, says he, is the true emblem of your condition: keep together, and you are safe; divide, and you are undone.

Aesop

DESTINIES

Like warp and woof all destinies
Are woven fast,
Link'd in sympathy like the
keys of an organ vast;
Pluck one thread, and the web
ye mar;
Break but one
Of a thousand keys, and the
paining jar
Through all will run.
John Greenleaf Whittier

He who serves his brother
best
Gets nearer God than all the
rest.
Alexander Pope

All your strength is in your
union;
All your danger in discord;
Therefore be at peace henceforward
And as brothers live together.
Henry Wadsworth Longfellow

A hundred times every day I remind myself that my inner and outer life depend on the labors of other men, living and dead, and that I must exert myself in order to give in the same measure as I have received and am still receiving.
Albert Einstein

OPEN THE DOOR OF YOUR HEART

Open the door of your heart,
   my friend,
Heedless of class or creed,
When you hear the cry of a
   brother's voice,
The sob of a child in need.

To the shining heavens that
   o'er you bend
You need no map or chart,
But only the love the Master
   gave:
Open the door of your heart.
   Edward Everett Hale

HE'S YOUR BROTHER

And when with grief you see
   your brother stray,
Or in a night of error lose
   his way,
Direct his wandering and
   restore the day . . .
Leave to avenging Heaven
   his stubborn will.
For, O, remember, he's
   your brother still.
   Jonathan Swift

PRAYER

Teach me to feel another's woe,
   To hide the fault I see;
That mercy I to others show,
   That mercy show to me.
   Alexander Pope

If any life of mine may ease
   The burden of another,
God give me love and care and
   strength
To help my ailing brother.
   Anonymous

Give us, Lord, a chance to be
Our goodly best, brave, wise
   and free,
Our goodly best for ourselves
   and others,
Till all men learn to live as
   brothers.
   From an Old English Inn

ABOU BEN ADHEM

Abou Ben Adhem (may his tribe
   increase!)
Awoke one night from a deep
   dream of peace,
And saw within the moonlight
   in his room,
Making it rich, and like a
   lily in bloom,
An angel, writing in a book of
   gold;
Exceeding peace had made Ben
   Adhem bold,
And to the presence in the
   room he said,
"What writest thou?"—The
   vision raised his head,
And with a look made of all
   sweet accord,
Answer'd, "The names of those
   who love the Lord."
"And is mine one?" said Abou.
   "Nay, not so,"
Replied the angel. Abou spoke
   more low,
But cheerily still; and said,
   "I pray thee, then,
Write me as one that loves
   his fellowmen."
The angel wrote and vanish'd.
   The next night
It came again, with a great
   wakening light,
And show'd the names whom love
   of God had bless'd,
And, lo! Ben Adhem's name
   led all the rest.
   Leigh Hunt

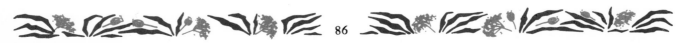

BRETHREN

The true Christian will recognize his brethren not necessarily in the Church or sect to which he belongs, but in all who live humbly, purely, and lovingly, in dependence on the Great Father of all living.

Arthur Christopher Benson

Study to be patient in bearing the defects of others and their infirmities be what they may: for thou hast many things which he must bear withal.

Thomas à Kempis

WHERE TO SEEK LOVE

I thought Love lived in the hot
    sunshine,
But O he lives in the moony
    light!
I thought to find Love in the
    heat of day,
But sweet Love is the comforter
    of night.

Seek Love in the pity of others'
    woe,
In the gentle relief of another's
    care,
In the darkness of night and the
    winter's snow,
In the naked and outcast, seek
    Love there.

William Blake

NO MAN IS AN ISLAND

No man is an island entire of itself: every man is a piece of the continent, a part of the main. If a clod be washed away by the sea, Europe is the less, as well as if a promontory were, as well as if a manor of thy friend's or of thine own were. Any man's death diminishes me, because I am involved in mankind. Therefore never send to know for whom the bell tolls. It tolls for thee.

John Donne

We must love men ere they will seem to us worthy of our love.

William Shakespeare

THE SWEETEST LIVES

The sweetest lives are those
    to duty wed,
Whose deeds, both great and
    small,
Are close-knit strands of un-
    broken thread
Where love ennobles all.
The world may sound no trumpets,
    ring no bells;
The book of life the shining
    record tells.

The love shall chant its own
    beatitudes
After its own life working.
A child's kiss
Set on thy sighing lips shall
    make thee glad;
A sick man helped by thee shall
    make thee strong;
Thou shalt be served thyself
    by every sense
Of service which thou renderest.
Elizabeth Barrett Browning

Be not disturbed at being misunderstood; be disturbed rather at not being understanding.

Chinese Proverb

You can't hold a man down without staying down with him.

Booker T. Washington

We must not only affirm the brotherhood of man; we must live it.

Henry Codman Potter

A BROTHER

For never man had a more faithful, loving, sincere servant than Friday was to me; without passions, sullenness, or designs, perfectly obliged and engaged; his very affections were tied to me, like those of a child to a father; and I dare say he would have sacrificed his life for the saving mine upon any occasion whatsoever; the many testimonies he gave me of this put it out of doubt and soon convinced me that I needed to use no precautions as to my safety on his account.

This frequently gave me occasion to observe, and that with wonder, that however it had pleased God, in His Providence, and in the government of the works of His hands, to take from so great a part of the world of His creatures the best uses to which their faculties and the powers of their souls are adapted; yet that He has bestowed upon them the same powers, the same reason, the same affections, the same sentiments of kindness and obligation, the same passions and resentments of wrongs, the same sense of gratitude, sincerity, fidelity, and all the capacities of doing good and receiving good that He has given to us; and that when He pleases to offer to them occasions of exerting these, they are as ready, nay, more ready to apply them to the right uses for which they were bestowed than we are. And this made me very melancholy sometimes, in reflecting, as the several occasions presented, how mean a use we make of all these, even though we have these powers enlightened by the great lamp of instruction, the Spirit of God, and by the knowledge of His Word, added to our understanding; and why it has pleased God to hide the like saving knowledge from so many millions of souls, who (if I might judge by this poor savage) would make a much better use of it than we did.

(From *Robinson Crusoe*)
Daniel DeFoe

Little friends may prove great friends.

Aesop

It is never too late to give up your prejudices.
Henry David Thoreau

Ay, we must all hang together, else we shall all hang separately.

Benjamin Franklin

THE ALMIGHTY WILL

The child, the seed, the grain
   of corn,
The acorn on the hill,
Each for some separate end is
   born
In season fit, and still
Each must in strength arise to
   work
The Almighty Will.
   Robert Louis Stevenson

Home

SONG

Stay, stay at home, my heart
  and rest;
Home-keeping hearts are happiest,
For those that wander they know
  not where
Are full of trouble and full
  of care;
To stay at home is best.

Weary and homesick and distressed,
They wander east, they wander
  west,
And are baffled and beaten and
  blown about
By the winds of the wilderness
  of doubt;
To stay at home is best.

Then stay at home, my heart,
  and rest;
The bird is safest in its nest,
Over all that flutter their
  wings and fly
A hawk is hovering in the sky;
To stay at home is best.
Henry Wadsworth Longfellow

Home is where the heart is.

Pliny the Elder

A house is built of logs and
  stone,
Of tiles and posts and piers;
A home is built of loving deeds
That stand a thousand years.
Victor Hugo

SITTIN' ON THE PORCH

Sittin' on the porch at night
  when all the tasks are done,
Just restin' there and talkin',
  with my easy slippers on,
An' my shirt band thrown wide
  open an' my feet upon the rail,
Oh, it's then I'm at my richest,
  with a wealth that cannot fail;
For the scent of early roses
  seems to flood the evening air,
An' a throne of downright
  gladness is my wicker rocking
  chair.

The dog asleep beside me, an'
  the children rompin' round,
With their shrieks of merry
  laughter, oh, there is no
  gladder sound
To the ears o' weary mortals
  spite of all the scoffers say,
Or a grander bit of music than
  the children at their play!
An' I tell myself times over,
  when I'm sittin' there at night,
That the world in which I'm
  livin' is a place o' real delight.

Then the moon begins its climbin'
  an' stars shine overhead,
An' the mother calls the children
  an' she takes 'em up to bed,
An' I smoke my pipe in silence
  an' I think o' many things,
An' balance up my riches with
  the lonesomeness o' kings,
An' I come to this conclusion,
  an' I'll wager that I'm right—
That I'm happier than they are
  sittin' on my porch at night.
Edgar Guest

WHEN MAMA CRIED

I do not believe in letting homesickness take over, when we have to make radical changes in our lives. There is no use crying over spilt milk, Mama used to say firmly. And when she said it, it was not a cliché but a pronouncement. Raised in New England, she managed to rush all over the country and live in Mexico besides while Father whipped about on his mining engineering jobs. I never heard her utter one word of complaint. If we holed up in a shack or in an adobe hut, she set packing boxes up and somehow made a home. Nobody ever had to feel sorry for her. But now, looking back, I can see that there were times when she read and re-read letters from home. But she always made any place seem gay. If we had to live out of suitcases, she made little chests of them, covered with cretonne or frills of leftover material from dresses she stitched up.

Even during the desperate days when Father vanished into Mexico and we were stranded in Texas in a boardinghouse and no letters or money came in, she made a good life for me. I have the happiest memories of that time when the landlady began to think Mama had no husband at all and was about to turn us out! It was a respectable boardinghouse, she said, and I had no idea what that meant. Mama took me on walks and we looked at everything. We ate sandwiches and had a picnic. She was too proud to write back to New England to the family for help, for this would diminish Father's stature. She simply kept me happy, and waited.

When he finally turned up, having been held up in the mountains of Mexico, I thought it strange that Mama cried. But all I heard her say was "Rufus, I am so thankful you are back, and safe."

I guess Father was pretty lucky.

He was weathered and wore a sombrero and swept me up in his arms and laughed. Paid the bill, charmed the landlady. I ate myself sick on the meals we had then. It was a special Christmas out of season with presents and Father singing funny Spanish songs while Mama mended his clothes and packed for a return to what was called "home."

Very often, I think, people are homesick for the past instead of for a place. Or simply for a different way of life than the one they are currently leading. No matter where childhood is spent or how much difficulty growing up has involved, it is easy later on to think of it as an eternal meadow filled with flowers. Surely birds sang daylong and air was always honeysuckle-sweet. In the same way when people move from East to West or West to East or South to North or North to South, the country left behind glows in the memory with a light never seen on any land.

Gladys Taber

ALLEGIANCE

God gave all men all earth to
     love,
But since our hearts are small,
Ordained for each one spot
     should prove
Beloved over all.
Rudyard Kipling

Nature

PART OF NATURE

We must go out and re-ally ourselves to Nature every day. We must make root, send out some little fibre at least, even every winter day. I am sensible that I am imbibing health when I open my mouth to the wind. Staying in this house is in this sense a hospital. A night and a forenoon is as much confident to those wards as I can stand. I am aware that I recover some sanity which I had lost the instant that I come abroad.

Henry David Thoreau

Nature, to be commanded, must be obeyed.

Francis Bacon

THE HEART OF THE TREE

What does he plant who plants
a tree?
He plants the friend of sun
and sky;
He plants the flag of breezes
free;
The shaft of beauty towering
high.

Henry C. Bunner

BUSY LITTLE BEE

How doth the busy little bee
Improve each shining hour,
And gather honey all the day
From every opening flower!

Isaac Watts

GOD'S GARDEN

The kiss of the sun for pardon,
The song of the birds for mirth,
One is nearer God's Heart in
a garden
Than anywhere else on earth.

Dorothy F. Gurney

ON WALDEN POND

I sit in my boat on Walden, playing the flute this evening, and see the perch, which I seem to have charmed, hovering around me, and the moon traveling over the bottom, which is strewn with the wrecks of the forest, and feel that nothing but the wildest imagination can conceive of the manner of life we are living. Nature is a wizard. The Concord nights are stranger than the Arabian nights.

Henry David Thoreau

THE MANUSCRIPTS OF GOD

And nature, the old nurse, took
The child upon the knee,
Saying, "Here is a story book
My father hath writ for thee.
Come, wander with me," she said,
"In regions yet untrod
And read what is still unread
In the manuscripts of God."

Henry Wadsworth Longfellow

NATURE REACHES OUT

Nature reaches out to us with welcoming arms,
and bids us enjoy her beauty; but we dread her
silence and rush into the crowded cities, there to
huddle like sheep fleeing from a ferocious wolf.
Kahlil Gibran

WHEN I HEARD
THE LEARN'D ASTRONOMER

When I heard the learn'd astron-
    omer;
When the proofs, the figures,
    were ranged in columns
    before me;
When I was shown the charts
    and diagrams, to add, divide,
    and measure them;
When I, sitting, heard the as-
    tronomer where he lectured
    with much applause in the
    lecture-room,
How soon, unaccountable, I became
    tired and sick;
Till rising and gliding out, I
    wander'd off by myself,
In the mystical moist night
    air, and from time to time,
Look'd up in perfect silence
    at the stars.
Walt Whitman

NOTHING GOLD CAN STAY

Nature's first green is gold,
Her hardest hue to hold.
Her early leaf's a flower;
But only so an hour.
Then leaf subsides to leaf.
So Eden sank to grief,
So dawn goes down to day.
Nothing gold can stay.
Robert Frost

THE FOREST PRIMEVAL

This is the forest primeval.
The murmuring pines and the
    hemlocks,
Bearded with moss, and in
    garments green, indistinct in
    the twilight,
Stand like Druids of eld,
    with voices sad and prophetic,
Stand like harpers hoar, with
    beards that rest on their
    bosoms.
Loud from its rocky caverns,
    the deep-voiced neighboring
    ocean
Speaks, and in accents dis-
    consolate answers the wail
    of the forest.
(From *Evangeline*)
Henry Wadsworth Longfellow

BY THE STREAM

I know a bank where the wild
    thyme blows,
Where oxslips and the nodding
    violet grows,
Quite over-canopied with lus-
    cious woodbine,
With sweet musk-roses and with
    eglantine.
William Shakespeare

Beauty seen is never lost,
God's colors all are fast;
The glory of this sunset heaven
Into my soul has passed.
Alfred, Lord Tennyson

THE HANDIWORK OF GOD

I believe in the brook as it
    wanders
From hillside into glade;
I believe in the breeze as it
    whispers
When evening's shadows fade.
I believe in the roar of the
    river
As it dashes from high cascade
I believe in the cry of the
    tempest
'Mid the thunder cannonade.
I believe in the light of
    shining stars,
I believe in the sun and the
    moon;
I believe in the flash of
    lightning,
I believe in the night-bird's
    croon.
I believe in the faith of the
    flowers,
I believe in the rock and sod,
For in all of these appeareth
    clear
The handiwork of God.
Author Unknown

THE OCEAN

And I have loved thee, Ocean!
    and my joy
Of youthful sports was on thy
    breast to be
Borne, like thy bubbles, on-
    ward: from a boy
I wanton'd with thy breakers—
    they to me
Were a delight; and if the
    freshening sea
Made them a terror—'twas a
    pleasing fear,
For I was as it were a child
    of thee,
And trusted to thy billows
    far and near,
And laid my hand upon thy
    mane—as I do here.
George Gordon, Lord Byron

All art is but imitation of nature.
Seneca

UNDER THE GREENWOOD TREE

Under the greenwood tree
Who loves to lie with me,
And turn his merry note,
Unto the sweet bird's throat,
Come hither, come hither, come
    hither!
Here shall he see
No enemy
But winter and rough weather.

Who doth ambition shun
And loves to live i' the sun,
Seeking the food he eats
And pleased with what he gets—
Come hither, come hither, come
    hither!
Here shall he see
No enemy
But winter and rough weather.
William Shakespeare

THE SPIDER

The spider holds a silver ball
In unperceived hands
And dancing softly to himself
His yarn of pearl unwinds.
Emily Dickinson

WOODLANDS

There is a serene and settled majesty to woodland scenery that enters into the soul and delights and elevates it, and fills it with noble
inclinations.

Washington Irving

TO A BUTTERFLY

I've watched you now a full
      half-hour,
Self-poised upon that yellow
      flower;
And, little Butterfly! indeed
I know not if you sleep or
      feed.
How motionless!—not frozen
      seas
More motionless! and then
What joy awaits you, when the
      breeze
Hath found you out among the
      trees,
And calls you forth again!

This plot of orchard-ground is
      ours;
My trees they are, my Sister's
      flowers;
Here rest your wings when they
      are weary;
Here lodge as in a sanctuary!
Come often to us, fear no wrong;
Sit near us on the bough!
We'll talk of sunshine and of
      song,
And summer days, when we were
      young;
Sweet childish days, that were
      as long
As twenty days are now.
            William Wordsworth

FROM WHERE I STAND

The tree which moves some to tears of joy is
in the eyes of others only a green thing which
stands in the way. Some see Nature all ridicule
and deformity, and by these I shall not regulate
my proportions; and some scarce see Nature at
all. But to the eyes of a man of imagination,
Nature is Imagination itself. As a man is, so he
sees.

            William Blake

OUT IN THE FIELDS WITH GOD

The little cares that fretted me,
I lost them yesterday,
Among the fields above the sea,
Among the winds at play,
Among the lowing of the herds,
The rustling of the trees,
Among the singing of the birds,
The humming of the bees.

The foolish fears of what might
      pass
I cast them all away
Among the clover-scented grass
Among the new-mown hay,
Among the rustling of the
      corn
Where drowsy poppies nod.
Where ill thoughts die and
      good are born—
Out in the fields with God!
      Elizabeth Barrett Browning

One touch of nature makes the whole world kin.
            William Shakespeare

Nature is the living, visible garment of God.
            Johann Wolfgang von Goethe

MUSIC OF THE SPHERES

There's music in the sighing
      of a reed;
There's music in the gushing
      of a rill;
There's music in all things,
      if men had ears;
The earth is but the music of
      the spheres.
      George Gordon, Lord Byron

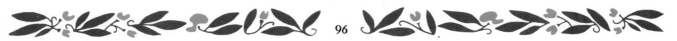

THE BROOK

I come from haunts of coot and
    hern,
I make a sudden sally
And sparkle out among the fern,
To bicker down a valley.

By thirty hills I hurry down,
Or slip between the ridges,
By twenty thorps, a little
    town,
And half a hundred bridges.

Till last by Philip's farm I
    flow
To join the brimming river,
For men may come and men may
    go,
But I go on forever.

I chatter over stony ways,
In little sharps and trebles,
I bubble into eddying bays,
I babble on the pebbles.

With many a curve my banks I
    fret
By many a field and fallow,
And many a fairy foreland set
With willow-weed and mallow.

I chatter, chatter, as I flow
To join the brimming river,
For men may come and men may
    go,
But I go on forever.
        Alfred, Lord Tennyson

He who plants a tree plants hope.
        Lucy Larcom

God almighty first planted a garden. And, indeed, it is the purest of human pleasures.
        Francis Bacon

IN LOVE WITH THIS WORLD

The longer I live the more my mind dwells upon the beauty and wonder of the world. . . .

I have loved the feel of the grass under my feet, and the sound of the running streams by my side. The hum of the wind in the treetops has always been good music to me, and the face of the fields has often comforted me more than the faces of men.

I am in love with this world. . . . I have tilled its soil, I have gathered its harvests, I have waited upon its seasons, and always have I reaped what I have sown.

I have climbed its mountains, roamed its forests, sailed its waters, crossed its deserts, felt the sting of its frosts, the oppression of its heats, the drench of its rains, the fury of its winds, and always have beauty and joy waited upon my goings and comings.
        John Burroughs

GOD'S WORLD

O world, I cannot hold thee
    close enough!
Thy winds, thy wide gray
    skies!
Thy mists, that roll and rise!
Thy woods, this autumn day,
    that ache and sag
And all but cry with color!
    That gaunt crag
To crush! To lift the lean
    of that black bluff!
World, world! I cannot get
    thee close enough!

Long have I known a glory in
    it all
But never knew I this,
Here such a passion is
As stretcheth me apart. Lord,
    I do fear
Thou'st made the world too
    beautiful this year.
My soul is all but out of me—
    let fall
No burning leaf; prithee, let
    no bird call.
        Edna St. Vincent Millay

A LOVELY MORNING

By the shore of Gitche Gumee,
By the shining Big-Sea Water,
At the doorway of his wigwam,
In the pleasant summer morning,
Hiawatha stood and waited.
All the air was full of
  freshness,
All the earth was bright and
  joyous,
And before him, through
  the sunshine,
Westward toward the neighbor-
  ing forest
Passed in golden swarms the
  Ahmo,
Passed the bees, the honey-
  makers,
Burning, singing in the sun-
  shine.
Bright above him shone the
  heavens,
Level spread the lake before
  him;
From its bosom leaped the
  sturgeon,
Sparkling, flashing in the
  sunshine;
On its margin the great
  forest
Stood reflected in the water,
Every tree-top had its
  shadow,
Motionless beneath the water.
                (From *Hiawatha*)
Henry Wadsworth Longfellow

NO MAN IS POOR

What riches are ours in the world of nature, from the majesty of a distant peak to the fragile beauty of a tiny flower, and all without cost to us, the beholders! No man is poor who has watched a sunrise or who keeps a mountain in his heart.

Esther Baldwin York

THE DANCING CRANES

Jody stood a moment to watch his father make an expert cast across the pond. He marveled at the skill of the knotted hands. The bob lay at the edge of a cluster of lily pads. Penny began to jerk it slowly across the water. It dipped and bobbed with the irregular rhythm of a live insect. There was no strike and Penny drew in his line and cast again in the same place. He called to an invisible fish, lurking near the weedy bottom.

"Now Grandpappy, I kin see you settin' there on your stoop." He jerked the bob more slowly. "You better lay down your pipe and come git your dinner."

Jody tore himself from the fascination of his father's performance and moved to his end of the pond. He cast badly for a time, tangling his line and laying his bob in the most unlikely places; over-reaching the narrow pond and en-meshing the hook in the tough saw-grass. Then something of harmony came to him. He felt his arm swing in a satisfying arc. His wrist flexed at the proper moment. He laid the bob exactly where he had meant to, at the edge of a patch of switch-grass.

Penny called, "Mighty nice, son. Leave it lay jest a minute. Then git ready the first second you jerk it."

He had not known his father was watching. He was tense. He jerked his pole cautiously and the bob flipped across the water. There was a swirl, a silver form shot half clear of the water, an open mouth as big as a cook-pot enveloped the bob.

A weight like a millstone dropped at the end of his line, fought like a wildcat, and pulled him off-balance. He braced himself against the frenzy to which he was irrevocably attached.

Penny called, "Take it easy. Don't let him git under them bonnets. Keep the tip o' your pole up. Don't give him no slack."

Penny left him to the struggle. His arms ached from the strain. He was afraid to tug too hard for fear of breaking the line. He dared not yield an inch for fear a sudden slackness would tell of the loss of the giant. He longed for magic words from his father, indicating some miracle by which he might land his fish and be done with the torment. The bass was sulking. It made a dash for the grasses, where it might tangle the line around their stems and so rip free. It came to Jody that if he walked around the edge of the pond, keeping a taut line, he might lead the bass into shallow water and flounder him at the edge. He worked cautiously. He was tempted to drop the pole and clutch the line itself and come to grips with his adversary. He began to walk away from the pond. He gave his pole a heave and landed the bass, flouncing, in the grass. He dropped the pole and ran, to move the catch to a final safety. The bass would weigh ten pounds. Penny came to him.

"Boy, I'm proud of you. Nobody couldn't of handled him better."

Jody stood panting. Penny thumped him on the back, as excited as he. He looked down, unbelieving, at the stout form and the great maw.

"I feel as good as if 'twas ol' Slewfoot," he said, and they grinned together and pummeled each other's backs.

"Now I got to go beat you," Penny said.

They took separate ponds. Penny called that he was licked and beaten. He began fishing for Ma Baxter's bream with a hand-line and bonnet worms. Jody cast and cast again, but there was never the mad swirl of waters, the great leap, the live and struggling weight. He caught a small bass and held it up to show his father.

"Throw him back," Penny called. "We don't need him for eatin'. Leave him to grow up big as t'other one. Then we'll come back again and ketch him."

Jody put the small fish back reluctantly and watched it swim away. His father was stern about not taking more of anything, fish or game, than could be eaten or kept. Hope of another monster dwindled as the sun finished its spring arc of the daylight sky. He cast leisurely, taking his pleasure in his increasing dexterity of arm and wrist. The moon was now wrong. It was no longer feed-time. The fish were not striking. Suddenly he heard his father whistle like a quail. It was the signal they used together in squirrel hunting. Jody laid down his pole and looked back to make sure he could identify the tuft of grass where he had covered his bass from the rays of the sun. He walked cautiously to where his father beckoned.

Penny whispered, "Foller me. We'll ease up clost as we dare."

He pointed. "The whoopin' cranes is dancin'."

Jody saw the great white birds in the distance. His father's eye, he thought, was like an eagle's. They crouched on all fours and crept forward slowly. Now and then Penny dropped flat on his stomach and Jody dropped behind him. They reached a clump of high saw-grass and Penny motioned for concealment behind it. The birds were so close that it seemed to Jody he might touch them with his long fishing pole. Penny squatted on his haunches and Jody followed. His eyes were wide. He made a count of the whooping cranes. There were sixteen.

The cranes were dancing a cotillion as surely as it was danced at Volusia. Two stood apart, erect and white, making a strange music that was part cry and part singing. The rhythm was irregular, like the dance. The other birds were in a circle. In the heart of the circle, several moved counter-clockwise. The musicians made their music. The dancers raised their wings and lifted their feet, first one and then the other. They sunk their heads deep in their snowy breasts, lifted them and sunk again. They moved soundlessly, part awkwardness, part grace. The dance was solemn. Wings fluttered, rising and falling like outstretched arms. The outer circle shuffled around and around. The group in the center attained a slow frenzy.

Suddenly all motion ceased. Jody thought the dance was over, or that the intruders had been discovered. Then the two musicians joined the circle. Two others took their places. There was a pause. The dance was resumed. The birds were reflected in the clear marsh water. Sixteen white shadows reflected the motions. The evening breeze moved across the saw-grass. It bowed and fluttered. The water rippled. The setting sun lay rosy on the white bodies. Magic birds were dancing in a mystic marsh. The grass swayed with them, and the shallow waters, and the earth fluttered under them. The earth was dancing with the cranes, and the low sun, and the wind and sky.

Jody found his own arms lifting and falling with his breath, as the cranes' wings lifted. The sun was sinking into the saw-grass. The marsh was golden. The whooping cranes were washed with gold. The far hammocks were black. Darkness came to the lily pads, and the water blackened. The cranes were whiter than any clouds, or any white bloom of oleander or of lily. Without warning, they took flight. Whether the hour-long dance was, simply, done, or whether the long nose of an alligator had lifted above the water to alarm them, Jody could not tell, but they were gone. They made a great circle against the sunset, whooping their strange rusty cry that sounded only in their flight.

Then they flew in a long line into the west, and vanished. Penny and Jody straightened and stood up. They were cramped from the long crouching. Dusk lay over the saw-grass, so that the ponds were scarcely visible. The world was shadow, melting into shadow. They turned to the north. Jody found his bass. They cut to the east, to leave the marsh behind them, then north again. The trail was dim in the growing darkness. It joined the scrub road and they turned once more east, continuing now in a certainty, for the dense growth of the scrub bordered the road like walls. The scrub was black and the road was a dark gray strip of carpet, sandy and soundless. Small creatures darted across in front of them and scurried in the bushes. In the distance, a panther screamed. Bullbats shot low over their heads. They walked in silence.

At the house, bread was baked and waiting, and hot fat was in the iron skillet. Penny lighted a fat-wood torch and went to the lot to do his chores. Jody scaled and dressed the fish at the back stoop, where a ray of light glimmered from the fire on the hearth. Ma Baxter dipped the pieces in meal and fried them crisp and golden. The family ate without speaking.

She said, "What ails you fellers?"

They did not answer. They had no thought for what they ate nor for the woman. They were no more than conscious that she spoke to them. They had seen a thing that was unearthly. They were in a trance from the strong spell of its beauty.

(From *The Yearling*)
Marjorie Kinnan Rawlings

THE GEESE

My father was the first to hear
The passage of the geese each
    fall,
Passing above the house so
    near
He'd hear within his heart
    their call.

And then at breakfast time
    he'd say:
"The geese were heading south
    last night,"
For he had lain awake till
    day,
Feeling his earthbound soul
    take flight.

Knowing that winter's wind
    comes soon
After rushing of those wings,
Seeing them pass before the
    moon,
Recalling the lure of faroff
    things.

Richard Peck

ALL-EMBRACING LOVE

Love all God's creation, both the whole and every grain of sand. Love every leaf, every ray of light. Love the animals, love the plants, love each separate thing. If thou love each thing thou will perceive the mystery of God in all; and when once thou perceive this, thou wilt thenceforward grow every day to a fuller understanding of it: until thou come at last to love the whole world with a love that will then be all embracing and universal.

Fyodor Dostoevski

THE GIFT

Anything that God makes is worth looking at. We live in no chance world. It has been all thought out.

Everywhere work has been spent on it lavishly —thought and work—loving thought and exquisite work. All its parts together, and every part separately, are stamped with skill, beauty, and purpose.

As the mere work of a Great Master we are driven to look—deliberately and long—at the things which are seen.

More than that, God made me to look at them. He who made light made the eye. It is a gift of the Creator.

The whole mechanism of man is made with reference to the temporal world—the eye for seeing it, the ear for hearing it.

Also God has made the world conspicuous; the whole temporal world clamors for observation.

Nature is never and nowhere silent. The bird will call to you, the sea will change her mood for you, the flower looks up appealingly from the wayside, and the sun, before he sets with irresistible coloring, will startle you into attention.

Had God feared the visible world had been a mere temptation to us, He would have made it less conspicuous.

Henry Drummond

Go forth, under the open sky, and listen to Nature's teachings.

William Cullen Bryant

COMPOSED AT WESTMINSTER BRIDGE

Earth has not anything to show
    more fair:
Dull would he be of soul who could
    pass by
A sight so touching in its
    majesty:
This city now doth, like a
    garment, wear
The beauty of the morning;
    silent, bare,
Ships, towers, domes, theatres,
    and temples lie
Open unto the fields, and to
    the sky;
All bright and glittering in
    the smokeless air.
Never did sun more beautifully
    steep
In his first splendour, valley,
    rock, or hill;
Ne'er saw I, never felt, a calm
    so deep!
The river glideth at his own
    sweet will:
Dear God! the very houses
    seem asleep;
And all that mighty heart is
    lying still!

William Wordsworth

Nothing is more beautiful than the loveliness of the woods before sunrise.

George Washington Carver

For in the true nature of things, if we will rightly consider, every green tree is far more glorious than if it were made of gold and silver.
Martin Luther

If I can put one thought of rosy sunset into the life of any man or woman, I shall feel that I have worked with God.

George Macdonald

Loveliest of lovely things
are they on earth, that
soonest pass away.
The rose that lives its little
hour is prized beyond the
sculptured flower.
William Cullen Bryant

The sky is that beautiful old parchment in which the sun and the moon keep their diary.
Alfred Kreymborg

Nature is painting for us, day after day, pictures of infinite beauty if only we have eyes to see them.

John Ruskin

SUNSET

But beauty seen is never lost,
God's colors all are fast;
The glory of this sunset heaven
Into my soul has passed.
John Greenleaf Whittier

Silently, one by one, in the
infinite meadows of heaven,
Blossomed the lovely stars,
the forget-me-nots of the angels.
Henry Wadsworth Longfellow

What is lovely never dies,
But passes into other loveliness.
Thomas Bailey Aldrich

Flowers always make people better, happier, and more helpful; they are sunshine, food and medicine to the soul.

Luther Burbank

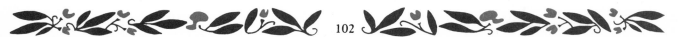

In the society of many men or in the midst of what is called success, I find my life of no account, and my spirits rapidly fall. I would rather be the barrenest pasture lying fallow than cursed with the compliments of kings, than be the sulphurous and accursed desert where Babylon once stood. But when I have only a rustling oak leaf, or the faint metallic cheep of a tree sparrow, for variety in my winter walk, my life becomes continent and sweet as the kernel of a nut. I would rather hear a single shrub oak leaf at the end of a wintry glade rustle of its own accord at my approach, than receive a shipload of stars and garters from the strange kings and peoples of the earth.

Henry David Thoreau

Worship

We say we want to find God—well—suppose we did! We say we long to be assured that the Lord is with us—Well, suppose suddenly you reached out your hand and felt Him!

Suppose suddenly you lifted up your eyes and saw Him looking down at you.

What would you do?

Peter Marshall

BY THY LIFE I LIVE

I love, my God, but with no
   love of mine,
For I have none to give;
I Love Thee, Lord, but all the
   love is Thine,
For by Thy life I live.
I am as nothing, and rejoice to
   be
Emptied and lost and swallowed
   up in Thee.

Thou, Lord, alone art all Thy
   children need,
And there is none beside;
From Thee the streams of blessed-
   ness proceed;
In Thee the blest abide.

Fountain of life, and all-abounding
   grace,
Our source, our center, and our
   dwelling place!

Madame Jeanne Marie Guyon

Saviour, I've no one else to
   tell
And so I trouble Thee,
I am the one forgot Thee so.
Dost Thou remember me?

Emily Dickinson

LET US WITH A GLADSOME MIND

Let us with a gladsome mind
Praise the Lord, for he is kind;
For his mercies aye endure,
Ever faithful, ever sure.

He, with all commanding might,
Filled the new-made world with
   light;
For his mercies aye endure,
Ever faithful, ever sure.

He the golden tressed sun
Caused all day his course to
   run;
For his mercies aye endure,
Ever faithful, ever sure.

All things living he doth feed;
His full hand supplies their
   need;
For his mercies aye endure,
Ever faithful, ever sure.

The horned moon to shine by
   night,
'Mid her spangled sisters
   bright;
For his mercies aye endure,
Ever faithful, ever sure.

Let us with a gladsome mind
Praise the Lord, for he is
   kind;
For his mercies aye endure,
Ever faithful, ever sure.

John Milton

Grant us grace, Almighty Father, so to pray as to deserve to be heard.

Jane Austen

CAN I BE SILENT?

Doth not all nature around me praise God? If I were silent, I should be an exception to the universe. Doth not the thunder praise Him as it rolls like drums in the march of the God of armies? Do not the mountains praise Him when the woods upon their summits wave in adoration? Does not the lightning write His name in letters of fire? Hath not the whole earth a voice? And shall I, can I, silent be?

Charles H. Spurgeon

DENOMINATIONS

We come to God by devious ways,
And who am I to say
That the road I take is the
    only road,
My way, the better way?

The earnest seeker after God
Can find Him like a flame,
Down any road, no matter what
His creed, or what his name.

So whether we may pause to pray
Where great cathedrals shine,
Or in some little weathered
    church,
Or at a wayside shrine,

The sincere traveler will
    arrive
Where the welcoming home
    lights shine,
Although the countless
    thousands take
A different road from mine.

Grace Noll Crowell

Prayer begins where human capacity ends.

Norman Vincent Peale

Here, Lord, is my life. I place it on the altar today. Use it as You will.

Albert Schweitzer

THE SOUL'S SINCERE DESIRE

Prayer is the soul's sincere
    desire,
Uttered or unexpressed;
The motion of a hidden fire,
That trembles in the breast.

Prayer is the burden of a sigh,
The falling of a tear,
The upward glancing of an eye,
When none but God is near.

James Montgomery

FOOTPRINTS

I have loved to hear my Lord spoken of, and wherever I have seen the print of His shoe in the earth, there have I coveted to put mine also.

John Bunyan

MATINS

Flowers rejoice when night is
    done,
Lift their heads to greet the
    sun;
Sweetest looks and odours raise,
In a silent hymn of praise.

So my heart would turn away
From the darkness to the day;
Lying open in God's sight
Like a flower in the light.

Henry Van Dyke

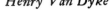

ON HIS BLINDNESS

When I consider how my light
  is spent,
Ere half my days, in this dark
  world and wide,
And that one Talent which is
  death to hide,
Lodg'd with me useless, though
  my soul more bent
To serve therewith my Maker,
  and present
My true account, lest he returning chide;
Doth God exact day-labour,
  light deny'd,
I fondly ask; But Patience, to
  prevent
That murmur, soon replies, God
  doth not need
Either man's work or his own
  gifts: who best
Bear his mild yoke, they serve
  him best: his State
Is kingly. Thousands at his
  bidding speed
And post o'er land and ocean
  without rest:
They also serve who only stand
  and wait.

John Milton

GOD BE IN MY HEAD

God be in my head,
And in my understanding;

God be in my eyes,
And in my looking;

God be in my mouth,
And in my speaking;

God be in my heart,
And in my thinking;

God be at my end,
And my departing.

Sarum Primer

There are times in a man's life when, regardless of the attitude of the body, the soul is on its knees in prayer.

Victor Hugo

IN THE GARDEN OF THE LORD

The word of God came unto me,
Sitting alone among the multitudes;
And my blind eyes were touched
  with light.
And there was laid upon my lips
  a flame of fire.

I laugh and shout for life is
  good,
Though my feet are set in
  silent ways.
In merry mood I leave the
  crowd
To walk in my garden. Ever as
  I walk
I gather fruits and flowers in
  my hands.
And with joyful heart I bless
  the sun
That kindles all the place with
  radiant life.

I run with playful winds that
  blow the scent
Of rose and jasmine in eddying
  whirls.
At last I come where tall lilies
  grow,
Lifting their faces like white
  saints to God.
While the lilies pray, I kneel
  upon the ground;
I have strayed into the holy
  temple of the Lord.

Helen Keller

Eyes raised toward Heaven are always beautiful,
whatever they be.

Joseph Joubert

Before Thee, Father,
In righteousness and humility,

With Thee, Brother,
In faith and courage,

In Thee, Spirit,
In stillness.

Dag Hammarskjöld

Our Father which art in heaven, Hallowed be
thy name. Thy Kingdom come. Thy will be
done in earth, as it is in heaven. Give us this
day our daily bread.

And forgive us our debts, as we forgive our
debtors.

And lead us not into temptation, but deliver
us from evil: For thine is the kingdom, and the
power, and the glory, for ever. Amen.

Matthew 6:9–13,
King James Version

GENTLE JESUS

Gentle Jesus, meek and mild,
Look upon a little child;
Pity my simplicity,
Suffer me to come to Thee.

Lamb of God, I look to Thee;
Thou shalt my example be;
Thou art gentle, meek and mild;
Thou wast once a little child.

Fain I would be as Thou art;
Give me Thy obedient heart.
Thou art pitiful and kind,
Let me have Thy loving mind.

Loving Jesus, gentle Lamb,
In Thy gracious hands I am:
Make me, Saviour, what Thou art;
Live Thyself within my heart.

Charles Wesley

MORTAR

Prayer is the mortar that holds our house
together.

St. Theresa of Ávila

WALKING WITH GOD

O for a closer walk with God,
A calm and heavenly frame,
A light to shine upon the road
That leads me to the Lamb!

Where is the blessedness I knew
When first I saw the Lord?
Where is the soul-refreshing
    view
Of Jesus and His word?

What peaceful hours I once
    enjoy'd!
How sweet their memory still!
But they have left an aching
    void,
The world can never fill.

Return, O holy Dove, return,
Sweet messenger of rest:
I hate the sins that made Thee
    mourn,
And drove Thee from my breast.

The dearest idol I have known,
Whate'er that idol be,
Help me to tear it from Thy
    throne,
And worship only Thee.

So shall my walk be close with
    God,
Calm and serene my frame;
So purer light shall mark the
    road
That leads me to the Lamb.

William Cowper

Communion with God is a great sea that fits
every bend in the shore of human need.

Harry Emerson Fosdick

THE HOLY SPIRIT OF PROMISE

Lord, what a change within us
  one short hour
Spent in Thy presence will pre-
  vail to make!
What heavy burdens from our
  bosoms take,
What parched grounds refresh
  as with a shower!
We kneel, and all around us
  seems to lower;
We rise, and all, the distant
  and the near,
Stands forth in sunny outline
  brave and clear;
We kneel, how weak! we rise,
  how full of power!

Why, therefore, should we do
  ourselves this wrong,
Or others, that we are not
  always strong,
That we are ever overborne
  with care,
That we should ever weak or
  heartless be,
Anxious or troubled, when with
  us is prayer,
And joy and strength and courage are with Thee!

Richard Chenevix Trench

In times of quietness our hearts should be like
trees, lifting their branches to the sky to draw
down strength which they will need to face
the storms that will surely come.

Toyohiko Kagawa

THE SECRET PLACE

Each soul has its secret place,
Where none may enter in
Save it and God—to them alone
What goeth on therein is known—
To it and God alone.

John Oxenham

THE LORD IS GOOD

Make a joyful noise unto the Lord,
  all ye lands.
Serve the Lord with gladness:
  come before his presence with
  singing.
Know ye that the Lord, he is God:
  it is he that hath made us,
  and not we ourselves;
  we are his people,
  and the sheep of his pasture.
Enter into his gates with
  thanksgiving,
  and into his courts with praise:
  be thankful unto him,
  and bless his name.
For the Lord is good;
  his mercy is everlasting;
  and his truth endureth to all
  generations.

Psalm 100,
King James Version

MORE THINGS ARE WROUGHT
BY PRAYER

More things are wrought by
  prayer
Than this world dreams of.
Wherefore let thy voice
Rise like a fountain for me
  night and day.
For what are men better than
  sheep or goats
That nourish a blind life
  within the brain,
If, knowing God, they lift not
  hands of prayer
Both for themselves and those
  who call them friend?
For so the whole round earth
  is every way
Bound by gold chains about the
  feet of God.

Alfred, Lord Tennyson

Morning

MY MORNING SONG

O Lord of life, Thy quickening voice awakes my morning song! In gladsome words I would rejoice that I to Thee belong. I see Thy light, I feel Thy wind; the world, it is Thy word;

Whatever wakes my heart and mind Thy presence is, My Lord.

Therefore I choose my highest part, and turn my face to Thee;

Therefore I stir my inmost heart to worship fervently.

George Macdonald

LOOK TO THIS DAY

Listen to the Exhortation of
the Dawn!
Look to this Day!
For it is Life, the very Life
of Life.

In its brief Course lie all the
Verities and Realities of your
Existence:

The Bliss of Growth,
The Glory of Action,
The Splendour of Beauty;
For Yesterday is but a Dream
And Tomorrow is only a Vision;
But Today well-lived makes
Every Yesterday a Dream of
Happiness,
And every Tomorrow a Vision of
Hope.

Look well therefore to this
Day!
Such is the Salutation of the
Dawn!

From the Sanskrit

SUNRISE

Now the king of day plays at bo-peep round the world's corner, and every cottage window smiles a golden smile—a very picture of glee. I see the water glistening in the eye. The smothered breathing of awakening day strikes the ear with an undulating motion over hill and dale, pasture and woodland, come they to me, and I am at home in the world.

Henry David Thoreau

My voice shalt thou hear in
the morning, O Lord;
in the morning will I direct
my prayer unto thee, and
will look up.

*Psalm 5:3,
King James Version*

The morning stars sang together, and all the sons of God shouted for joy.

*Job 38:7,
King James Version*

PRAYER

Oh, God, the King Eternal, who dividest the day from the darkness, and turnest the shadow of death into the morning; drive far off from us all wrong desires, incline our hearts to keep thy law, and guide our feet into the way of peace; that having done thy will with cheerfulness while it was day, we may, when the night cometh, rejoice to give thee thanks; through Jesus Christ our Lord. Amen.

From The Book of Common Prayer

Evening

A NIGHT-PIECE

The sky is overcast
With a continuous cloud of
    texture close,
Heavy and wan, all whitened
    by the Moon,
Which through that veil is
    indistinctly seen,
A dull, contracted circle,
    yielding light
So feebly spread, that not
    a shadow falls,
Chequering the ground—
    from rock, plant, tree or
    tower.

At length a pleasant
    instantaneous gleam
Startles the pensive traveller
    while he treads
His lonesome path, with unob-
    serving eye
Bent earthwards; he looks up—
    the clouds are split Asunder,—
    and above his head he sees
The clear Moon, and the glory
    of the heavens.
There, in a black-blue vault
    she sails along,
Followed by multitudes of
    stars, that, small
And sharp, and bright, along
    the dark abyss
Drive as she drives: how fast
    they wheel away,
Yet vanish not!—the wind is
    in the tree,
But they are silent;—
    still they roll along
Immeasurably distant; and the
    vault,
Built around by those white
    clouds, enormous clouds,
Still deepens its unfathomable
    depth.

At length the Vision closes;
    and the mind,
Not undisturbed by the delight
    it feels,
Which slowly settles into
    peaceful calm,
Is left to muse upon the
    solemn scene.
                William Wordsworth

ON THE SETTING SUN

We often praise the evening
    clouds,
And tints so gay and bold,
But seldom think upon our God,
Who tinged these clouds with
    gold.
                Sir Walter Scott

CRADLE SONG

Sleep, baby, sleep!
Thy father's watching the
    sheep,
Thy mother's shaking the
    dreamland tree,
And down drops a little dream
    for thee,
Sleep, baby, sleep!
                Elizabeth Prentiss

PRAYER AT NIGHT

O Lord, support us all the day long, until the shadows lengthen and the evening comes, and the busy world is hushed, and the fever of life is over, and our work is done. Then in thy mercy grant us a safe lodging, and a holy rest, and peace at the last. Amen.

From *The Book of Common Prayer*

GRACE BEFORE SLEEP

How can our minds and bodies be
Grateful enough that we have
    spent
Here in this generous room, we
    three,
This evening of content?
Each one of us has walked
    through storm
And fled the wolves along the
    road;
But here the hearth is wide
    and warm,
And for this shelter and this
    light
Accept, O Lord, our thanks
    tonight.

Sara Teasdale

How sweet the moonlight sleeps
    upon this bank!
Here will we sit, and let the
    sounds of music
Creep in our ears: soft still-
    ness and the night
Become the touches of sweet
    harmony.

William Shakespeare

THE LAND OF STORY-BOOKS

At evening when the lamp is
    lit,
Around the fire my parents sit;
They sit at home and talk and
    sing,
And do not play at anything.

Now, with my little gun, I
    crawl
All in the dark along the wall,
And follow round the forest
    track
Away behind the sofa back.

There, in the night, where none can
    spy,
All in my hunter's camp I lie,
And play at books that I have
    read
Till it is time to go to bed.

These are the hills, these are
    the woods,
These are my starry solitudes;
And there the river by whose
    brink
The roaring lions come to drink.

O see the others far away
As if in firelit camp they lay,
And I, like to an Indian scout,
Around their party prowled about.

So, when my nurse comes in for
    me,
Home I return across the sea,
And go to bed with backward
    looks
At my dear land of Story-books.

Robert Louis Stevenson

When the day returns, call us up with morning faces and with morning hearts, eager to labor, happy if happiness be our portion and if the day be marked for sorrow, strong to endure.

Robert Louis Stevenson

The Simple Life

TO ME, MY FARM IS...

My farm to me is not just land
Where bare, unpainted buildings
  stand.
To me my farm is nothing less
Than all created loveliness.
My farm is not where I must
  soil
My hands in endless, dreary
  toil,
But where, through seed and
  swelling pod,
I've learned to walk and talk
  with God.

My farm to me is not a place
Outmoded by a modern race.
I like to think I just see less
Of evil, greed and selfishness.
My farm's not lonely, for all
  day
I hear my children shout and
  play,
And here, when age comes, free
  from fears,
I'll live again, long joyous
  years.

My farm's a heaven—here dwells
  rest,
Security and happiness.
Whate'er befalls the world outside
Here faith and hope and love
  abide.

And so my farm is not just land
Where bare, unpainted buildings
  stand.
To me my farm is nothing less
Than all God's hoarded loveliness.
        Author Unknown

THE CRY OF THE HILL-BORN

I am homesick for my mountains—
My heroic mother hills—
And the longing that is on me
No solace ever stills.
        Bliss Carman

SUCH THINGS ARE BEAUTIFUL

What are the natural features which make a township handsome? A river, with its waterfalls and meadows, a lake, a hill, a cliff or individual rocks, a forest, and ancient trees standing singly. Such things are beautiful; they have a high use which dollars and cents never represent. If the inhabitants of a town were wise they would seek to preserve these things, though at a considerable expense; for preachers, or any at present recognized system of school education. I do not think him fit to be the founder of a state or even a town who does not foresee the use of these things, but legislates chiefly for oxen, as it were.

        Henry David Thoreau

SONG OF THE OPEN ROAD

I think that I shall never see
A billboard lovely as a tree.
Indeed, unless the billboards
  fall
I'll never see a tree at all.
        Ogden Nash

The country is both the philosopher's garden and library, in which he reads and contemplates the power, wisdom, and goodness, of God.
        William Penn

The Busy Life

THE HOUSE BY THE SIDE OF THE ROAD

There are hermit souls that
    live withdrawn
In the place of their self-
    content;
There are souls like stars,
    that dwell apart,
In a fellowless firmament;
There are pioneer souls that
    blaze their paths
Where highways never ran—
But let me live by the side of
    the road
And be a friend to man.

Let me live in a house by the
    side of the road,
Where the race of men go by—
The men who are good and the
    men who are bad,
As good and as bad as I.
I would not sit in the scorner's
    seat,
Or hurl the cynic's ban—
Let me live by the side of the
    road
And be a friend to man.

I see from my house by the
    side of the road,
By the side of the highway of
    life,
The men who press with the
    ardor of hope,
The men who are faint with the
    strife.
But I turn not away from their
    smiles nor their tears,
Both parts of an infinite plan—
Let me live in a house by the
    side of the road
And be a friend to man.

I know there are brook-gladdened
    meadows ahead

And mountains of wearisome
    height;
That the road passes on through
    the long afternoon
And stretches away to the night.
But still I rejoice when the
    travelers rejoice,
And weep with the strangers
    that moan,
Nor live in my house by the
    side of the road
Like a man who dwells alone.

Let me live in my house by the
    side of the road—
It's here the race of men go by.
They are good, they are bad,
    they are weak, they are strong
Wise, foolish—so am I;
Then why should I sit in the
    scorner's seat,
Or hurl the cynic's ban?
Let me live in my house by the
    side of the road
And be a friend to man.
        Sam Walter Foss

The fog comes on little cat
    feet.
It sits looking
Over the harbor and city
on silent haunches
and then, moves on.
        Carl Sandburg

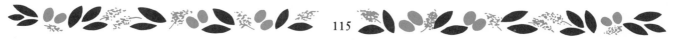

Purpose

STRENGTH IS THE BASIS

Strength is the firm basis on which is built the temple of the Triumphant Life. Without a central motive and fixed resolve, your life will be a poor, weak, drifting, unstable thing. Let the act of the moment be governed by the deep abiding purpose of the heart. You will act differently at different times, but the act will not be wrong if the heart is right. You may fall and go astray at times, especially under great stress, but you will quickly regain yourself, and will grow wiser and stronger thereby so long as you guide yourself by the moral compass within . . .

Err on the side of strength rather than weakness. The measures you adopt may not be the best, but if they are the best you know, then your plain duty is to carry them out; by so doing you will discover the better way, if you are anxious for progress, and are willing to learn. . . .

Rise up in your divine strength, and spurn from your mind and life all meanness and weakness. Do not live the false life of a puling slave, but live the true life of a conquering master.

James Allen

THE WINDS OF FATE

One ship drives east and another
   drives west
With the selfsame winds that
   blow.
'Tis the set of the sails
And not the gales
Which tells us the way to go.

Like the winds of the sea are
   the ways of fate,
As we voyage along through life:
'Tis the set of a soul
That decides its goal,
And not the calm or the strife.

Ella Wheeler Wilcox

THE UNMARRED PAGE

Let us not forget the revelry
   and the din
That ushered in the New Year
   late last night;
Let us be mindful that God
   hands us each
A beautiful white page on
   which to write
Our record of the days He
   gives, and He
Asks only that we live them
   worthily.

Grace Noll Crowell

THE POET'S PRAYER

If there be some weaker one,
   Give me strength to
     help him on;
If a blinder soul there be,
   Let me guide him nearer
     Thee;
Make my mortal dreams
   come true
   With the work I fain would
     do;
Clothe with life the weak
   intent,
   Let me be the thing I
     meant;
Let me find in Thy employ,
   Peace that dearer is than joy;
Out of self to love be led,
   And to heaven acclimated,
Until all things sweet and
   good
   Seem Thy natural habitude.

John Greenleaf Whittier

For me the solitude of the early morning is the most precious time of the day . . . The early morning hours symbolize for me a rebirth; the anxieties, frustrations, and woes of the preceding day seem to have been washed away during the night. God has granted another day of life. He has granted another chance to do something worthwhile for humanity.

Dr. Michael E. DeBakey

WILL

The human will, that force un-
    seen,
The offspring of a deathless
    soul,
Can hew the way to any goal,
Though walls of granite inter-
    vene.

Ella Wheeler Wilcox

ONLY ONE

I am only one,
But still I am one.
I cannot do everything,
But still I can do something;
And because I cannot do
    everything
I will not refuse to do the
    something that I can do.
Edward Everett Hale

SOWERS

We must not hope to be mowers,
And to gather the ripe and
    gold ears,
Unless we have first been
    sowers
And watered the furrows with
    tears.

It is not just as we take it,
This mystical world of ours,

Life's field will yield as
    we make it
A harvest of thorns or of
    flowers.

Johann Wolfgang von Goethe

WHAT IS LIFE?

Life is a sojourn here on earth
Which begins the day God gives
    us birth,
We enter this world
    from the Great Unknown
And God gives each Spirit
A form of its own
And endows this form
With a heart and a soul
To spur man on to his
    ultimate goal—
And through the senses
Of feeling and seeing
God makes man into a human
    being
So he may experience a mortal
    life
And through this period
Of smiles and strife
Prepare himself to Return as
    he Came,
For birth and death
Are in essence the same,
For both are fashioned by God's
    mighty hand
And, while we cannot understand,
We know we are born to die and
    arise
For beyond this world in beauty
    lies
The purpose of living
And the ultimate goal
God gives at birth to each seek-
    ing soul—
So enjoy your sojourn on earth
    and be glad
That God gives you a Choice
Between Good Things and Bad,
And only be sure that you Heed
    God's Voice
Whenever life asks you to make
    a choice.

Helen Steiner Rice

AIM FOR A STAR

Aim for a star!
   Never be satisfied
With a life that is less
   than the best,
Failure lies only
   in not having tried—
In keeping the soul
   suppressed.

Aim for a star!
   Look up and away,
And follow its
   beckoning beam,
Make each tomorrow
   a better Today—
And don't be afraid
   to dream.

Aim for a star, and keep
   your sights high!
With a heartful of faith
   within,
Your feet on the ground,
   and your eyes on the sky,
Some day you are bound
   to win!
     Helen Lowrie Marshall

When a man's pursuit gradually makes his face shine and grow handsome, be sure it is a worthy one.

     William James

RIGHT BEGINNINGS

Life is full of beginnings. They occur every day and every hour to every person. Most beginnings are small and appear trivial and insignificant, but in reality they are the most important things in life.

See how in the material world everything proceeds from small beginnings. The mightiest river is at first a rivulet over which the grasshopper could leap; the great flood commences with a few drops of rain; the sturdy oak, that has endured the storms of a thousand winters, was once an acorn.

Consider how in the spiritual world the greatest things proceed from the smallest beginnings. A light fancy may be the inception of a wonderful invention or an immortal work of art; a spoken sentence may turn the tide of history; a pure thought entertained may lead to the exercise of a worldwide regenerative power. . . .

There are right beginnings and wrong beginnings, followed by effects of like nature. You can, by careful thought, avoid wrong beginnings and make right beginnings, and so escape evil results and enjoy good results. . . .

Loving, gentle, kind, unselfish, and pure thoughts are right beginnings, leading to blissful results. This is so simple, so plain, so absolutely true; and yet how neglected, how evaded, and how little understood!

Your whole life is a series of effects, having their cause in thought—in your own thought. All conduct is made and molded by thought; all deeds, good or bad, are thoughts made visible.

     James Allen

AFFECTION NEVER WAS WASTED

Talk not of wasted affection!
  affection never was wasted;
If it enrich not the heart of
  another,
it's waters, returning back to
  their springs, like the rain
shall fill them full of refreshment:
That which the fountain sends
  forth returns again to the
  fountain.
Henry Wadsworth Longfellow

LOVE'S FIRST KISS

First time he kissed me, he
  but only kissed
The fingers of this hand
  wherewith I write;
And ever since, it grew more
  clean and white,
Slow to world-greetings, quick
  with its "Oh, list,"
When the angels speak. A ring
  of amethyst
I could not wear here, plainer
  to my sight,
Than that first kiss. The
  second passed in height
The first, and sought the
  forehead, and half missed,
Half falling on the hair. O
  beyond meed!
That was the chrism of love,
  which love's own crown,
With sanctifying sweetness,
  did precede.
The third upon my lips was
  folded down
In perfect, purple state; since
  when, indeed,
I have been proud and said,
  "My love, my own."
Elizabeth Barrett Browning

We are shaped and fashioned by what we love.
Johann Wolfgang von Goethe

FAULTS

They came to tell your faults
  to me,
They named them over one by
  one;
I laughed aloud when they were
  done,
I knew them all so well before—
Oh, they were blind, too
  blind to see
Your faults had made me love
  you more.

        Sara Teasdale

To love is to find pleasure in the happiness of
the person loved.
Gottfried Wilhelm von Leibnitz

MY SOUL PREACHED

My soul preached to me and taught me to love
that which the people abhor and befriend him
whom they revile.

My soul showed me that Love prides itself
not only in the one who loves, but also in the
beloved.

Ere my soul preached to me, Love was in
my heart as a tiny thread fastened between two
pegs.

But now Love has become a halo whose beginning is its end, and whose end is its beginning. It surrounds every being and extends
slowly to embrace all that shall be.

        Kahlil Gibran

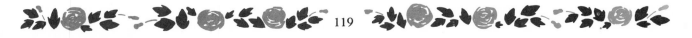

TWO

Two shall be born a whole wide world apart
and one day out of darkness they shall stand
and read life's meaning in each other's eyes.

Author Unknown

ALL IN ALL

In Love, if Love be Love,
    if Love be ours,
Faith and unfaith can ne'er be
    equal powers:
Unfaith in aught is want of
    faith in all.

It is the little rift within
    the lute,
That by and by will make the
    music mute,
And ever widening slowly silence
    all.

The little rift within the
    lover's lute,
Or little pitted speck in
    garner'd fruit,
That rotting inward slowly
    moulders all.

It is not worth the keeping:
    let it go:
But shall it? answer, darling,
    answer, no.
And trust me not at all or
    all in all.

Alfred, Lord Tennyson

Love spends his all, and still has store.

Philip James Bailey

Love is blind, the phrase runs. Nay, I would
rather say, love sees as God sees, and with
infinite wisdom has infinite pardon.

Ouida

In all things we learn only from those we love.

Johann Wolfgang von Goethe

It is difficult to know at what moment love
begins; it is less difficult to know that it has
begun.

Henry Wadsworth Longfellow

EVE TO ADAM

"With thee conversing, I for-
    get all time,
All seasons, and their change;
    all please alike.
Sweet is the breath of Morn,
    her rising sweet,
With charm of earliest birds;
    pleasant the Sun,
When first on this delightful
    land he spreads
His orient beams, on herb,
    tree, fruit, and flower,
Glistening with dew;
    fragant the fertil Earth
After soft showers;
    and sweet the coming on
Of grateful Evening mild,
    then silent Night,
With this her solemn bird,
    and this fair Moon,
And these the gems of Heaven,
    her starry train:
But neither breath of Morn,
    when she ascends
With charm of earliest birds;
    nor rising Sun
On this delightful land;
    nor herb, fruit, flower,
Glistening with dew;
    nor fragrance after showers;
Nor grateful Evening mild;
    nor silent Night,
With this her solemn bird;
    nor walk by moon,
Or glittering star-light,
    without thee is sweet."

John Milton

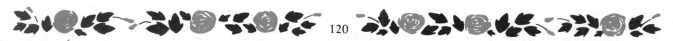

TO LIVE IN LOVE

To transmute everything into Happiness and Joy, this is supremely the work and duty of the Heavenly minded man. To reduce everything to wretchedness and deprivation is the process which the world-minded unconsciously pursue. To live in Love is to work in Joy. Love is the magic that transforms all things into power and beauty. It brings plenty out of poverty, power out of weakness, loveliness out of deformity, sweetness out of bitterness, light out of darkness, and produces all blissful conditions out of its own substantial but indefinable essence.

He who loves can never want. The universe belongs to Goodness, and it therefore belongs to the good man. It can be possessed by all without stint or shrinking, for Goodness, and the abundance of Goodness (material, mental, and spiritual abundance), is inexhaustible. Think lovingly, speak lovingly, act lovingly, and your every need shall be supplied; you shall not walk in desert places, . . . no danger shall overtake you.

Love sees with faultless vision, judges true judgment, acts in wisdom. Look through the eyes of Love, and you shall see everywhere the Beautiful and True; judge with the mind of Love, and you shall not err, shall wake no wail of sorrow; act in the spirit of Love, and you shall strike undying harmonies upon the Harp of Life.

James Allen

Let us not love in word, neither in tongue; but in deed and in truth.

1 John 3:18,
King James Version

What we love we shall grow to resemble.
Bernard of Clairvaux

Love is the doorway through which the human soul passes from selfishness to service and from solitude to kinship with all mankind.

Anonymous

THE MORE YOU LOVE

The more you love, the more
    you'll find
That life is good and friends
    are kind . . .
For only what we give away
Enriches us from day to day.
Helen Steiner Rice

Love is good above all others,
    which alone maketh every
    burden light.
Love is watchful, and
    whilst sleeping still
    keeps watch; though fatigued
    is not weary;
    though pressed is not
    forced.
Love is sincere, gentle,
    strong, patient, faithful,
    prudent, long-suffering,
    manly.
Love is circumspect, humble,
    upright; not weary, not
    fickle, nor intent on vain
    things; sober, chaste,
    steadfast, quiet, and
    guarded in all the senses
Thomas à Kempis

INSCRIPTION ON A SUNDIAL

Time flies,
Suns rise,
And shadows fall.
Let time go by.
Love is forever over all.
Author Unknown

The pains of love be sweeter far
Than all other pleasures are.
John Dryden

HE LOVETH ALL

He prayeth best, who loveth
  best
All things both great and
  small;
For the dear God who loveth us,
He made and loveth all.
Samuel Taylor Coleridge

To be loved, love.
Decimus Magnus Ausonius

GIVE ALL TO LOVE

Give all to love;
Obey thy heart;
Friends, kindred, days,
Estate, good-fame,
Plans, credit and the Muse,—
Nothing refuse.

'Tis a brave master;
Let it have scope;
Follow it utterly,
Hope beyond hope;
High and more high
It dives into noon,
With wings unspent,
Untold intent;
But it is god,
Knows its own path
And the outlets of the sky.

It was never for the mean;
It requireth courage stout.
Souls above doubt,
Valor unbending,
It will reward,—
They shall return
More than they were,
And ever ascending.

Leave all for love;
Yet, hear me, yet,
One word more thy heart behoved,
One pulse more of firm en-
  deavor,—
Keep thee to-day,
To-morrow, forever,
Free as an Arab
Of thy beloved.

Cling with life to the maid;
But when the surprise,
First vague shadow of surmise
Flits across her bosom young,
Of a joy apart from thee,
Free be she, fancy-free;
Nor thou detain her vesture's hem,
Nor the palest rose she flung
From her summer diadem.

Though thou loved her as thy-
  self,
As a self of purer clay,
Though her parting dims the
  day,
Stealing grace from all alive;
Heartily know,
When half-gods go,
The gods arrive.
Ralph Waldo Emerson

THY HEART IN MINE

Go from me. Yet I feel that I
  shall stand
Henceforward in thy shadow.
  Nevermore
Alone upon the threshold of my
  door
Of individual life, I shall
  command
The uses of my soul, nor lift
  my hand
Serenely in the sunshine as
  before,
Without the sense of that which
  I forbore—
Thy touch upon the palm. The
  widest land
Doom takes to part us, leaves
  thy heart in mine
With pulses that beat double.
  What I do
And what I dream include thee,
  as the wine
Must taste of its own grapes.
  And when I sue
God for myself, He hears that
  name of thine,
And sees within my eyes the
  tears of two.
Elizabeth Barrett Browning

SHALL I COMPARE THEE TO A SUMMER'S DAY?

Shall I compare thee to a summer's day?
Thou art more lovely and more
temperate:
Rough winds do shake the darling
buds of May,
And summer's lease hath all too
short a date:
Sometime too hot the eye of
heaven shines,
And often is his gold com-
plexion dimm'd;
And every fair from fair sometime declines,
By change or nature's changing
course untrimm'd;
But thy eternal summer shall
not fade
Nor lose possession of that
fair thou owest;
Nor shall Death brag thou
wander'st in his shade,
When in eternal lines to time
thou growest;
So long as men can breathe or
eyes can see,
So long lives this and this
gives life to thee.

William Shakespeare

IN MEMORIAM

I hold it true, whate'er be-
fall;
I feel it, when I sorrow most;
'Tis better to have loved and
lost
Than never to have loved at
all.

Alfred, Lord Tennyson

MY LUVE

O, my luve is like a red, red
rose,
That's newly sprung in June:
O, my luve is like the melodie,
That's sweetly played in tune.

As fair art thou, my bonnie
lass,
So deep in luve am I;
And I will luve thee still, my
dear,
Till a' the seas gang dry.

Till a' the seas gang dry, my
dear,
And the rocks melt wi' the
sun;
And I will luve thee still, my
dear,
While the sands o' life shall
run.

Robert Burns

A BIRTHDAY

My heart is like a singing
bird
Whose nest is in a water'd
shoot;
My heart is like an apple-
tree
Whose boughs are bent with
thick-set fruit;
My heart is like a rainbow
shell
That paddles in a halcyon sea;
My heart is gladder than
all these,
Because my love is come to
me.

Raise me a dais of silk and
down:
Hang it with fair and purple
dyes;
Carve it in doves and pomegran-
ates,
And peacocks with a hundred
eyes;
Work it in gold and silver
grapes,
In leaves and silver fleurs-
de-lys;
Because the birthday of my
life
Is come, my love is come to me,

Christina Rossetti

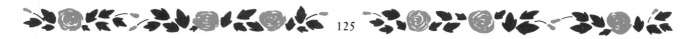

ONENESS

I would live henceforth with some gentle soul such a life as may be conceived, double for variety, single for harmony—two, only that we might admire at our oneness—one, because indivisible. Such community to be a pledge of holy living. How could aught unworthy be admitted into our society? To listen with one ear to each summer sound, to behold with one eye each summer scene, our visual rays so to meet and mingle with the object as to be one bent and doubled; with two tongues to be wearied, and thought to spring ceaselessly from a double fountain.

Henry David Thoreau

The deepest truth blooms only from the deepest love.

Heinrich Heine

LOVE'S NOT TIME'S FOOL

Let me not to the marriage of
    true minds
Admit impediments. Love is not
    love
Which alters when it al-
    teration finds,
Or bends with the remover to
    remove.
O, no! it is an ever-fixed
    mark,
That looks on tempests and is
    never shaken;
It is the star to every wan-
    dering bark,
Whose worth's unknown, al-
    though his height be taken.
Love's not Time's fool, though
    rosy lips and cheeks
Within his bending sickle's
    compass come;
Love alters not with his brief
    hours and weeks,
But bears it out even to the
    edge of doom.
If this be error and upon me
    proved,
I never writ, nor no man ever
    loved.

William Shakespeare

Love is never lost. If not reciprocated, it will flow back and soften and purify the heart.

Washington Irving

Love is a smoke raised with the
    fume of sighs;
Being purged, a fire sparkling
    in lovers' eyes;
Being vex'd, a sea nourish'd with
    lovers' tears:
What is it else? a madness most
    discreet,
A choking gall and persevering
    sweet.

William Shakespeare

Of all earthly music, that which reaches the farthest into heaven is the beating of a loving heart.

Henry Ward Beecher

OF MARRIAGE

Here love begins to render the prose of Life into hymns and canticles of praise with music that is set by night, to be sung in the day. Here Love's longing draws back the veil, and illumines the recesses of the heart, creating a happiness that no other happiness can surpass but that of the Soul when she embraces God.

Marriage is the union of two divinities that a third might be born on earth. It is the union of two souls in a strong love for the abolishment of separateness. It is that higher unity which fuses the separate unities within the two spirits. It is the golden ring in a chain whose beginning is a glance, and whose ending is Eternity. It is the pure rain that falls from an umblemished sky to fructify and bless the fields of divine Nature.

As the first glance from the eyes of the beloved is like a seed sown in the human heart, and the first kiss of her lips like a flower upon the branch of the Tree of Life, so the union of two lovers in marriage is like the first fruit of the first flower of that seed.

Kahlil Gibran

THE GIFT

A wise lover values not so much the gift of the lover as the love of the giver.

Thomas à Kempis

COME, CIVIL NIGHT

Spread thy close curtain, love-
    performing night,
That runaways' eyes may wink,
    and Romeo
Leap to these arms, untalk'd of
    and unseen.
Lovers can see to do their
    amorous rites
By their own beauties; or, if
    love be blind,
It best agrees with night. Come,
    civil night,
Thou sober-suited matron, all
    in black,
And learn me how to lose
    a winning match,
Play'd for a pair of stainless
    maidenhoods:
Hood my unmann'd blood bating
    in my cheeks
With thy black mantle, till
    strange love grown bold
Think true love acted simple
    modesty.
Come, night, come, Romeo, come,
    thou day in night;
For thou wilt lie upon the
    wings of night
Whiter than new snow on a
    raven's back.
Come, gentle night, come, loving,
    black-brow'd night,
Give me my Romeo; and, when he
    shall die,
Take him and cut him out in
    little stars,
And he will make the face of
    heaven so fine,
That all the world will be in
    love with night,
And pay no worship to the garish
    sun.

O, I have bought the mansion of
    a love,
But not possess'd it, and, though
    I am sold,
Not yet enjoy'd; so tedious is this day
As is the night before some
    festival
To an impatient child that hath
    new robes
And may not wear them.

      (From *Romeo and Juliet*)
      William Shakespeare

The greatest happiness of life is the conviction that we are loved, loved for ourselves, or rather loved in spite of ourselves.

Victor Hugo

THE HOUR OF LOVE

Oh, God, thank you for this beautiful hour of love.

My dear is asleep now, but I am too filled with the wonder and joy of it to sleep just yet.

I stand at the window gazing up at your star-riddled sky. I lean on the sill and gaze upon your quiet earth.

How rich and fruitful it smells, how fragrant with life and the promise of life.

I see your trees reaching out as if to each other. For even trees must have mates to mature. Then they cast down their seeds and the rich fertile earth receives them to bear afresh.

I see the fireflies winking, hear the crickets and the locusts and the frogs. All are calling, calling, insistently, almost comically, "Here I am! Come. Come to me!"

"Male and female created he them," I think. For everything must have its opposite and meet with its opposite to be fulfilled.

Marjorie Holmes

Is love possible? Every man knows that for himself. For me it is.

Ernest Hemingway

THE HIGHWAYMAN

Part One

The wind was a torrent of darkness among the gusty trees,
The moon was a ghostly galleon
   tossed upon cloudy seas,
The road was a river of moonlight
   over the purple moor,
And the highwayman came riding—
    Riding—riding—
The highwayman came riding, up
   to the old-inn door.

He'd a French cocked-hat on his
   forehead, a bunch of lace
   at his chin,
A coat of the claret velvet,
   and breeches of brown doeskin:
They fitted with never a
   wrinkle; his boots were up to
   the thigh!
And he rode with a jewelled
   twinkle,
    His pistol butts a-twinkle,
His rapier hilt a-twinkle, under
   the jewelled sky.

Over the cobbles he clattered
   and clashed in the dark innyard,
And he tapped with his whip on
   the shutters, but all was locked and barred:
He whistled a tune to the window,
   and who should be waiting there
But the landlord's black-
   eyed daughter,
    Bess, the landlord's daughter,
Plaiting a dark red love-knot
   into her long black hair.

And dark in the dark old inn-
   yard a stable wicket creaked
Where Tim, the ostler, listened;
   his face was white and peaked,
His eyes were hollows of madness,
   his hair like moldy hay;
But he loved the landlord's
   daughter,
    The landlord's red-lipped
    daughter:
Dumb as a dog he listened, and
   he heard the robber say—

"One kiss, my bonny sweetheart,
   I'm after a prize tonight,
But I shall be back with the
   yellow gold before the morning
   light.
Yet if they press me sharply,
   and harry me through the day,
Then look for me by moonlight,
    Watch for me by moonlight:
I'll come to thee by moonlight,
   though Hell should bar the way."

He rose upright in the stirrups,
   he scarce could reach her hand;
But she loosened her hair i'
   the casement! His face burnt like a brand
As the black cascade of perfume
   came tumbling over his breast;
And he kissed its waves in the
   moonlight,
    (Oh, sweet black waves in the
   moonlight)
Then he tugged at his reins in
   the moonlight, and galloped
   away to the West.

Part Two

He did not come in the dawning;
   he did not come at noon;
And out of the tawny sunset, before the rise o' the moon,
When the road was a gypsy's
   ribbon, looping the purple moor,
A red coat troop came marching—
    Marching—marching—
King George's men came marching, up
   to the old inn-door.

They said no word to the landlord,
   they drank his ale instead;
But they gagged his daughter and
   bound her to the foot of her
   narrow bed.
Two of them knelt at her
   casement, with muskets at the side!
There was death at every
   window;
    And Hell at one dark window;
For Bess could see, through her
   casement, the road that he would ride.

They had tied her up to attention, with many a sniggering jest:
They had bound a musket beside
  her,
with the barrel beneath her
  breast!
"Now keep good watch!" and
  they kissed her.
    She heard the dead man say—

Look for me by moonlight;
    Watch for me by moonlight;
I'll come to thee by moonlight,
    though Hell should bar the way!

She twisted her hands behind her;
  but all the knots held good!
She writhed her hands till her
  fingers were wet with sweat or blood!
They stretched and strained in
  the darkness, and the
  hours crawled by like years;
Till, now, on the stroke of
  midnight,
    Cold, on the stroke of midnight,
The tip of one finger touched
  it! The trigger at least was hers!

The tip of one finger touched
  it; she strove no more for the
  rest!
Up, she stood up to attention,
  with the barrel beneath her
  breast,
She would not risk their hearing:
  she would not strive again;
For the road lay bare in the moonlight,
    Blank and bare in the moonlight;
And the blood of her veins in
  the moonlight throbbed to her Love's refrain.

Tlot-tlot, tlot-tlot! Had
  they heard it? The horse
  hoofs ringing clear—
Tlot-tlot, tlot-tlot, in the
  distance? Were they deaf that they did
  not hear?
Down the ribbon of moonlight,
  over the brow of the hill,
The highwayman came riding,
    Riding, riding!
The red-coats looked to their
  priming! She stood up
  straight and still!

Tlot-tlot, in the frosty
  silence! *Tlot-tlot,* in the echoing night!
Nearer he came and nearer! Her face was like
  a light!
Her eyes grew wide for a moment;
  she drew one last deep breath,
Then her finger moved in the
  moonlight,
    Her musket shattered the moon-
  light,
Shattered her breast in the
  moonlight and warned him—with her death.

He turned; he spurred him Westward;
  he did not know who stood
Bowed with her head o'er the
  musket, drenched with her
  own red blood!
Not till the dawn he heard it,
  and slowly blanched to hear
How Bess, the landlord's
  daughter,
    The landlord's black-eyed daughter,
Had watched for her Love in the
  moonlight; and died in the darkness there.

Back, he spurred like a madman,
  shrieking a curse to the sky,
With the white road smoking
  behind him, and his rapier
  brandished high!
Blood-red were his spurs i' the
  golden noon; wine-red was his velvet coat;
When they shot him down on the
  highway,
    Down like a dog on the highway,
And he lay in his blood on the
  highway, with the bunch of lace at his
  throat.

And still of a winter's night, they
  say, when the wind is in the trees,
When the moon is a ghostly
  galleon tossed upon
  cloudy seas,
When the road is a ribbon of
  moonlight over the purple moor,
A highwayman comes riding—
    Riding—riding—
A highwayman comes riding, up
  to the old inn-door.

Over the cobbles he clatters
and clangs in the dark inn-yard;
And he taps with his whip on
the shutters, but all is
locked and barred:
He whistles a tune to the
window, and who should be
waiting there
But the landlord's black-
eyed daughter,
Bess, the landlord's daughter,
Plaiting a dark red love-knot
into her long black hair.

Alfred Noyes

Do not be afraid of showing affection. Be warm and tender, thoughtful and affectionate. Men are more helped by sympathy than by service. Love is more than money, and a kind word will give more pleasure than a present.

Sir John Lubbock

Love comforteth like sunshine after rain.

William Shakespeare

As the bow unto the cord is
So unto the man is woman.
Though she bends him, she obeys him,
Though she draws him, yet she follows,
Useless each without the other.

Henry Wadsworth Longfellow

If I were to speak with the combined eloquence of men and angels I should stir men like a fanfare of trumpets or the crashing of cymbals, but unless I had love, I should do nothing more. If I had the gift of foretelling the future and had in my mind not only all human knowledge but the secrets of God, and if, in addition, I had that absolute faith which can move mountains, but had no love, I tell you I should amount to nothing at all. If I were to sell all my possessions to feed the hungry and, for my convictions, allowed my body to be burned, and yet had no love, I should achieve precisely nothing.

This love of which I speak is slow to lose patience—it looks for a way of being constructive. It is not possessive: it is neither anxious to impress nor does it cherish inflated ideas of its own importance.

Love has good manners and does not pursue selfish advantage. It is not touchy. It does not compile statistics of evil or gloat over the wickedness of other people. On the contrary, it is glad with all good men when Truth prevails.

Love knows no limit to its endurance, no end to its trust, no fading of its hope: it can outlast anything. It is, in fact, the one thing that still stands when all else has fallen.

I Corinthians 13:1–8,
J. B. Phillips,
The New Testament
in Modern English

THE MAGIC OF LOVE

Love is like magic
And it always will be,
For love still remains
Life's sweet mystery!

Love works in ways
That are wondrous and strange
And there's nothing in life
That love cannot change!

Love can transform
The most commonplace
Into beauty and splendor
And sweetness and grace!

Love is unselfish,
Understanding and kind,
For it sees with its heart
And not with its mind!

Love is the answer
That everyone seeks—
Love is the language
That every heart speaks—

Love can't be bought,
It is priceless and free,
Love like pure magic
Is a sweet mystery!

Helen Steiner Rice

Love cannot be forced, love cannot be coaxed and teased. It comes out of Heaven, unasked and unsought.

Pearl Buck

WHEN, IN DISGRACE
WITH FORTUNE AND MEN'S EYES

When, in disgrace with fortune
　　and men's eyes,
I all alone beweep my outcast
　　state,
And trouble deaf heaven with my
　　bootless' cries,
And look upon myself, and curse
　　my fate,
Wishing me like to one more
　　rich in hope,
Featured like him, like him
　　with friends possessed,
Desiring this man's art,
　　and that man's scope,
With what I most enjoy con-
　　tented least;
Yet in these thoughts myself
　　almost despising,
Haply I think on thee, and
　　then my state,
Like to the lark at break
　　of day arising
From sullen earth, sings hymns
　　at heaven's gate;
For thy sweet love remembered
　　such wealth brings
That then I scorn to change my
　　state with kings.
　　　　William Shakespeare

He who comes to do good knocks at the gate; he who loves finds the door open.

Rabindranath Tagore

What the heart has once owned and had, it shall never lose.

Henry Ward Beecher

WHAT IS LOVE?

What is love?
No words can define it,
It's something so great
Only God could design it . . .

Wonder of Wonders,
Beyond man's conception,
And only in God
Can love find true perfection,
For love means much more
Than small words can express,
For what man calls love
Is so very much less
Than the beauty and depth
And the true richness of
God's gift to mankind—
His compassionate love . . .
For love has become
A word that's misused,
Perverted, distorted
And often abused,
To speak of "light romance"
Or some affinity for
A passing attraction
That is seldom much more
Than a mere interlude
Of inflamed fascination,
A romantic fling
Of no lasting duration . . .
But love is enduring
And patient and kind,
It judges all things
With the heart not the mind,
And love can transform
The most commonplace
Into beauty and splendor
And sweetness and grace . . .
For love is unselfish,
Giving more than it takes,
And no matter what happens
Love never forsakes,
It's faithful and trusting
And always believing,
Guileless and honest
And never deceiving . . .
Yes, love is beyond
What man can define,
For love is Immortal
And God's Gift is Divine!
　　　　Helen Steiner Rice

LEARNING TO LOVE

Is life not full of opportunities for learning love? Every man and woman every day has a thousand of them. The world is not a playground; it is a schoolroom. Life is not a holiday, but an education. And the one eternal lesson for us all is how better we can love. What makes a man a good artist, a good sculptor, a good musician? Practice. What makes a man a good man? Practice. Love is not a thing of enthusiastic emotion. It is a rich, strong, manly, vigorous expression of the whole Christian character—the Christ-like nature in its fullest development. And the constituents of this great character are only to be built up by ceaseless practice.

Henry Drummond

God is love; and he that dwelleth in love dwelleth in God, and God in him.

I John 4:16,
King James Version

Once I knew the depth where no hope was and darkness lay on the face of all things. Then love came and set my soul free. Once I fretted and beat myself against the wall that shut me in. My life was without a past or future, and death a consummation devoutly to be wished. But a little word from the fingers of another fell into my hands that clutched at emptiness, and my heart leaped up with the rapture of living. I do not know the meaning of the darkness, but I have learned the overcoming of it.

Helen Keller

If thou neglectest thy love to thy neighbor, in vain thou professest thy love to God; for by thy love to God, the love to thy neighbor is begotten, and by the love to thy neighbor, thy love to God is nourished.

Francis Quarles

No one perfectly loves God who does not perfectly love some of his creatures.

Marguerite de Valois

THE PUP

He tore the curtains yesterday,
And scratched the paper on
    the wall;
Ma's rubbers, too, have gone
    astray—
She says she left them in the
    hall;
He tugged the table cloth and
    broke
A fancy saucer and a cup;
Though Bud and I think it a
    joke
Ma scolds a lot about the pup.

The sofa pillows are a sight,
The rugs are looking somewhat
    frayed,
And there is ruin, left and
    right,
That little Boston bull has
    made.
He slept on Buddy's counter-
    pane—
Ma found him there when she
    woke up.
I think it needless to explain
She scolds a lot about the pup.

And yet he comes and licks her
    hand
And sometimes climbs into her
    lap
And there, Bud lets me under-
    stand,
He very often takes his nap.
And Bud and I have learned to
    know
She wouldn't give the rascal
    up:
She's really fond of him, al-
    though
She scolds a lot about the pup.

Edgar Guest

Look round our world; behold the
    chain of love
Combining all below and all above.

Alexander Pope

THE MAN AND THE CHILD

It is the man in us who works;
Who earns his daily bread and
  anxious scans
The evening skies to know to-
  morrow's plans;
It is the man who hurries as he
  walks;
Finds courage in a crowd; shouts
  as he talks;
Who shuts his eyes and bur-
  rows through his task;
Who doubts his neighbor and
  who wears a mask;
Who moves in armor and who
  hides his tears.
It is the man in us who fears.

It is the child in us who plays;
Who sees no happiness beyond
  today's;
Who sings for joy; who wonders,
  and who weeps;
It is the child in us at night
  who sleeps.
It is the child who silent
  turns his face,
Open and maskless, naked of
  defense,
Simple with trust, distilled of
  all pretense,
To sudden beauty in another's
  face—
It is the child in us who loves.
          Anne Morrow Lindbergh

A new commandment I give unto you, That ye love one another; as I have loved you, that ye also love one another.

John 13:34,
King James Version

If we love one another, God dwelleth in us, and his love is perfected in us.

1 John 4:12,
King James Version

Blessed is the servant who loves his brother as much when he is sick and useless as when he is well and can be of service to him. And blessed is he who loves his brother as well when he is afar off as when he is by his side, and who would say nothing behind his back he might not, in love, say before his face.

St. Francis of Assisi

Alexander, Caesar, Charlemagne, and myself founded empires; but on what foundation did we rest the creations of our genius? Upon force. Jesus Christ founded an empire upon love; and at this hour millions of men would die for Him.

Napoleon Bonaparte

Love does not consist in gazing at each other, but in looking outward together in the same direction.

Antoine de Saint-Exupéry

For God so loved the world, that he gave his only begotten Son, that whosoever believeth in Him should not perish, but have everlasting life.

John 3:16,
King James Version

Forgiveness

THE FOOL'S PRAYER

The royal feast was done; the
  King
Sought some new sport to banish
  care,
And to his jester cried: "Sir
  Fool,
Kneel now, and make for us a
  prayer!"

The jester doffed his cap and
  bells,
And stood the mocking court
  before;
They could not see the bitter
  smile
Behind the painted grin he wore.

He bowed his head, and bent his
  knee
Upon the monarch's silken
  stool;
His pleading voice arose: "O
  Lord,
Be merciful to me, a fool!

"No pity, Lord, could change
  the heart
From red with wrong to white
  as wool;
The rod must heal the sin:
  but, Lord,
Be merciful to me, a fool!

"Tis not by guilt the onward
  sweep
Of truth and right, O Lord,
  we stay;
'Tis by our follies that so
  long
We hold the earth from heaven
  away.

"These clumsy feet, still in
  the mire,
Go crushing blossoms without
  end;

These hard, well-meaning hands
  we thrust
Among the heart-strings of a
  friend.

"The ill-timed truth we might
  have kept—
Who knows how sharp it pierced
  and stung?
The word we had not sense to
  say—
Who knows how grandly it had
  rung?

"Our faults no tenderness should
  ask,
The chastening stripes must
  cleanse them all;
But for our blunders—oh, in
  shame
Before the eyes of heaven we
  fall.

"Earth bears no balsam for
  mistakes.
Men crown the knave, and
  scourge the tool
That did his will; but Thou,
  O Lord,
Be merciful to me, a fool!"

The room was hushed; in
  silence rose
The King, and sought his
  gardens cool,
And walked apart, and murmured
  low,
"Be merciful to me, a fool!"
Edward Rowland Sill

In the presence of God, nothing stands between
Him and us—we are forgiven. But we cannot
feel His presence if anything is allowed to
stand between ourselves and others.
Dag Hammarskjöld

THE DELIVERANCE OF ROBINSON CRUSOE

In the morning I took the Bible, and beginning at the New Testament, I began seriously to read it and imposed upon myself to read a while every morning and every night, not tying myself to the number of chapters, but as long as my thoughts should engage me. It was not long after I set seriously to this work but I found my heart more deeply and sincerely affected with the wickedness of my past life. The impression of my dream revived, and the words, "All these things have not brought thee to repentance," ran seriously in my thoughts. I was earnestly begging of God to give me repentance, when it happened providentially the very day that reading the Scripture, I came to these words, "He is exalted a Prince and a Saviour, to give repentance, and to give remission." I threw down the book and with my heart as well as my hands lifted up to Heaven, in a kind of ectasy of joy, I cried out aloud, "Jesus, Thou Son of David, Jesus, Thou exalted Prince and Saviour, give me repentance!"

This was the first time that I could say, in the true sense of the words, that I prayed in all my life; for now I prayed with a sense of my condition, and with a true Scripture view of hope founded on the encouragement of the Word of God; and from this time, I may say, I began to have hope that God would hear me.

Now I began to construe the words mentioned above, "Call on Me, and I will deliver you," in a different sense from what I had ever done before; for then I had no notion of anything being called deliverance but my being delivered from the captivity I was in, for though I was indeed at large in the place, yet the island was certainly a prison to me, and that in the worst sense in the world; but now I learned to take it in another sense. Now I looked back upon my past life with such horror, and my sins appeared so dreadful, that my soul sought nothing of God but deliverance from the load of guilt that bore down all my comfort. As for my solitary life, it was nothing; I did not so much as pray to be delivered from it or think of it; it was all of no consideration in comparison to this; and I added this part here to hint to whoever shall read it, that whenever they come to a true sense of things, they will find deliverance from sin a much greater blessing than deliverance from affliction.

(From *Robinson Crusoe*)
Daniel DeFoe

FORGIVENESS

My heart was heavy, for its
   trust had been
Abused, its kindness answered
   with foul wrong;
So, turning gloomily from my
   fellow-men,
One summer Sabbath day I
   strolled among
The green mounds of the village
   burial-place;
Where, pondering how all human
   love and hate
Find one sad level; and how,
   soon or late,
Wronged and wrongdoer, each
   with meekened face,
And cold hands folded over a
   still heart,
Pass the green threshold of our
   common grave,
Whither all footsteps tend,
   whence none depart,
Awed for myself, and pitying my
   race,
Our common sorrow, like a
   mighty wave,
Swept all my pride away, and
   trembling I forgave!
John Greenleaf Whittier

Peace

PEACE

With eager heart and will on
    fire,
I fought to win my great desire
"Peace shall be mine," I said;
    but life
Grew bitter in the weary strife.

My soul was tired, and my
    pride
Was wounded deep: to Heaven I
    cried,
"God grant me peace or I must
    die,
The dumb stars glittered no
    reply.

Broken at last, I bowed my
    head,
Forgetting all myself, and
    said,
"Whatever comes, His will be
    done;"
And in that moment peace was
    won.

Henry Van Dyke

LORD, MAKE ME AN INSTRUMENT OF YOUR PEACE

Lord, make me an instrument of Your peace;
where there is hatred, let me sow love; where
there is injury, pardon; where there is discord,
union; where there is doubt, faith; where there
is despair, hope; where there is darkness, light;
and where there is sadness, joy.

O Divine Master, grant that I may not so
much seek to be consoled as to console, to be
understood as to understand, to be loved as to
love; for it is in giving that we receive, it is in par-
doning that we are pardoned, and it is in dying
that we are born to eternal life.

St. Francis of Assisi

THE ULTIMATE TRIUMPH

He only finds peace who conquers himself, who
strives, day by day, after greater self-possession,
greater self-control, greater calmness of mind.
One can only be a joy to himself and a blessing
to others in the measure that he has command
of himself; and such self-command is gained
only by persistent practice. A man must conquer
his weaknesses by daily effort; he must understand them and study how to eliminate them
from his character; and if he continues to strive,
not giving way, he will gradually become vic-
torious; and each little victory gained (though
there is a sense in which no victory can be called
little) will be so much more calmness acquired
and added to his character as an eternal possession. He will thus make himself strong and
capable and blessed, fit to perform his duties
faultlessly, and to meet all events with an un-
troubled spirit. . . .

The mind of the calm man is like the surface
of a still lake; it reflects life and things of life
truly. Whereas the troubled mind, like the troubled surface of a lake, gives back a distorted
image of all things which fall upon it. Gazing
into the serene depths within him, the self-
conquered man sees a just reflection of the
universe. He sees the Cosmic Perfection; sees the
equity in his own lot; even those things which
are regarded by the world as unjust and grievous
(and which formerly appeared so to him) are
now known to be the effects of his own past
deeds, and are therefore joyfully accepted as
portions of the perfect whole. Thus his calmness
remains with him with its illimitable fund of re-
source in joy and enlightment. . . .

Where the calm mind is, there is strength and
rest, there is love and wisdom; there is one who
has fought successfully innumerable battles
against self, who, after long toil in secret against
his own failings has triumphed at last.

James Allen

DEAR LORD AND FATHER
OF MANKIND

Dear Lord and Father of
   mankind!
Forgive our foolish ways!
Reclothe us in our rightful
   mind,
In purer lives Thy service find,
In deeper reverence, praise.

In simple trust like theirs who
   heard,
Beside the Syrian sea,
The gracious calling of the
   Lord,
Let us, like them, without
   a word,
Rise up and follow Thee.

O Sabbath rest by Galilee!
O calm of hills above,
Where Jesus knelt to share
   with Thee
The silence of eternity
Interpreted by love!

With that deep hush subduing
   all
Our words and works that drown
The tender whisper of Thy call,
As noiseless let Thy blessing
   fall
As fell Thy manna down.

Drop Thy still dews of quietness,
Till all our striving cease;
Take from our souls the
   strain and stress,
And let our ordered lives confess
The beauty of Thy peace.

Breathe through the heats of
   our desire
Thy coolness and Thy balm;
Let sense be dumb; let flesh
   retire;
Speak through the earthquake,
   wind and fire,
O still small voice of calm!
         John Greenleaf Whittier

ODE ON SOLITUDE

Happy is the man whose wish and
   care
A few paternal acres bound,
Content to breate his native
   air
In his own ground.

Whose herds with milk, whose
   fields with bread,
Whose flocks supply him with
   attire,
Whose trees in summer yield
   him shade,
In winter fire.

Bless'd who can unconcern'dly
   find
Hours, days, and years slide
   soft away,
In health of body, peace of
   mind,
Quiet by day;

Sound sleep by night: study
   and ease
Together mix'd; sweet
   recreation;
And innocence, which most
   does please,
With meditation.

Thus let me live, unseen,
   unknown,
Thus unlamented let me die;
Steal from the world, and
   not a stone
Tell where I lie.
         Alexander Pope

"I WAS RADIANT"

My greatest interest, when I was eleven, lay in the Church. . . . I'd watch the grown-ups praying and would get the same feeling they had of elation, exaltation, of being carried above and beyond oneself.

The beauty that came into the tired faces of the very old men and women excited me. All week long so many of them were confused and inarticulate. But on Sunday, in the church, they had no difficulty expressing themselves both in song and talk. The emotion that had invaded them was so much bigger than they. Some would rock. Some would cry. Some would talk with eloquence and fire, their confusions and doubts dispelled. And, oh, those hymns!

It began to dawn on me that if sordidness left a deep and lasting mark, so could the goodness in life. The big thing in my life was the feeling that I was getting close to God. Not that I could accept all the doctrines preached. My logic, my reasoning powers made me question much of the doctrine.

For example, as a little girl I was told to ask God to forgive my sins. But what sins could a little girl commit?

My search for God and my finding of Him were to begin in one of those Protestant churches where they were having a children's revival. It was there I came truly to know and to reverence Christ, the Redeemer.

All my girl friends in the neighborhood were going to this children's revival. I went religiously, every day. When the preacher, the Reverend R. J. Williams, called those who wished to repent and be saved, all my gang would go up there to the mourners' bench and kneel down—but not for long. They would pop up quick as hot cakes and as though they had brand new souls. But we stout hearts in the back knew they hadn't been cleansed of sin but were just trying to attract attention.

"Come up and shake my hand," the Reverend R. J. Williams would say in his booming voice. "Don't you want to be little soldiers of the Lord?"

Two or three times I did go up and shake his hand. Then I'd return to my seat. I wasn't sure I wanted to be saved. "What can I ask God?" I kept thinking. "What have I got to say to Him?"

One night there were only three of us youngsters still left unsaved in the whole congregation. All the rest had gone to the mourners' bench and been redeemed.

"Come!" cried the Reverend R. J. Williams, an inspired and fiery preacher. "Get down on your knees and pray to our Lord!"

So I thought, "I will get down on my knees and pray just to see what happens." I prayed, "O Lord! I don't know what to ask of You!"

I did this every night. Every night I was on my knees—and nothing happened. I didn't feel purged of sin or close to the Lord. I didn't feel what some of the others felt so sincerely. It was this way with me right through the last night of the children's revival meeting.

I was the only one left who was still unsaved, and the preacher looked at me. He looked at me and announced he would continue the revival, if necessary, for three more nights—just to save me. I like to think that the Reverend R. J. Williams saw something special and fervent in me, something deep and passionate struggling toward salvation and spiritual expression.

On the last night of the three extra nights of the meeting I got down on the mourners' bench, down on my knees once more. And I told myself, "If nothing happens tonight, I'll not come back again."

Nobody had come that night to the meeting, nobody but the very old people who were always there. I was praying hard and hopefully, asking God, "What am I seeking here? What do I want of You? Help me! If nothing happens, I can't come back here any more!"

And then it happened! The peace of heart and mind, the peace I had been seeking all my life.

I know that never again, so long as I live, can I experience that wonderful reaction I had that night in the little church. Love flooded my heart and I knew I had found God and that now and for always I would have an ally, a friend close by to strengthen me and cheer me on.

I don't know exactly what happened or when I got up. I don't even know whether I talked. But the people who were there that night were astounded. Afterward they told me that I was radiant and like one transfixed. They said that the light in my face electrified the whole church. And I did feel full of light and warmth.

Ethel Waters

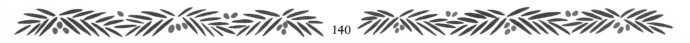

THE GOOD TIME COMING

War in men's eyes shall be
A monster of iniquity
In the good time coming.
Nations shall not quarrel
   then,
To prove which is the stronger;
Nor slaughter men for glory's
   sake;—
Wait a little longer.
           Charles Mackay

MOMENTS OF AWARENESS

So much of life we all
   pass by
With heedless ear,
   and careless eye.
Bent with our cares
   we plod along,
Blind to the beauty,
   deaf to the song.

But moments there are
   when we pause to rest
And turn our eyes from
   the goal's far crest.
We become aware of
   the wayside flowers,
And sense God's hand
   in this world of ours.

We hear a refrain,
   see a rainbow's end,
Or we look into the heart
   of a friend.
We feel at one with
   mankind. We share
His griefs and glories,
   joy and care.

The sun flecks gold thru the
   sheltering trees,
And we shoulder our burdens
   with twice the ease.
Peace and content and
   a world that sings
The moment of true
   awareness brings.
        Helen Lowrie Marshall

A PRAYER

Teach me, Father, how to go
Softly as the grasses grow;
Hush my soul to meet the
   shock
Of the wild world as a rock;
But my spirit, propt with
   power,
Make as simple as a flower.

Let the dry heart fill its
   cup,
Like a poppy looking up;
Let life lightly wear her
   crown,
Like a poppy looking down,
When its heart is filled
   with dew,
And its life begins anew.

Teach me, Father, how to be
Kind and patient as a tree.
Joyfully the crickets croon
Under shady oak at noon;
Beetle, on his mission bent,
Tarries in that cooling tent.
Let me, also, cheer a spot,
Hidden field or garden
   grot—
Place where passing souls
   can rest
On the way and be their best.
        Edwin Markham

How beautiful upon the mountains are the feet
of him that bringeth good tidings, that pub-
lisheth peace.

        Isaiah 52:7,
        King James Version

Blessed are the peacemakers.

        Matthew 5:9,
        King James Version

Patriotism is not enough. I must have no hatred
or bitterness towards anyone.

        Edith Cavell

THE PEACE
OF MEDITATION

So we may know God better
    And feel His quiet power,
Let us daily keep in silence
    A Meditation Hour—
For to understand God's
    greatness
And to use His gifts each day
The soul must learn to meet
    Him
In a meditative way,
So let us plan with prayerful
    care
To always allocate
A certain portion of each day
To be still and meditate . . .
For when everything is quiet
And we're lost in meditation,
Our soul is then preparing
For a deeper dedication
That will make it wholly
    possible
To quietly endure
The violent world around us—
For in God we are secure.

Helen Steiner Rice

It shall come to pass in the latter days that the mountain of the house of the Lord shall be established as the highest of the mountains, and shall be raised up above the hills; and peoples shall flow to it, and many nations shall come, and say: "Come, let us go up to the mountain of the Lord, to the house of the God of Jacob; that he may teach us his ways and we may walk in his paths." For out of Zion shall go forth the law, and the word of the Lord from Jerusalem. He shall judge between many peoples, and shall decide for strong nations afar off; and they shall beat their swords into plowshares, and their spears into pruning hooks; nation shall not lift up sword against nation, neither shall they learn war any more; but they shall sit every man under his vine and under his fig tree, and none shall make them afraid; for the mouth of the Lord of hosts has spoken.

Micah 4:1–4,
Revised Standard Version

Peace hath her victories
No less renown'd than war.
John Milton

Christmas

AND THE WORD WAS MADE FLESH

Light looked down and beheld
 Darkness.
"Thither will I go," said
 Light.
Peace looked down and beheld
 War.
"Thither will I go," said
 Peace.
Love looked down and beheld
 Hate.
"Thither will I go," said
 Love.
So came Light and shone.
So came Peace and gave rest.
So came Love and brought Life.
Laurence Housman

In the beginning was the Word, and the Word
was with God, and the Word was God. The
same was in the beginning with God. All things
were made by him; and without him was not
any thing made that was made. In him was life;
and the life was the light of men. . . . And
the Word was made flesh, and dwelt among us,
(and we beheld his glory, the glory as of the
only begotten of the Father,) full of grace and
truth.

John 1:1–4,14,
King James Version

BY HIM

What comfort by Him do we win
Who made Himself the price of
 sin
To make us heirs of glory?
To see this Babe, all innocence,
A Martyr born in our defence:
Can man forget this Story?
Ben Jonson

AWAY IN A MANGER

Away in a manger, no crib for
 a bed,
The little Lord Jesus laid down
 his sweet head,
The stars in the sky looked down
 where He lay,
The little Lord Jesus, asleep
 on the hay.

The cattle are lowing, the
 Baby awakes,
But little Lord Jesus, no
 crying He makes.
I love Thee Lord Jesus, look
 down from the sky,
And stay by my cradle till
 morning is nigh.

Be near me, Lord Jesus, I ask
 Thee to stay
Close by me for ever, and
 love me, I pray.
Bless all the dear children
 in Thy tender care,
And fit us for heaven to live
 with Thee there.
Martin Luther

THE CHRISTMAS STAR

Stars rise and set, that star
 shines on:
Songs fail, but still that
 music beats
Through all the ages come
 and gone,
In lane and field and city
 streets.
And we who catch the Christmas
 gleam,
Watching with children on the
 hill,
We know, we know it is no
 dream—
He stands among us still!
Nancy Byrd Turner

WE, TOO, ARE BIDDEN

The angel of the Lord said to the shepherds, "And this shall be a sign unto you: Ye shall find the babe wrapped in swaddling clothes, lying in a manger."

They made haste to go to Bethlehem to see the thing which had come to pass. "For unto you," the angel said, "is born this day in the city of David a Saviour, which is Christ the Lord."

But as they journeyed to Bethlehem they fell into a discussion as to just how they should find the place where the infant lay. The shepherds were not familiar with the town, even though it lay a short journey from the fields in which they tended their flocks. Besides, they knew that many from the country roundabout had gone to Bethlehem in compliance with the decree of Caesar Augustus that all the world should be taxed. Indeed, one of the group grumbled, "In Bethlehem there be many mangers, and how are we to find the one?"

And the youngest shepherd said, "It will be made known to us."

The night was bright with stars and the way more easy than they had expected. In spite of the late hour many walked in the narrow streets of Bethlehem and from all the houses there came a clatter. The shepherds stood for a moment in perplexity as to the appointed place. The noises of the town were confusing to men who had been standing silent under starlight.

And suddenly the volume of voices increased, and down the street there came a caravan of camels. Upon the backs of the beasts sat great bearded men, and with them they brought sacks of precious stuffs and huge treasure chests from different kingdoms. The air was filled with the pungent tang of spice and perfume.

The startled shepherds stood against the wall to let the cavalcade of the mighty pass by. And these wise men and kings seemed to have no doubt as to their destination. They swept past the inn and dismounted at the door of the stable.

"It is there the Child lies in the manger," said one of the shepherds and made as if to follow,

but his fellows were abashed and said among themselves, "It is not meet that we should crowd in upon the heels of the mighty."

"We, too, are bidden," insisted the youngest shepherd. "For us, as well, there was the voice of the angel of the Lord."

And timidly the men from the fields followed after and found places near the door. They watched as the men from distant countries came and silently placed their gifts at the foot of the manger where the Child lay sleeping. And the shepherds stood aside and let the great of the earth go out into the night to take up again their long journey.

Presently they were alone, but as they had no gifts to lay beside the gold and frankincense they turned to go back to their flocks. But Mary, the mother, made a sign to the youngest shepherd to come closer. And he said, "We are shepherds, and we have come suddenly from the fields whence an angel summoned us. There is naught which we could add to the gifts of wise men and of kings."

Mary replied, "Before the throne of God, who is a king and who is a wise man, you have brought with you a gift more precious than all the others. It lies within your heart."

And suddenly it was known to the shepherd the meaning of the words of Mary. He knelt at the foot of the manger and gave to the Child his prayer of joy and of devotion.

Heywood Broun

A SON IS BORN

For unto us a child is born, unto us a son is given: and the government shall be upon his shoulder: and his name shall be called Wonderful, Counsellor, The mighty God, The everlasting Father, The Prince of Peace.

Isaiah 7:14;9:6,
King James Version

GOD REST YOU MERRY, GENTLEMEN

God rest you merry, gentlemen,
Let nothing you dismay,
For Jesus Christ, our
      Saviour,
Was born upon this day,
To save us all from Satan's
      power
When we were gone astray.
O tidings of comfort and joy!
For Jesus Christ, our Saviour,
Was born on Christmas Day.
Now to the Lord sing praises,
All you within this place,
And with true love and brother-
      hood
Each other now embrace;
This holy tide of Christmas
All others doth deface.
O tidings of comfort and joy!
For Jesus Christ, our Saviour,
Was born on Christmas Day.

Anonymous

"A MERRY CHRISTMAS, UNCLE!"

"A merry Christmas, uncle! God save you!" cried a cheerful voice. It was the voice of Scrooge's nephew, who came upon him so quickly that this was the first intimation he had had of his approach.

"Bah!" said Scrooge. "Hum-bug!"

He had so heated himself with rapid walking in the fog and frost, this nephew of Scrooge's that he was all in a glow; his face was ruddy and handsome; his eyes sparkled, and his breath smoked again.

"Christmas is a humbug, uncle!" said Scrooge's nephew. "You don't mean that, I am sure?"

"I do," said Scrooge. "Merry Christmas! What right have you to be merry? What reason have you to be merry? You're poor enough."

"Come then," returned the nephew gaily. "What right have you to be dismal? What reason have you to be morose? You're rich enough."

Scrooge, having no better answer ready on the spur of the moment, said "Bah!" again; and followed it up with "Humbug!"

"Don't be cross, uncle!" said the nephew.

"What else can I be," returned the uncle, "when I live in such a world of fools as this? Merry Christmas! Out upon merry Christmas! What's Christmas-time to you but a time for paying bills without money; a time for finding yourself a year older, and not an hour richer; a time for balancing your books, and having every item in 'em through a round dozen of months presented dead against you? If I could work my will," said Scrooge indignantly, "every idiot who goes about with 'Merry Christmas' on his lips should be boiled with his own pudding, and buried with a stake of holly through his heart. He should!"

"Uncle!" pleaded the nephew.

"Nephew!" returned the uncle sternly, "keep Christmas in your own way, and let me keep it in mine."

"Keep it!" repeated Scrooge's nephew. "But you don't keep it."

"Let me leave it alone, then," said Scrooge. "Much good may it do you! Much good it has ever done you!"

"There are many things from which I might have derived good by which I have not profited, I dare say," returned the nephew, "Christmas among the rest. But I am sure I have always thought of Christmas-time, when it has come around—apart from the veneration due to its sacred name and origin, if anything belonging to it can be apart from that—as a good time; a kind, forgiving, charitable, pleasant time; the only time I know of, in the long calendar of the year, when men and women seem by one consent to open their shut-up hearts freely, and to think of people below them as if they really were fellow-passengers to the grave, and not another race of creatures bound on other journeys. And therefore, uncle, though it has never put a scrap of gold or silver in my pocket, I believe that it has done me good, and will do me good; and I say, God bless it!"

(From *A Christmas Carol*)
Charles Dickens

SUMMERTIME CHRISTMAS

Sometimes, when I was still a child, Christmas came for me in the summer, when we visited my father's folks in Mississippi.

. . . There were beautiful "summer Christmas trees" on the front lawn, adorned with velvety white magnolia blossoms. I remember the heavily-loaded fig tree just outside our bedroom window, and how I reached out and touched it. This was Christmas, too, in our hearts, for there was an abundance of peace and love for God and each other.

I learned that Christmas could come on a summer's day. Christmas could come at any season, if that sense of love were strong in the family.

Dale Evans Rogers

JOURNEY OF THE MAGI

'A cold coming we had of it,
Just the worst time of the year
For a journey, and such
    a long journey:
The ways deep and
    the weather sharp,
The very dead of winter.'
And the camels galled,
    sore-footed, refractory,
Lying down in the melting snow.
There were times we regretted
The summer palaces
    on slopes, the terraces,
And the silken girls
    bringing sherbet.
Then the camel men cursing
    and grumbling
And running away, and wanting
    their liquor and women,
And the night-fires going out,
    and the lack of shelters,
And the cities hostile
    and the towns unfriendly
And the villages dirty and
    charging high prices:
A hard time we had of it.
At the end we preferred to
    travel all night,

Sleeping in snatches,
With the voices singing in our
    ears, saying
That this was all folly.
Then at dawn we came down to a
    temperate valley,
Wet, below the snow line,
    smelling of vegetation;
With a running stream and a
    water-mill beating the
darkness,
And three trees on the low sky,
And an old white horse gal-
    loped away in the meadow.
Then we came to a tavern with
    vine-leaves over the lintel,
Six hands at an open door
    dicing for pieces of silver,
And feet kicking the empty
    wine-skins.
But there was no information,
    and so we continued
And arrived at evening, not a
    moment too soon
Finding the place; it was (you
    may say) satisfactory.

All this was a long time ago,
    I remember,
And I would do it again, but
    set down
This set down
This: were we led all that
    way for
Birth or Death? There was a
    Birth, certainly,
We had evidence and no doubt.
I had seen birth and death,
But had thought they were
    different; this Birth was
Hard and bitter agony for us,
    like Death, our death.
We returned to our places,
    these Kingdoms,
But no longer at ease here,
    in the old dispensation,
With an alien people clutching
    their gods,
I should be glad of another
    death.

T. S. Eliot

CHRISTMAS IN THE HEART

We always think of Christmas as a time of snow and icicles hanging from the old well and snow over the valley. But I had a friend who was newly married and went to live in the tropics. She felt sorry for herself as Christmas drew near. She wept. And then her husband brought in some tropical flowers, to decorate the house, he said. And it came to her suddenly that Christmas was not a place, nor was it weather, it was a state of mind. After all, she thought, Christ was not born in the North, he was born in a stable in Bethlehem. And so she got a small palm tree and put flowers on the flat leaves, and was gay and merry. It was, she said, one of the best Christmases ever, although they afterward moved back to New England where the snow fell and the pine trees were silvered.

It is certainly true that Christmas is only seasonal in the heart. The snow may be clean and deep outside, or you may be in a dingy city apartment or you may be in a steaming tropical country. But it is still Christmas. Whether you serve the plump crispy turkey, or something exotic wrapped in pandanus leaves, the feeling of Christmas is there. It is in the mind and in the heart. The faith we have in the good rises like a tide and wherever we are, we feel it. Christmas graces any board and gives a new lift to our life, and as we hear once more the familiar carols, we thank God for the birth of His son. "O little town of Bethlehem, how still we see thee lie—Above thy dark and dreamless streets the silent stars go by."

As always when the old house creaks into quiet, I snuff the Christmas candles, and check to be sure nobody has left a turkey bone where the Irish could get it. The colored ribbons and tissues are swept up, the fire has died down, and I let the cockers and Irish out for a last run in the new-fallen snow. They take nips of it, roll in it.

And now, as always, I have a special reunion with my Honey, a golden cocker who died a time ago. I hear her paws softly padding beside me as I put the house to bed. I can see her golden feather of tail wagging happily. Some might say this is foolish for she was, after all, only a dog, and she is dead. But the fourteen years of love and loyalty she gave me are very much alive as I say "Good night, Honey."

The house talks, as old houses do. A beam settles. A chair rocks. A floor creaks with unseen footsteps. I like this, for it reminds me of all the lives that have been lived under this roof, and I feel their friendly presence as I poke the embers. Christmas is over. It is time to burn the wrappings, write the thank-you notes, return the calls, set the house in order for the New Year. It is also time to consider where our lives are bound, what purpose steadies our course. How much have we helped our fellow men this year, and what good have we accomplished? Has the world been better because we were in it? If Christmas means anything, it means good will to all. I doubt many of us truly live up to that, but we can try again.

As I let the dogs back in, I smell the snow. The walk is silver, the picket fence wears pointed caps. Night herself is luminous with the falling snow. A flurry comes in with the dogs and melts on the wide floor boards. No two snowflakes, I am told, are exactly alike and this is a mystery. Now the intricate shapes are gone, and only a spot of water remains. It is not very practical to stand in the open door at midnight and let the snow blow in. But it has been my habit for years to close Christmas Day just so, sending my blessing out to all the people in the world, those I know well and love greatly, and those I shall never see. And as I close the door, I repeat again my Christmas blessing. "God rest you merry, gentlemen."

Gladys Taber

O Father, may that holy star
  Grow every year more bright,
And send its glorious beams afar
  To fill the world with light.
    William Cullen Bryant

GUESSING TIME

It's guessing time at our house;
   every evening after tea
We start guessing what old
   Santa's going to leave us
   on our tree.
Everyone of us holds secrets
   that the others try to
   steal,
And that eyes and lips are
   plainly having trouble
   to conceal.
And a little lip that quivered
   just a bit the other night
Was a sad and startling warning
   that I mustn't guess it right.

"Guess what you will get for
   Christmas!" is the cry
   that starts the fun.
And I answer: "Give the letter
   with which the name's begun."
Oh, the eyes that dance around
   me and the joyous faces there
Keep me nightly guessing wildly:
   "Is it something I can wear?"
I implore them all to tell me
   in a frantic sort of way
And pretend that I am puzzled,
   just to keep them feeling gay.

Oh, the wide and knowing glances
   that across the table fly
And the winks exchanged with
   mother, that they think I
   never spy;
Oh, the whispered confidences
   that are poured into her ear,
And the laughter gay that follows
   when I try my best to hear!
Oh, the shouts of glad decision
   when I bet that it's a cane,
And the merry answering chorus:
   "No, it's not. Just guess
   again!"
It's guessing time at our house,
   and the fun is running fast,
And I wish somehow this contest
   of delight could always last,
For the love that's in their faces
   and their laughter ringing
   clear
Is their dad's most precious
   present when the Christmas
   time is near.
And soon as it is over, when
   the tree is bare and plain,
I shall start in looking forward
   to the time to guess again.

Edgar Guest

Easter

"HE HAS RISEN"

They took Jesus away. As they went, they met a man named Simon, from Cyrene, who was coming into the city from the country. They seized him, put the cross on him and made him carry it behind Jesus. A large crowd of people followed him; among them were some women who were weeping and wailing for him. Jesus turned to them and said: "Women of Jerusalem! Don't cry for me, but for yourselves and your children. For the days are coming when people will say, 'How lucky are the women who never had children, who never nursed them:' That will be the time when people will say to the mountains, 'Fall on us!' and to the hills, 'Hide us!' For if such things as these are done when the wood is green, what will it be like when it is dry?" They took two others also, both of them criminals, to be put to death with Jesus. When they came to the place called "The Skull," they nailed Jesus to the cross there and the two criminals, one on his right and one on his left. Jesus said, "Forgive them, Father! For they don't know what they are doing." They divided his clothes among themselves by throwing dice. The people stood there watching, while the Jewish leaders made fun of him: "He saved others; let him save himself, if he is the Messiah whom God has chosen!" The soldiers also made fun of him; they came up to him and offered him wine, and said, "Save yourself, if you are the king of the Jews!" These words were written above him: "This is the King of the Jews." One of the criminals hanging there threw insults at him: "Aren't you the Messiah? Save yourself and us!" The other one, however, rebuked him, saying: "Don't you fear God? Here we are all under the same sentence. Ours, however, is only right, for we are getting what we deserve for what we did; but he has done no wrong."

And he said to Jesus, "Remember me, Jesus, when you come as King!" Jesus said to him, "I tell you this: today you will be in Paradise with me."

It was about twelve o'clock when the sun stopped shining and darkness covered the whole country until three o'clock; and the curtain hanging in the temple was torn in two. Jesus cried out in a loud voice, "Father! In your hands I place my spirit!" He said this and died. The army officer saw what had happened and he praised God saying, "Certainly he was a good man!" When the people who had gathered there to watch the spectacle saw what happened, they all went back home beating their breasts. All those who knew Jesus personally, including the women who had followed him from Galilee, stood off at a distance to see these things. There was a man named Joseph from the Jewish town of Arimathea. He was a good and honorable man, and waited for the coming of the Kingdom of God. Although a member of the Council, he had not agreed with their decision and action. He went into the presence of Pilate and asked for the body of Jesus. Then he took the body down, wrapped it in a linen sheet, and placed it in a grave which had been dug out of the rock—a grave which had never been used. It was Friday, and the Sabbath was about to begin.

The women who had followed Jesus from Galilee went with Joseph and saw the grave and how Jesus' body was laid in it. Then they went back home and prepared spices and ointments for his body.

On the Sabbath they rested, as the Law commanded.

Very early on Sunday morning the women went to the grave carrying the spices they had prepared. They found the stone rolled away from the entrance to the grave, so they went on in; but they did not find the body of the Lord Jesus. They stood there, uncertain about this, when suddenly two men in bright shining

clothes stood by them. Full of fear, the women bowed down to the ground, as the men said to them: "Why are you looking among the dead for one who is alive? He is not here; he has risen. Remember what he said to you while he was in Galilee: The Son of Man must be handed over to sinful men, be nailed to the cross and be raised to life on the third day." Then the women remembered his words, returned from the grave, and told all these things to the eleven disciples and all the rest. The women were Mary Magdalene, Joanna, and Mary the mother of James; they and the other women with them told these things to the apostles. But the apostles thought that what the women said was nonsense, and did not believe them. But Peter got up and ran to the grave; he bent down and saw the grave clothes and nothing else. Then he went back home wondering at what had happened.

Luke 23:26–24:12,
The New Testament
in Today's English

"WHY SHOULD HE DIE FOR SUCH AS I"

In everything both great and
    small
We see the hand of God in all,
And in the miracles of Spring
When everywhere in everything
His handiwork is all around
And every lovely sight and
    sound
Proclaims the God of earth and
    sky
I ask myself "just who am I"
That God should send His only
    Son
That my salvation should be won
Upon a cross by a sinless man
To bring fulfillment to God's
    plan—
For Jesus suffered, bled and
    died
That sinners might be
    sanctified,
And to grant God's children
    such as I
Eternal life in that home on
    high.

Helen Steiner Rice

NO MANGER FOR EASTER

He stirs—He moves—in the
    lifting gloom
He wakes, and searching through
    the tomb
Finds no one waiting at night's
    end;
Only Himself—no other friend.

Where are the heralding angels
    now?
Where the donkey and the cow
That warmed Him when the night
    was deep?
Where are the shepherds, the
    kindly sheep?

Where that star of Christmas
    skies?
Where the kingly and the wise?
Where are the righteous, those
    in sin?
And where is the keeper of the
    inn?

He folds the linen clothes
    away,
Then facing the sunrise side
    of day,
Steps into Easter, a lonely
    stranger
Longing for old friends round
    His manger.

Ralph W. Seager

EASTER

I got me flowers to strew
    Thy way,
I got me boughs off many a
    tree;
But Thou wast up by break of day,
And brough'st Thy sweets along
    with Thee.
Yet though my flowers be lost,
    they say
A heart can never come too
    late;
Teach it to sing Thy praise
    this day,
And then this day my life
    shall date.

George Herbert

EVIL DAYS

When He was entering Jerusalem
During that last week
He was hailed with thunderous
    hosannas;
The people ran in His wake,
    waving palm branches.

Yet the days were becoming
    ever more ominous, more grim.
There was no stirring the
    hearts of men through love:
Their eyebrows knit in disdain.
And now, the epilogue. Finis.

The heavens lay heavy over the
    houses,
Crushing with all of their
    leaden weight.
The Pharisees were seeking
    evidence against Him,
Yet cringed before Him like
    foxes.

Then the dark forces of the
    Temple
Gave Him up to be judged by the
    offscourings.
And, with the same fervor with
    which they once sang His praises,
Men now reviled Him.

The rabble from the vicinity
Was peering in at the gateway.
They kept jostling as they bided
    the outcome,
Surging, receding.

The neighborhood crawled with
    sly whispers
And rumors crept in from all
    sides:
He recalled the flight into
    Egypt and His childhood
But recalled them now as in a
    dream.

He remembered the majestic
    cliffside in the wilderness
And that exceeding high mountain
Whereon Satan had tempted Him,
Offering Him all the kingdoms
    of the world.
And the marriage feast at
    Cana
And the guests in great
    admiration over the miracle.
And the sea on which, in a
    mist,
He had walked to the boat as
    if over dry land.

And the gathering of the poor
    in a hovel
And His going down into a
    cellar by the light of a taper
Which had suddenly gone out
    in affright
When the man risen from the
    dead was trying to get to
    his feet.

                    Boris Pasternak

Eternity

WHAT DEATH IS LIKE

I asked what death is like
And saw the eventide
Stoop down caressing earth
All sad and lone and tired.

I asked what death is like
And saw a fresh sunrise
That came expelling night
And waking sleeping eyes.

I asked what death is like
And saw a shadowed face
Of One I recognized,
A friend I should embrace.
Perry Tanksley

O LOVE THAT WILT NOT LET ME GO

O Love that wilt not let me
go,
I rest my weary soul in Thee;
I give thee back the life I
owe,
That in Thine ocean depths
its flow
May richer, fuller be.

O Light that followest all
my way,
I yield my flickering torch
to Thee;
My heart restores its borrowed
ray,
That in Thy sunshine's blaze
its day
May brighter, fairer be.
George Matheson

THE BIVOUAC OF THE DEAD

The muffled drum's sad roll has
beat
The soldier's last tattoo;
No more on life's parade shall meet
The brave and fallen few.
On Fame's eternal camping-ground
Their silent tents are spread,
And Glory guards, with solemn
ground,
The bivouac of the dead.
Theodore O'Hara

UPHILL

Does the road wind uphill all
the way?
Yes, to the very end.
Will the day's journey take
the whole long day?
From morn to night, my friend.

But is there for the night a
resting-place?
A roof for when the slow, dark
hours begin.
May not the darkness hide it
from my face?
You cannot miss that inn.

Shall I meet other wayfarers
at night?
Those who have gone before.
Then must I knock, or call when
just in sight?
They will not keep you waiting
at the door.

Shall I find comfort, travel-
sore and weak?
Of labour you shall find the sum.
Will there be beds for me and
all who seek?
Yea, beds for all who come.
Christina Rossetti

WE ARE SEVEN

A simple Child,
That lightly draws its breath,
And feels its life in every limb,
What should it know of death?

I met a little cottage Girl:
She was eight years old, she said;
Her hair was thick with many
  a curl
That clustered round her head.

She had a rustic, woodland air,
And she was wildly clad:
Her eyes were fair, and very
  fair;
Her beauty made me glad.

"Sisters and brothers, little Maid,
How many may you be?"
"How many? Seven in all,"
  she said
And wondering looked at me.

"And where are they? I pray you
  tell."
She answered, "Seven are we;
And two of us at Conway dwell,
And two are gone to sea.

"Two of us in the church-yard
  lie,
My sister and my brother;
And, in the church-yard cottage,
  I
Dwell near them with my mother."

"You say that two at Conway
  dwell,
And two are gone to sea,
Yet ye are seven! I pray you
  tell,
Sweet Maid, how this may be."

Then did the little Maid reply,
"Seven boys and girls are we;
Two of us in the church-yard lie,
Beneath the church-yard tree."

"You run about, my little Maid,
Your limbs they are alive;
If two are in the church-yard laid,
  Then ye are only five."

"Their graves are green, they
  may be seen,"
The little Maid replied,
"Twelve steps or more from my
  mother's door,
And they are side by side.

"My stockings there I often
  knit,
My kerchief there I hem;
And there upon the ground I
  sit,
And sing a song to them.

"And often after sunset, Sir,
When it is light and fair,
I take my little porringer,
And eat my supper there.

"The first that died was sister
  Jane;
In bed she moaning lay,
Till God released her of her
  pain;
And then she went away.

"So in the church-yard she
  was laid
And, when the grass was dry,
Together round her grave we
  played
My brother John and I.

And when the ground was white
  with snow,
And I could run and slide,
My brother John was forced
  to go,
And he lies by her side."

"How many are you, then,"
  said I,
"If they are two in heaven?"
Quick was the little Maid's
  reply,
"O Master! we are seven."

"But they are dead; those
  two are dead!
Their spirits are in heaven!"
'T was throwing words away;
  for still
The little Maid would have
  her will,
And said, "Nay, we are seven!"
William Wordsworth

TOWARD ETERNITY

Because I could not stop for
    Death,
He kindly stopped for me;
The carriage held but just our-
    selves
And Immortality.

We slowly drove, he knew no
    haste,
And I had put away
My labor, and my leisure too,
For his civility.

We passed the school where
    children played
At wrestling in a ring;
We passed the fields of gazing
    grain,
We passed the setting sun.

We paused before a house that
    seemed
A swelling of the ground;
The roof was scarcely visible,
The cornice but a mound.

Since then 'tis centuries;
    but each
Feels shorter than the day
I first surmised the horses'
    heads
Were toward eternity.

Emily Dickinson

Be of good cheer; I have overcome the world.

John 16:33,
King James Version

If God hath made this world
so fair
Where sin and death abound,
How beautiful beyond compare
Will paradise be found.

James Montgomery

BE STILL AND KNOW

Oh, God, death is so still, so utterly still.

Death is more still than the quietest meadow on a summer day. Stiller than the whitest snows of a winter hillside. More deeply still than the deepest stillness of a starry night.

There is such peace in death, for the spirit is lost in the bliss of some absolute dream.

Death is the perfect knowing.

"Be still and know that I am God," you said. The living can never attain that absolute perfection of stillness and knowing. Only the dead.

But so profound is their stillness this we do know: In you they live.

Marjorie Holmes

JUDGMENT DAY

Every day is Judgment Day,
Count on no to-morrow.
He who will not, when he may,
Act to-day, to-day, to-day,
Doth but borrow
Sorrow.

John Oxenham

JOYFUL EXPECTATION

I do not fear death. Often I wake in the night and think of it. I look forward to it with a thrill of joyful expectation and anticipation, which would become impatience were it not that Jesus is my Master, as well as my Savior. I feel I have work to do for Him that I would not shirk, and also that His time to call me home will be the best and right time, and therefore I am content to wait.

I could not do without Jesus. I cannot and I do not live without Him. It is a new and different life, and this life which takes away all fear of death is what I want others to have and enjoy.

Frances Ridley Havergal

156

LUCY GRAY

Oft I had heard of Lucy Gray:
And, when I crossed the wild,
I chanced to see at break of
    day
The solitary child.

No mate, no comrade Lucy knew;
She dwelt on a wide moor,
The sweetest thing that ever
    grew
Beside a human door!

You yet may spy the fawn at
    play,
The hare upon the green;
But the sweet face of Lucy
    Gray
Will never more be seen.

"To-night will be a stormy
    night—
You to the town must go;
And take a lantern, child, to
    light
Your mother through the
    snow."

"That, Father, will I gladly
    do!
'Tis scarcely afternoon—
The minster-clock has just
    struck two,
And yonder is the moon!"

At this the Father raised his
    hook,
And snapped a faggot-band;
He plied his work;—and Lucy
    took
The lantern in her hand.

Not blither is the mountain roe:
With many a wanton
    stroke
Her feet disperse the powdery
    snow,
That rises up like smoke.

The storm came on before its
    time:
She wandered up and down;
And many a hill did Lucy
    climb;
But never reached the town.

The wretched parents all that
    night
Went shouting far and wide;
But there was neither sound
    nor sight
To serve them for a guide.

At day-break on a hill they
    stood
That overlooked the moor;
And thence they saw the
    bridge of wood,
A furlong from their door.

They wept, and, turning
    homeward cried.
"In heaven we all shall meet!"
—When in the snow the mother
    spied
The print of Lucy's feet.

Then downward from the steep
    hill's edge
They tracked the footmarks small;
And through the broken hawthorn
    hedge,
And by the long stone wall;

And then an open field they
    crossed;
The marks were still the same;
They tracked them on, nor ever
    lost;
And to the bridge they came.

They followed from the snowy
    bank
Those footmarks, one by one,
Into the middle of the plank;
And further there were none!

—Yet some maintain that to
    this day
She is a living child;
That you may see sweet Lucy Gray
Upon the lonesome wild.

O'er rough and smooth she trips
    along,
And never looks behind;
And sings a solitary song
That whistles in the wind.
        William Wordsworth

DEATH IS THE DOOR
TO LIFE EVERMORE

We live a short while on Earth
    below,
Reluctant to die for we do not
    know
Just what "dark death" is all
    about
And so we view it with fear and
    doubt,
Not certain of what is around
    the bend
We look on death as the final
    end
To all that made us a mortal
    being
And yet there lies just beyond
    our seeing
A beautiful life so full and
    complete
That we should leave with
    hurrying feet
To walk with God by sacred
    streams
Amid beauty and peace beyond
    our dreams—
For all who believe in the
    risen Lord
Have been assured of this
    reward
And death for them is just
    "graduation"
To a higher realm of wide
    elevation—
For life on earth is a transient
    affair,
Just a few brief years in which
    to prepare
For a life that is free from
    pain and tears
Where time is not counted by
    hours or years—
For death is only the method
    God chose
To colonize heaven with the
    souls of those
Who by their apprenticeship on
    Earth
Proved worthy to dwell in the
    land of new birth—

So death is not sad . . . it's a
    time for elation,
A joyous transition . . . the
    soul's emigration
Into a place where the soul's
    safe and free
To live with God through
    eternity!
      Helen Steiner Rice

REQUIEM

Under the wide and starry sky,
Dig the grave and let me lie.
Glad did I live and gladly die,
And I laid me down with a will.

This be the verse you grave for
    me:
Here he lies where he longed to
    be;
Home is the sailor, home from
    sea,
And the hunter home from the
    hill.
      Robert Louis Stevenson

CONSOLATION

He is not dead, this friend;
    not dead,
But, in the path we mortals
    tread,
Gone some few, trifling steps
    ahead,
And nearer to the end;
So that you, too, once past
    the bend,
Shall meet again, as face to
    face, this friend
You fancy dead.
      Robert Louis Stevenson

WHEN THE STARS ARE GONE

The stars shine over the
  mountains,
The stars shine over the sea,
The stars look up to the mighty
  God,
The stars look down on me;
The stars shall last for a
  million years,
A million years and a day,
But God and I will live and
  love
When the stars have passed away.
Robert Louis Stevenson

PROMISES OF GOD

We have the promises of God as thick as daisies
in summer meadows, that death, which men
most fear, shall be to us the most blessed of experiences, if we trust in Him. Death is un-
clasping; joy, breaking out in the desert; the
heart, come to its blossoming time! Do we call
it dying when the bud bursts into flower?
Henry Ward Beecher

HE SHALL COME

I cannot tell if it be soon or
  late
When he shall come, for whom
  my spirit yearns:
I only know that, breathlessly,
I wait until the moment when
  my Lord returns;
Until he comes, and I, at
  last, may look through all
  eternity upon that face
That I have found so
  precious in the Book
Where God records the story
  of his Grace.
Helen Frazee-Bower

LIFE AND DEATH

Beyond this vale of tears
There is a life above.
Unmeasured by the flight of
  years;
And all that life is love.
James Montgomery

AWAY

I cannot say, and I will not
  say
That he is dead. He is just
  away
With a cheery smile, and a
  wave of the hand,
He has wandered into an unknown land.

And left us dreaming how very
  fair
It needs must be since he
  lingers there.

And you—O you, who the
  wildest yearn
For the old-time step and the
  glad return—

Think of him faring on, as
  dear
In the love of there as the
  love of here;

Think of him still as the
  same, I say;
He is not dead, he is just away.
James Whitcomb Riley

Let us learn like a bird for a
  moment to take
Sweet rest on a branch that is
  ready to break;
She feels the branch tremble,
  yet gaily she sings.
What is it to her? She has
  wings, she has wings!
Victor Hugo

THE KING'S RING

Once in Persia reigned a king,
Who upon his signet ring
Graved a maxim true and wise,
Which, if held before his
    eyes,
Gave him counsel, at a glance,
Fit for every change or chance:
Solemn words, and these are they:
"Even this shall pass away!"

Trains of camels through the
    sand
Brought him gems from Samarcand;
Fleets of galleys through the
    seas
Brought him pearls to rival
    these.
But he counted little gain
Treasures of the mine or main.
"What is wealth?" the king would
    say;
"Even this shall pass away."

In the revels of his court,
At the zenith of his sport,
When the palms of all his
    guests
Burned with clapping at his
    jests,
He, amid his figs and wine,
Cried, "O loving friends of
    mine!
Pleasure comes, but does not stay;
'Even this shall pass away.' "

Lady fairest ever seen
Was the bride he crowned his
    queen.
Pillowed on the marriage-bed,
Whispering to his soul, he said,
"Though a bridegroom never
    pressed
Dearer bosom to his breast,
Mortal flesh must come to clay:
'Even this shall pass away.' "

Fighting on a furious field,
Once a javelin pierced his
    shield.
Soldiers with a loud lament
Bore him bleeding to his tent.
Groaning from his tortured side,
"Pain is hard to bear," he cried,

"But with patience day by day,
'Even this shall pass away.' "

Towering in the public square
Twenty cubits in the air,
Rose his statue carved in stone,
Then the king, disguised,
    unknown,
Gazing at his sculptured name,
Asked himself, "And what is fame?
Fame is but a slow decay:
'Even this shall pass away.' "

Struck with palsy, sere and old,
Waiting at the Gates of Gold,
Spake he with his dying breath,
"Life is done, but what is
    Death?"
Then, in answer to the king,
Fell a sunbeam on his ring,
Showing by a heavenly ray—
"Even this shall pass away."
                    Theodore Tilton

SOLDIER REST!

Soldier rest! thy warfare o'er,
Dream of fighting fields no more;
Sleep the sleep that knows not
    breaking,
Morn of toil, nor night of
    waking.
                    Sir Walter Scott

The glory of the star, the glory of the sun—we
must not lose either in the other. We must not
be so full of the hope of heaven that we cannot
do our work on the earth; we must not be so lost
in the work of the earth that we shall not be
inspired by the hope of heaven.
                    Phillips Brooks

THERE IS NO DEATH

For years I have been recording a series of incidents which bear out the conviction that life, not death, is the basic principle of our universe. From them I have gained the unshakable belief that there is no death, that here and hereafter are one. When I reached this conclusion, I found it to be the most satisfying and convincing philosophy of my entire life. Following are the experiences which convinced me that human spirits on both sides of death live in a fellowship that continues unbroken.

H. B. Clarke, an old friend of mine, was of a scientific turn of mind, restrained, factual, unemotional. I was called one night by his physician, who expected him to live only a few hours. His heart action was slow. He had no reflex action at all.

I began to pray for him, as did others. The next day his eyes opened and after a few days he recovered his speech. His heart action returned to normal. After he recovered strength he said, "At some time during my illness something very peculiar happened to me. It seemed that I was a long distance away, in the most beautiful and attractive place I have ever seen. There were lights all about me. I saw faces dimly revealed—kind faces they were—and I felt peaceful and happy. In fact I never felt happier.

"The thought came, 'I must be dying.' Then it occurred to me, 'Perhaps I have died.' I almost laughed out loud, and asked myself, 'Why have I been afraid of death all my life? There is nothing to be afraid of in this.'"

"Did you want to live?" I asked.

He smiled and said, "It did not make the slightest difference. If anything, I think I would have preferred to stay in that beautiful place."

Hallucination? A dream? A vision? I do not believe so. I have spent too many years talking to people who have come to the edge of "something" and had a look across, who unanimously have reported beauty, light and peace, to have any doubt in my mind.

A member of my church, Mrs. Bryson Kalt, tells of an aunt whose husband and three children were burned to death when their house was destroyed by fire. The aunt was badly burned but lived for three years. When finally she lay dying, a radiance suddenly came over her face. "It is all so beautiful," she said. "They are coming to meet me. Fluff up my pillows and let me go to sleep."

Friends of mine, Mr. and Mrs. William Sage, lived in New Jersey and I was often in their home. Will Sage died first. A few years later, when Mrs. Sage was on her deathbed, the most surprised look passed across her face. It lighted up in a wonderful smile as she said, "Why, it is Will!" That she saw him those about her bed had no doubt whatsoever.

Arthur Godfrey tells of being asleep in his bunk on a destroyer when he was in the Navy. Suddenly his father stood beside him, put out his hand, smiled and said, "So long, son." Godfrey answered, "So long, Dad." Later he learned of his father's death. The time of his passing had been the precise period during which Godfrey in his sleep "saw" his father.

The late Rufus Jones, one of the most famous spiritual leaders of our time, had a son, Lowell, the apple of his eye. The boy became sick when Dr. Jones was on the ocean bound for Europe. The night before entering Liverpool, while lying in his bunk, Dr. Jones experienced an indefinable, unexplainable sadness. Then, he said, he seemed to be enveloped in the arms of God. A great feeling of peace and a sense of profound possession of his son came to him.

Upon landing in Liverpool, he was advised that his son had died; the death occurred at the exact moment when Dr. Jones had felt God's presence and the everlasting nearness of his son.

A boy serving in Korea wrote to his mother, saying, "The strangest things happen to me. Once in a while at night, when I am afraid, Dad seems to be with me." His father had been dead for ten years. "Do you think that Dad can actually be with me here on these Korean battlefields?"

Why not? How can we not believe that this could be true? Again and again proofs are offered that this universe is a great spiritual sounding house, alive and vital.

My mother was a great soul, and her influence on me will ever stand out in my life as an experience that cannot be surpassed. During my adult years whenever I had the opportunity I went home to see her. It was always an exciting experience.

Then came her death, and in the fullness of summertime we tenderly laid her body in the beautiful little cemetery at Lynchburg in southern Ohio, a town where she had lived as a girl.

It came autumn, and I felt that I wanted to be with my mother again. I was lonely without her, so I went to Lynchburg. The weather was cold and the sky overcast as I walked to the cemetery. I pushed through the old iron gates and my feet rustled in the leaves as I walked to her grave, where I sat sad and lonely. But of a sudden the clouds parted and the sun came through.

Then I seemed to hear her voice. The message was clear and distinct, stated in her beloved old-time tone: "Why seek ye the living among the dead? I am not here. I am with you and my loved ones always."

In a burst of inner light I became wondrously happy. I knew that what I had heard was the truth. I stood up and put my hand on the tombstone and saw it for what it was: only a place where mortal remains lay. But she, that gloriously lovely spirit, is still with us, her loved ones.

The New Testament teaches the indestructibility of life. It describes Jesus after His crucifixion in a series of disappearances and reappearances. This indicates He is trying to tell us that when we do not see Him it does not mean He is not there. Out of sight does not mean out of life.

The mystical appearances which some of us today experience indicate the same truth: that He is nearby. Did He not say, "Because I live, ye shall live also"? In other words, our loved ones who have died in this faith are also nearby, and occasionally draw near to comfort us.

The Bible gives us other insights into the great question, "What happens when a man leaves this world?" And it wisely tells us that we know these truths by faith. The surest way into truth, says Henri Bergson, the philosopher, is by perception, by intuition; by reasoning to a certain point, then taking a "mortal leap." You come to that glorious moment when you simply "know" the truth.

Of these deep and tender matters I have no doubt whatsoever. I firmly believe in the continuation of life after what we call death takes place. I believe there are two sides to the phenomenon known as death: this side where we now live, and the other side where we shall continue to live. Eternity does not start with death. We are in eternity now. We merely change the form of the experience called life—and that change, I am persuaded, is for the better.

Norman Vincent Peale

May you live all the days of your life.

Jonathan Swift

AT THE MID-HOUR OF NIGHT

At the mid-hour of night,
  when stars are weeping, I
  fly
To the lone vale we loved, when
  life shone warm in thine
  eye;
And I think oft if spirits can
  steal from the regions of
  air,
To revisit past scenes of
  delight, thou wilt come to
  me there,
And tell me our love is remembered, even in the sky!

Then I sing the wild song 'twas
  once such a pleasure to hear,
When our voices, commingling,
  breathed, like one, on the
  ear,
And, as Echo far off through
  the vale my sad orison rolls,
I think, O my love! 't is thy
  voice from the Kingdom of
  Souls,
Faintly answering still the
  notes that once were so dear.

Thomas Moore

AT LAST

When on my day of life the
　night is falling,
And, in the winds from unsunned
　spaces blown,
I hear far voices out of dark-
　ness calling
My feet to paths unknown,

Thou who hast made my home of
　life so pleasant,
Leave not its tenant when its
　walls decay;
O Love Divine, O Helper ever
　present,
Be Thou my strength and stay!

Be near me when all else is from
　me drifting;
Earth, sky, home's pictures,
　days of shade and shine,
And kindly faces to my own
　uplifting
The love which answers mine.

I have but Thee, my Father! let
　Thy spirit
Be with me then to comfort and
　uphold;

No gate of pearl, no branch of
　palm I merit,
Nor street of shining gold.

Suffice it if—my good and ill
　unreckoned,
And both forgiven through Thy
　abounding grace—
I find myself by hands familiar
　beckoned
Unto my fitting place.

Some humble door among Thy
　many mansions,
Some sheltering shade where sin
　and striving cease,
And flows forever through
　heaven's green expansions
The river of Thy peace.

There, from the music round about
　me stealing,
I fain would learn the new and
　holy song,
And find at last, beneath Thy
　trees of healing,
The life for which I long.

John Greenleaf Whittier

Family

WHERE THERE IS LOVE

Where there is love the heart
  is light,
Where there is love the day
  is bright,
Where there is love there
  is a song
To help when things are going
  wrong . . .
Where there is love there is
  a smile
To make all things seem more
  worthwhile
Where there is love there's
  quiet peace,
A tranquil place where turmoils
  cease . . .
Love changes darkness into
  light
And makes the heart take "wing-
  less flight" . . .
And Mothers have a special way
Of filling homes with love each
  day,
And when the home is filled
  with love
You'll always find God spoken
  of,
And when a family "prays to-
  gether,"
That family also "stays to-
  gether" . . .
And once again a Mother's
  touch
Can mold and shape and do so
  much
To make this world a better
  place
For every color, creed and race—
For when man walks with God
  again,
There shall be peace on earth
  for men.

Helen Steiner Rice

Except the Lord build the house,
they labour in vain that build
  it:
except the Lord keep the city,
the watchman waketh but in vain.
It is vain for you to rise up
  early,
to sit up late,
to eat the bread of sorrows:
for so he giveth his beloved
  sleep.
Lo, children are an heritage
  of the Lord:
and the fruit of the womb is
  his reward.
As arrows are in the hand of
  a mighty man;
so are children of the youth.
Happy is the man that hath his
  quiver full of them:
they shall not be ashamed,
but they shall speak with the
  enemies in the gate.

Psalm 127,
King James Version

WE AND THEY

Father, Mother and Me,
Sister and Auntie say
All the people like us are We
And everyone else is They.
Rudyard Kipling

Honour thy father and thy mother: that thy
days may be long upon the land which the Lord
thy God giveth thee.

Exodus 20:12,
King James Version

On the whole, ought I not to rejoice that God was pleased to give me such a father that from earliest years I had the example of a real man of God's own making continually before me? Let me learn of him. Let me write my books as he built his houses, and walk as blamelessly through this shadow world.

Thomas Carlyle

A baby is God's opinion that life should go on.

Carl Sandburg

A MOTHER'S PRAYER

Father in Heaven, make me wise,
So that my gaze may never meet
A question in my children's
    eyes;
God keep me always kind and
    sweet,

And patient, too, before their
    need;
Let each vexation know its
    place,
Let gentleness be all my creed,
Let laughter live upon my face!

A mother's day is very long,
There are so many things to do!
But never let me lose my song
Before the hardest day is
    through.

Margaret Sangster

Children begin by loving their parents; as they grow older they judge them; sometimes they forgive them.

Oscar Wilde

FATHER AND SON

Be more than his dad,
Be a chum to the lad;
Be a part of his life
Every hour of the day;
Find time to talk with him,
Take time to walk with him,
Share in his studies
And share in his play;
Take him to places,
To ball games and races,
Teach him the things
That you want him to know;
Don't live apart from him,
Don't keep your heart from him,
Be his best comrade,
He's needing you so!

Never neglect him,
Though young, still respect him,
Hear his opinions
With patience and pride;
Show him his error,
But be not a terror,
Grim-visaged and fearful,
When he's at your side.
Know what his thoughts are,
Know what his sports are,
Know all his playmates,
It's easy to learn to;
Be such a father
That when troubles gather
You'll be the first one
For counsel, he'll turn to.

You can inspire him
With courage, and fire him
Hot with ambition
For deeds that are good;
He'll not betray you
Nor illy repay you,
If you have taught him
The things that you should.
Father and son
Must in all things be one—
Partners in trouble
And comrades in joy.
More than a dad
Was the best pal you had;
Be such a chum
As you knew, to your boy.

Edgar Guest

THE BALLAD OF THE HARP-WEAVER

"Son," said my mother,
When I was knee high,
"You've need of clothes to
    cover you,
And not a rag have I.

"There's nothing in the
    house
To make a boy breeches,
Nor shears to cut a cloth
    with
Nor thread to take stitches.

"There's nothing in the
    house
But a loaf-end of rye,
And a harp with a woman's
    head
Nobody will buy."
And she began to cry.

That was in the early fall.
When came the late fall,
"Son," she said, "the sight
    of you
Makes your mother's blood
    crawl,—

"Little skinny shoulder-blades
Sticking through your clothes!
And where you'll get a jacket
    from
God above knows.

"It's lucky for me, lad,
Your daddy's in the ground.
And can't see the way I let
His son go around!"
And she made a queer sound.

That was in the late fall.
When the winter came,
I'd not a pair of breeches
Nor a shirt to my name.

I couldn't go to school,
Or out of doors to play.
And all the other little
    boys
Passed our way.

"Son," said my mother.
"Come, climb into my lap,

And I'll chafe your little
    bones
While you take a nap."

And, oh, but we were silly
For half an hour or more,
Me with my long legs
Dragging on the floor,

A-rock-rock-rocking
To a mother-goose rhyme!
Oh, but we were happy
For half an hour's time!

But there was I, a great boy,
And what would folks say
To hear my mother singing me
To sleep all day,
In such a daft way?

Men say the winter
Was bad that year;
Fuel was scarce,
And food was dear.

A wind with a wolf's head
Howled about our door,
And we burned up the chairs
And sat upon the floor.

All that was left us
Was a chair we couldn't
    break,
And the harp with a woman's
    head
Nobody would take,
For song or pity's sake.

The night before Christmas
I cried with the cold,
I cried myself to sleep
Like a two-year-old.

And in the deep night
I felt my mother rise,
And stare down upon me
With love in her eyes.

I saw my mother sitting
On the one good chair,
A light falling on her
From I couldn't tell where,

Looking nineteen,
And not a day older,

And the harp with a woman's
    head
Leaned against her shoulder.

Her thin fingers, moving
In the thin tall strings,
Were weav-weav-weaving
Wonderful things.

Many bright threads,
From where I couldn't see,
Were running through the
    harp-strings
Rapidly,

And gold threads whistling
Through my mother's hand.
I saw the web grow,
And the pattern expand.

She wove a child's jacket
And when it was done
She laid it on the floor
And wove another one.

She wove a red cloak
So regal to see,
"She's made it for a king's
    son,"
But I knew it was for me.

She wove a pair of breeches
Quicker than that!
She wove a pair of boots
And a little cocked hat.

She wove a pair of mittens,
She wove a little blouse,
She wove all night
In the still, cold house.

She sang as she worked,
And the harp-strings spoke;
Her voice never faltered,
And the thread never broke,
And when I awoke—

There sat my mother
With the harp against her
    shoulder,
Looking nineteen
And not a day older,

A smile about her lips,
And a light about her head,

And her hands in the harp-
    strings
Frozen dead.

And piled up beside her
And toppling to the skies,
Were the clothes of a king's
    son,
Just my size.
        Edna St. Vincent Millay

A good woman is a wondrous creature, cleaving
to the right and to the good under all change:
lovely in youthful comeliness, lovely all her life
long in comeliness of heart.
        Alfred, Lord Tennyson

Who can find a virtuous woman? for her price
is far above rubies.

        Proverbs 31:10,
        King James Version

MOTHER'S BEDTIME STORIES

When we boys were little, we used to go to
Mother's room Sunday evenings, on our way
upstairs to bed, and sit in a circle around her,
while she told us a story from the Bible or
talked to us about how good we ought to be
and how much we ought to love God. She
loved God herself as much as she dared to, and
she deeply loved us, and she was especially
tender and dear on those Sunday evenings. One
of my brothers told me years afterward how
much they had meant to him in those days, and
how he had cherished the memory of them all
his life.

        Clarence Day

SHOOTING-STARS

When I was five I was al-
    lowed to stay up late
On summer nights, to watch
    the shooting-stars;
"Meteors" were what the grown-
    ups called them.
My father and I would lean on
    the pasture-bars
And watch the stars fall,
    leaving trails of fire.
They were so beautiful! I can
    still recall
How bright each was, falling
    through black space,
And that my father and I
    shared in it all.
Now when I see a meteor descend
In flame, I quickly bridge
    the years behind
To those of the present; I am
    back again
In that old field; miraculous-
    ly find
My hand in my father's hand,
    gentle yet strong,
While we watch the shooting-
    stars' bright, fiery throng.
Pauline Havard

GOING TO THE OFFICE

If it was a rainy day, Father would prepare for rough weather by wearing a derby hat and a black rubber mackintosh over his usual tailed coat. (He seldom was informal enough to wear a sack suit in town except on warm days, or when he left New York to go to the country, in summer.) If the sun was out, he wore a silk hat and carried a cane, like his friends. When he and they passed each other on the street, they raised their canes and touched the brims of their hats with them, in formal salute.

Clarence Day

A wise son maketh a glad father.

Proverbs 10:1,
King James Version

ONLY A DAD

Only a dad with a tired face
Coming home from the daily race,
Bringing little of gold or
    fame
To show how well he has played
    the game;
But glad in his heart that his
    own rejoice
To see him come and to hear his
    voice.

Only a dad with a brood of four,
One of ten million men or more
Plodding along in the daily
    strife
Bearing the whips and the scorns
    of life,
With never a whimper of pain
    or hate,
For the sake of those who at
    home await.

Only a dad, neither rich nor
    proud,
Merely one of the surging
    crowd,
Toiling, striving from day to
    day,
Facing whatever may come his
    way,
Silent whenever the harsh con-
    demn,
And bearing it all for the
    love of them.

Only a dad but he gives his
    all,
To smooth the way for his
    children small,
Doing with courage stern and
    grim
The deeds that his father did
    for him.
This is the line that for him
    I pen:
Only a dad, but the best of
    men.

Edgar Guest

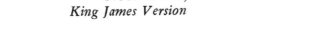

GRANDPA

My grandpa is the finest man
Excep' my pa. My grandpa can
Make kites an' carts an' lots
   of things
You pull along the ground with
   strings,
And he knows all the names of
   birds,
And how they call 'thout using
   words,
And where they live and what
   they eat,
And how they build their nests
   so neat.
He's lots of fun! Sometimes
   all day
He comes to visit me and play.
You see he's getting old, and
   so
To work he doesn't have to go,
And when it isn't raining, he
Drops in to have some fun with
   me.

He takes my hand and we go out
And everything we talk about.
He tells me how God makes the
   trees,
And why it hurts to pick up
   bees.
Sometimes he stops and shows to
   me
The place where fairies used
   to be;
And then he tells me stories,
   too,
And I am sorry when he's through.
When I am asking him for more
He says: "Why there's a candy
   store!
Let's us go there and see if
   they
Have got the kind we like to-
   day."
Then when we get back home my
   ma
Says: "You are spoiling Buddy,
   Pa."

My grandpa is my mother's pa,
I guess that's what all grandpas
   are

And sometimes ma, all smiles,
   will say:
"You didn't always act that way.
When I was little, then you
   said
That children should be sent to
   bed
And not allowed to rule the
   place
And lead old folks a merry
   chase."
And grandpa laughs and says:
   "That's true,
That's what I used to say to
   you.
It is a father's place to show
The young the way that they
   should go,
But grandpas have a different
   task,
Which is to get them all they
   ask."

When I get big and old and gray
I'm going to spend my time in
   play;
I'm going to be a grandpa, too,
And do as all the grandpas do.
I'll buy my daughter's children
   things
Like horns and drums and tops
   with strings,
And tell them all about the
   trees
And frogs and fish and birds
   and bees
And fairies in the shady glen
And tales of giants, too,
   and when
They beg of me for just one
   more,
I'll take them to the candy
   store;
I'll buy them everything they
   see
The way my grandpa does for me.
                Edgar Guest

I think, am sure, a brother's love exceeds all the
world's love in its unworldliness.
                Robert Browning

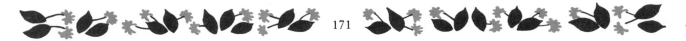

Days to Come

Look not mournfully into the Past. It comes not back again. Wisely improve the Present. It is thine. Go forth to meet the shadowy Future, without fear, and with a manly heart.

Henry Wadsworth Longfellow

I never think of the future,
It comes soon enough.

Albert Einstein

Every man's life is a plan of God.

Horace Bushnell

LIFE

Let me but live my life from
  year to year,
With forward face and un-
  reluctant soul;
Not hurrying to, nor turning
  from, the goal;
Not mourning for the things
  that disappear
In the dim past, nor holding
  back in fear
From what the future veils;
  but with a whole
And happy heart, that pays its toll
To Youth and Age, and
  travels on with cheer.

So let the way wind up the
  hill or down,
O'er rough or smooth, the
  journey will be joy:
Still seeking what I sought
  when but a boy,
New friendship, high adventure,
  and a crown,
My heart will keep the courage
  of the quest,
And hope the road's last turn
  will be the best.

Henry Van Dyke

RING OUT, WILD BELLS

Ring out, wild bells, to the
  wild sky,
The flying cloud, the frosty
  light:
The year is dying in the night;
Ring out, wild bells, and let
  him die.

Ring out the old, ring in the
  new,
Ring, happy bells, across the
  snow
The year is going, let him go;
Ring out the false, ring in the
  true.

Alfred, Lord Tennyson

The tissue of Life to be
We weave with colors all our
  own,
And in the field of Destiny
We reap as we have sown.

John Greenleaf Whittier

Ideals

MY AIM

I live for those who love me,
For those who know me true;
For the heaven that smiles
    above me,
And awaits my spirit too.
For the cause that lacks
    assistance,
For the wrong that needs re-
    sistance,
For the future in the distance,
And the good that I can do.

George Linnaeus Banks

THE DREAM

Ah, great it is to believe
    the dream
As we stand in youth by the
    stream;
But a greater thing is to fight
    life through,
And say at the end, "The dream
    is true!"

Edwin Markham

Finish every day and be done with it. You have done what you could. Some blunders and absurdities no doubt crept in; forget them as soon as you can. Tomorrow is a new day; begin it well and serenely and with too high a spirit to be cumbered with your old nonsense. This day is all that is good and fair. It is too dear, with its hopes and invitations, to waste a moment on the yesterdays.

Ralph Waldo Emerson

May I be no man's enemy, and may I be the friend of that which is eternal and abides. May I never quarrel with those nearest me; and if I do, may I never devise evil against any man; if any devise evil against me, may I escape uninjured and without the need of hurting him. May I love, seek, and attain only that which is good. May I wish for all men's happiness and envy none. May I never rejoice in the ill-fortune of one who has wronged me. When I have done or said what is wrong, may I never wait for the rebuke of others, but always rebuke myself until I make amends. . . . May I win no victory that harms either me or my opponent. . . . . May I reconcile friends who are wroth with one another. May I, to the extent of my power, give all needful help to my friends and to all who are in want. May I never fail a friend in danger. When visiting those in grief may I be able by gentle and healing words to soften their pain. . . . May I respect myself . . . May I always keep tame that which rages within me . . . May I accustom myself to be gentle, and never be angry with people because of circumstances. May I never discuss who is wicked and what wicked things he has done, but know good men and follow in their footsteps.

Eusebius

Be good; get good, and do good. Do all the good you can, to all the people you can, in all the ways you can, as often as ever you can, as long as you can.

Charles H. Spurgeon

The ideals which have always shone before me and filled me with the joy of living are goodness, beauty, and truth.

Albert Einstein

THREE GATES

If you are tempted to reveal
A tale to you someone has told
About another, make it pass,
Before you speak, three gates
  of gold.
These narrow gates: First,
  "Is it true?"
Then, "Is it needful?" In
  your mind
Give truthful answer. And the
  next
Is last and narrowest, "Is it
  kind?"
And if to reach your lips at
  last
It passes through these gate-
  ways three,
Then you may tell the tale,
  nor fear
What the result of speech may
  be.

From the Arabian

MY PHILOSOPHY OF LIFE...

To know the will of God is
  the greatest knowledge.
To suffer the will of God
  is the greatest heroism.
To do the will of God is the
  greatest achievement.
To have the approval of God
  on your work is the greatest
  happiness.

Albert Schweitzer

O God, grant us the serenity to accept what cannot be changed; The courage to change what can be changed; And wisdom to know one from the other.

Reinhold Niebuhr

To become Christlike is the only thing in the whole world worth caring for, the thing before which every ambition of man is folly and all lower achievement vain.

Henry Drummond

PRAYER

Grant me, O Lord, to know what I ought to know, to love what I ought to love, to praise what delights Thee most, to value what is precious in Thy sight, to hate what is offensive to Thee. Do not suffer me to judge according to the sight of my eyes, nor to pass sentence according to the hearing of the ears of ignorant men; but to discern with a true judgment between things visible and spiritual, and above all, always to inquire what is the good pleasure of Thy will.

Thomas à Kempis

THE CHRISTIAN GENTLEMAN

A Christian gentleman will be
  slow to lose patience—
  a Christian grace.
A Christian gentleman will look
  for a way to be constructive,
  even when provoked.
A Christian gentleman will not
  envy the good fortune of
  others.
A Christian gentleman will refrain from trying to impress
  others with his own importance.
A Christian gentleman will have
  good manners.
A Christian gentleman will not
  be "touchy,"
  even when he feels the right of
  resentment.
A Christian gentleman will think
  the best, not the worst, of
  others; he will try to be as
  wise as the serpent and harmless as a dove in handling others.
A Christian gentleman will not
  gloat over the wickedness
  of other people.
Above all else, a Christian
  gentleman will exhibit the
  love of Christ in his heart
  and life.

L. Nelson Bell

A PSALM OF LIFE

Tell me not, in mournful
   numbers,
Life is but an empty dream!—
For the soul is dead that
   slumbers,
And things are not what they
   seem.

Life is real! Life is earnest!
And the grave is not its goal;
Dust thou art, to dust return-
   est,
Was not spoken of the soul.

Not enjoyment, and not sorrow,
Is our destined end or way;
But to act, that each tomorrow
Find us farther than today.

Art is long, and Time is
   fleeting,
And our hearts, though stout
   and brave,
Still, like muffled drums,
   are beating
Funeral marches to the grave.

In the world's broad field of
   battle,
In the bivouac of life,
Be not dumb, driven cattle!
Be a hero in the strife!

Trust no Future, howe'er
   pleasant!
Let the dead Past bury its
   dead!
Act,—act in the living
   Present!
Heart within, and God o'erhead!

Lives of great men all remind
   us
We can make our lives sublime,
And, departing, leave behind us
Footprints on the sands of time;

Footprints that perhaps another,
Sailing o'er life's solemn
   main,
A forlorn and shipwrecked
   brother,

Seeing, shall take heart again.
Let us then be up and doing,
With a heart for any fate;
Still achieving, still pursuing,
Learn to labor and to wait.
    Henry Wadsworth Longfellow

RULES IN
QUEEN ELIZABETH'S COURT
The Spiritual Glass

Read distinctly.
Pray devoutly.
Sigh deeply.
Suffer patiently.
Make yourselves lowly.
Give not sentence hastily.
Speak but seldom, and that
   truly.
Present your speech discreetly
Observe Ten [1] diligently.
Flee from Seven [2] mightily.
Guide Five [3] circumspectly.
Resist temptation strongly.
Break that off quickly.
Weep bitterly.
Have compassion tenderly.
Do good deeds lustily.
Love heartily.
Love faithfully.
Love God only.
Love all others for him
   charitably.
Love in adversity.
Love in prosperity.
Think always on Love, which
   is nothing but God himself.
Thus Love bringeth the Lover
   to Love,
   which is God himself.

[1] *Commandments*
[2] *Deadly Sins*
[3] *Senses*

Whatsoever things are true,
Whatsoever things are honest,
Whatsoever things are just,
Whatsoever things are pure;
Whatsoever things are lovely,
Whatsoever things are of good
report; if there be any virtue,
and if there be any praise,
think on these things.

Philippians 4:8,
King James Version

THOMAS JEFFERSON'S DECALOGUE FOR THE PRACTICAL LIFE

1. Never put off till tomorrow
what you can do today.

2. Never trouble another for
what you can do yourself.

3. Never spend your money before
you have it.

4. Never buy what you do not
want, because it is cheap;
it will be dear to you.

5. Pride costs us more than
hunger, thirst and cold.

6. We never repent of having
eaten too little.

7. Nothing is troublesome
that we do willingly.

8. How much pain have cost us
the evils which have never
happened.

9. Take things always by
their smooth handle.

10. When angry, count ten,
before you speak; if
very angry, an hundred.

(From a letter to
Thomas Jefferson Smith,
February 21, 1825)

Live every day of your life as though you expected to live forever.

Douglas MacArthur

If we work upon marble, it will perish; if on
brass, time will efface it; if we rear temples,
they will crumple into dust; but if we work
upon immortal minds, and imbue them with
principles, with the just fear of God and love of
our fellow men, we engrave on those tablets
something that will brighten to all eternity.

Daniel Webster

We have committed the Golden Rule to memory; now let us commit it to life.

Edwin Markham

I have four things to learn
in life:
To think clearly without
hurry or confusion;
To love everybody sincerely
To act in everything with the
highest motives;
To trust in God unhesitatingly.

Helen Keller

I do not believe there is a problem in this country or the world today which could not be
settled if approached through the teaching of
the Sermon on the Mount.

Harry S. Truman

No man or woman of the humblest sort can
really be strong, gentle, pure, and good without
the world being better for it, without somebody being helped and comforted by the very
existence of that goodness.

Phillips Brooks

THE THINGS THAT NEVER DIE

The pure, the bright, the
  beautiful,
That stirred our hearts in
  youth,
The impulses to wordless
  prayer,
The dreams of love and truth;

The longings after something
  lost,
The spirit's yearning cry,
The strivings after better
  hopes—
These things can never die.

The timid hand stretched forth
  to aid
A brother in his need,
A kindly word in grief's dark
  hour
That proves a friend indeed;

The plea for mercy softly
  breathed,
When justice threatens nigh,
The sorrow of a contrite heart—
These things shall never die.

The cruel and bitter word,
That wounded as it fell;
The chilling want of sympathy
We feel, but never tell;
The hard repulse that chills
  the heart,
Whose hopes were bounding high,
In an unfading record kept—
These things shall never die.

Let nothing pass, for every
  hand
Must find some work to do;
Lose not a chance to waken
  love—

Be firm, and just, and true:
So shall a light that cannot
  fade
Beam on thee from on high,
And angel voices say to thee—
These things shall never die.
          Charles Dickens

THE BEATITUDES

Happy are those who know they are spiritually
  poor; the Kingdom of Heaven belongs to them!
Happy are those who mourn: God will com-
  fort them!
Happy are the meek: They will receive what
  God has promised.
Happy are those whose greatest desire is to do
  what God requires: God will satisfy them fully!
Happy are those who show mercy to others:
  God will show mercy to them.
Happy are the pure in heart: they will see
  God.
Happy are those who work for peace among
  men; God will call them his sons!
Happy are those who suffer persecution be-
  cause they do what God requires: The King-
  dom of Heaven belongs to them!
Happy are you when men insult and mistreat
  you and tell all kinds of evil lies against you
  because you are my followers.
Rejoice and be glad, because a great reward is
  kept for you in heaven. This is how men mis-
  treated the prophets who lived before you."
          Matthew 5:3–11,
          The New Testament
          in Today's English

Childhood

A child may be as new to the world as snow-drops in January, and yet already have a good and keen and deep understanding, a full mind and a hospitable heart. He may be able to think hard, imagine richly, face trouble, take good care of himself and of others, keep well, and live abundantly.

Walter de la Mare

The child is father of the man.

William Wordsworth

The secret of education lies in respecting the pupil.

Ralph Waldo Emerson

A LITTLE GIRL

There was a little girl
Who had a little curl
Right in the middle of her
   forehead,
And when she was good
She was very, very good,
And when she was bad she was
   horrid.

Henry Wadsworth Longfellow

The mother's heart is the child's schoolroom.

Henry Ward Beecher

LITTLE BOYS IN CHURCH

Small boys in the church pews
   grow
Very fast, the first you know
Ones only halfway up are older
And at their father's cheek
   or shoulder.

One day they are only bright
Heads that in the high church
   light
Look as if they were washed
   in dew,
Their ears and hair are all so
   new.

This Sunday only heads that
   dance,
Next Sunday heads and coats
   and pants,
All the boys have sprung uphill,
Heads are erect, and ears stand
   still.

One week they are boys, and
   then
Next week they are slim young
   men
Standing very still and lean,
Perilously scrubbed and clean.

Enjoy each small boy while you
   can,
Tomorrow there will be a man
Standing taller than belief,
Little boys in church are brief.

Robert P. Tristram Coffin

THE CHOIR BOY

In his white surplice there he
  stands,
A hymnal in his boyish hands;
The morning sun upon his hair
Suggests a halo circling there.

His voice as sweet and fresh
  to hear
As feathered songbird singing
  clear;
His eyes as innocent and blue
As skies with heaven shining
  through.

Is this the boy who all the
  week
Brought worried lines to father's
  cheek?
Is this the mischievous small
  lad
Whom teacher found so very bad?

It cannot be! but mother, who
Serenely listens from her pew,
Feels truly what the others
  miss—
At heart he always is like
  this!

Anne Campbell

I REMEMBER, I REMEMBER

I remember, I remember
The fir-trees dark and high;
I used to think their slender
  tops
Were close against the sky:
It was a childish ignorance,
But now 'tis little joy
To know I'm farther off from
  heav'n
Than when I was a boy.

Thomas Hood

Train up a child in the way he should go; and
when he is old, he will not depart from it.

Proverbs 22:6,
King James Version

We need love's tender lessons
  taught
As only weakness can;
God hath his small interpreters;
The child must teach the man.

John Greenleaf Whittier

THE SPIRIT OF A LITTLE CHILD

Our religion is one which challenges the or-
dinary human standards by holding that the
ideal of life is the spirit of a little child. We
tend to glorify adulthood and wisdom and
wordly prudence, but the Gospel reverses all
this. The Gospel says that the inescapable condition of entrance into the divine fellowship
is that we turn and become as a little child.
As against our natural judgment we must become tender and full of wonder and unspoiled
by the hard skepticism on which we so often
pride ourselves. But when we really look into
the heart of a child, willful as he may be, we
are often ashamed. God has sent children into
the world, not only to replenish it, but to serve
as sacred reminders of something ineffably
precious which we are always in danger of losing. The sacrament of childhood is thus a continuing revelation.

Elton Trueblood

I had a little daughter,
And she was given to me
To lead me gently backward
To the Heavenly Father's knee,
That I, by the force of nature,
Might in some dim wise divine
The depth of His infinite
  patience
To this wayward soul of mine.

James Russell Lowell

THE BAREFOOT BOY

Blessings on thee, little man,
Barefoot boy, with cheek of
  tan!
With thy turned-up pantaloons,
And thy merry whistled tunes;
With thy red lip, redder still
Kissed by strawberries on the
  hill;
With the sunshine on thy face,
Through thy torn brim's jaunty
  grace;
From my heart I give thee joy,
I was once a barefoot boy!
Prince thou art,—the grown up
  man
Only is republican.
Let the million-dollared ride!
Barefoot, trudging at his
  side,
Thou hast more than he can buy
In the reach of ear and eye,
Outward sunshine, inward joy:
Blessings on thee, barefoot
  boy!

Oh for boyhood's painless play,
Sleep that wakes in laughing
  day,
Health that mocks the doctor's
  rules,
Knowledge never learned in
  schools,
Of the wild bee's morning chase,
Of the wild-flower's time
  and place,
Flight of fowl and habitude
Of the tenants of the wood;
How the tortoise bears his
  shell,
How the woodchuck digs his cell,
And the ground-mole sinks his
  well;
How the robin feeds her young,
How the oriole's nest is
  hung;
Where the whitest lilies blow,
Where the freshest berries grow,
Where the ground-nut trails
  its vine,
Where the wood grape's clusters
  shine;

Of the black wasp's cunning
  way,
Mason of his walls of clay,
And the architectural plans
Of gray hornet artisans!
For, eschewing books and tasks,
Nature answers all he asks;
Hand in hand with her he walks,
Face to face with her he talks,
Part and parcel of her joy,
Blessings on thee barefoot boy!
        John Greenleaf Whittier

THE ROUGH LITTLE RASCAL

A smudge on his nose and a
  smear on his cheek
And knees that might not have
  been washed in a week;
A bump on his forehead, a scar
  on his lip,
A relic of many a tumble and
  trip:
A rough little, tough little
  rascal, but sweet,
Is he that each evening I'm
  eager to meet.

A brow that is beady with
  jewels of sweat;
A face that's as black as a
  visage can get;
A suit that at noon was a garment of white,
Now one that his mother declares
  is a fright:
A fun-loving, sun-loving rascal,
  and fine,
Is he that comes placing his
  black fist in mine.

A crop of brown hair that is
  tousled and tossed;
A waist from which two of the
  buttons are lost;
A smile that shines out through
  the dirt and the grime,
And eyes that are flashing delight all the time:
All these are the joys that I'm
  eager to meet
And look for the moment I get
  to my street.
        Edgar Guest

TOM SAWYER MEETS A STRANGER

The summer evenings were long. It was not dark, yet. Presently Tom checked his whistle. A stranger was before him—a boy a shade larger than himself. A newcomer of any age or either sex was an impressive curiosity in the poor little shabby village of St. Petersburg. This boy was well-dressed, too—well dressed on a weekday. This was simply astonishing. His cap was a dainty thing, his close-buttoned blue cloth roundabout was new and natty, and so were his pantaloons. He had shoes on—and it was only Friday. He even wore a neck tie, a bright bit of ribbon. He had a citified air about him that ate into Tom's vitals. The more Tom stared at the splendid marvel, the higher he turned up his nose at his finery and the shabbier and shabbier his own outfit seemed to him to grow. Neither boy spoke. If one moved, the other moved—but only sidewise, in a circle; they kept face to face and eye to eye all the time. Finally Tom said:

"I can lick you!"

"I'd like to see you try it."

"Well, I can do it."

"No you can't, either."

"Yes I can."

"No you can't."

"I can."

"You can't."

"Can!"

"Can't!"

An uncomfortable pause. Then Tom said:

"What's your name?"

"Tisn't any of your business, maybe."

"Well I 'low I'll *make* it my business."

"Well why don't you?"

"If you say much, I will."

"Much—much—*much*. There now."

"Oh, you think you're mighty smart, *don't* you? I could lick you with one hand tied behind me, if I wanted to."

"Well why don't you *do* it? You *say* you can do it."

"Well, I *will*, if you fool with me."

"Oh yes—I've seen whole families in the same fix."

"Smarty! You think you're *some*, now, *don't* you? Oh, what a hat!"

"You can lump that hat if you don't like it. I dare you to knock it off—and anybody that'll take a dare will suck eggs."

"You're a liar!"

"You're another."

"You're a fighting liar and dasn't take it up."

"Aw—take a walk!"

"Say—if you give me much more of your sass I'll take and bounce a rock off'n your head."

"Oh, of *course* you will."

"Well I *will*."

"Well why don't you *do* it then? What do you keep *saying* you will for? Why don't you *do* it? It's because you're afraid."

"I *ain't* afraid."

"You are."

"I ain't."

"You are."

Another pause, and more eyeing and sidling around each other. Presently they were shoulder to shoulder. Tom said:

"Get away from here!"

"Go away yourself!"

"I won't."

"I won't either."

So they stood each with a foot placed at an angle as a brace, and both shoving with might and main, and glowering at each other with hate. But neither could get an advantage. After struggling till both were hot and flushed, each relaxed his strain with watchful caution, and Tom said:

"You're a coward and a pup. I'll tell my big brother on you, and he can thrash you with his little finger, and I'll make him do it, too."

"What do I care for your big brother? I've got a brother that's bigger than he is—and what's more, he can throw him over that fence, too." (Both brothers were imaginary.)

"That's a lie."

"*Your* saying so don't make it so."

Tom drew a line in the dust with his big toe, and said:

"I dare you to step over that, and I'll lick you till you can't stand up. Anybody that'll take a dare will steal sheep."

The new boy stepped over promptly, and said:

"Now you said you'd do it, now let's see you do it."

"Don't you crowd me now; you better look out."

"Well, you *said* you'd do it—why don't you do it?"

"By jingo! for two cents I *will* do it."

The new boy took two broad coppers out of his pocket and held them out with derision. Tom struck them to the ground. In an instant both boys were rolling and tumbling in the dirt, gripped together like cats; and for the space of a minute they tugged and tore at each other's hair and clothes, punched and scratched each other's noses, and covered themselves with dust and glory. Presently the confusion took form and through the fog of battle Tom appeared, seated astride the new boy, and pounding him with his fists.

"Holler 'nuff!" said he.

The boy only struggled to free himself. He was crying, mainly from rage.

"Holler 'nuff!"—and the pounding went on.

At last the stranger got out a smothered "Nuff!" and Tom let him up and said:

"Now that'll learn you. Better look out who you're fooling with next time."

The new boy went off brushing the dust from his clothes, sobbing, snuffing, and occasionally looking back and shaking his head and threatening what he would do to Tom the "next time he caught him out." To which Tom responded with jeers, and started off in a high feather, and as soon as his back was turned the new boy snatched up a stone, threw it and hit him between the shoulders and then turned tail and ran like an antelope. Tom chased the traitor home, and thus found out where he lived. He then held a position at the gate for some time, daring the enemy to come outside, but the enemy only made faces at him through the window and declined. At last the enemy's mother appeared, and called Tom a bad, vicious, vulgar child, and ordered him away. So he went away; but he said he "lowed" to "lay" for that boy.

(From *Tom Sawyer*)
Mark Twain

LIVING ARROWS

You may give them your love
   but not your thoughts,
For they have their own
   thoughts.
You may house their bodies but
   not their souls,
For their souls dwell in the
   house of tomorrow
   which you cannot visit, not
   even in your dreams.
You may strive to be like them,
   but seek not to make them
   like you.
For life goes not backward nor
   tarries with yesterday.
You are the bows from which
   your children as living
   arrows are sent forth.
Kahlil Gibran

Challenge

EXCELSIOR!

The shades of night were falling
fast,
As through an Alpine village
passed
A youth, who bore, 'mid snow
and ice,
A banner with the strange
device—
Excelsior!

His brow was sad; his eye
beneath
Flashed like a falchion from
its sheath;
And like a silver clarion rung
The accents of that unknown
tongue—
Excelsior!

In happy homes he saw the light
Of household fires gleam warm
and bright:
Above, the spectral glaciers
shone,
And from his lips escaped a
groan—
Excelsior!

"Try not the pass," the old man
said:
"Dark lowers the tempest
overhead;
The roaring torrent is deep and
wide!"
And loud that clarion voice
replied,
Excelsior!

"O stay," the maiden said, "and
rest
Thy weary head upon this breast!"
A tear stood in his bright
blue eye,
But still he answered, with
a sigh,
Excelsior!

"Beware the pine-tree's withered
branch!
Beware the awful avalanche!"
This was the peasant's last
good-night:
A voice replied, far up the
height,
Excelsior!

At break of day, as heaven-
ward
The pious monks of Saint
Bernard
Uttered the oft-repeated
prayer,
A voice cried, through the
startled air,
Excelsior!

A traveller, by the faithful
hound,
Half-buried in the snow was
found,
Still grasping in his hand of
ice
That banner with the strange
device—
Excelsior!

There in the twilight cold and
gray,
Lifeless, but beautiful, he lay,
And from the sky, serene and
far,
A voice fell, like a falling
star—
Excelsior!
  Henry Wadsworth Longfellow

Great things are done when men and mountains meet.

  William Blake

THE ROAD IS ROUGH

You'll find the road is long and rough, with soft spots far apart, where only those can make the grade who have the Uphill Heart, And when they stop you with a thud or jolt you with a crack, Let Courage call the signals as you keep on coming back. Keep coming back, and though the world may romp across your spine, Let every game's end find you still upon the battling line: For when the One Great Scorer comes to make against your name, He writes—not that you won or lost—but how you played the game.

(From *"Alumnus Football"*)
Grantland Rice

Not only around our infancy
Doth heaven with all its
     splendors lie;
Daily, with souls that cringe
     and plot,
We Sinais climb and know it not.
James Russell Lowell

There is in every true woman's heart a spark of heavenly fire, which lies dormant in the broad daylight of prosperity; but which kindles up, and beams and blazes in the dark hour of adversity.

Washington Irving

THE CROW AND THE PITCHER

A crow, ready to die with thirst, flew with joy to a pitcher which he beheld at some distance. When he came, he found water in it indeed, but so near the bottom, that with all his stooping and straining, he was not able to reach it. Then he endeavoured to overturn the pitcher, that so at last he might be able to get a little of it; but his strength was not sufficient for this. At last, seeing some pebbles lie near the place, he cast them one by one into the pitcher; and thus, by degrees, raised the water up to the very brim, and satisfied his thirst.

Aesop

. . . Man holds in his hands the power to abolish all forms of human poverty and all forms of human life. And yet the same revolutionary beliefs for which our forebears fought are still at issue around the globe—the belief that the rights of man come not from the generosity of the state but from the hand of God.

. . . With a good conscience our only sure reward, with history the final judge of our deeds, let us go forth to lead the land we love, asking His blessing and His help, but knowing that here on earth God's work must truly be our own.

John F. Kennedy

BELIEVE ME, IF ALL THOSE ENDEARING YOUNG CHARMS

Believe me, if all those endearing young charms,
Which I gaze on so fondly
   to-day,
Were to change by to-morrow, and
   fleet in my arms,
Like fairy-gifts fading away,
Thou wouldst still be adored,
   as this moment thou art,
Let thy loveliness fade as it
   will,
And around the dear ruin each
   wish of my heart
Would entwine itself verdantly
   still.

It is not while beauty and youth
   are thine own,
And thy cheeks unprofaned by a
   tear,
That the fervor and faith of a
   soul may be known,
To which time will but make thee
   more dear!
No, the heart that has truly
   loved never forgets,
But as truly loves on to the
   close,
As the sunflower turns to her
   god when he sets
The same look which she turned
   when he rose!

Thomas Moore

I grow old learning something new every day.
Solon

To be seventy years young is sometimes far more cheerful and hopeful than to be forty years old.

Oliver Wendell Holmes

TO AGE

Welcome, old friend! These many
   years
Have we lived door by door;
The Fates have laid aside their
   shears
Perhaps for some few more.

I was indocile at an age
When better boys were taught,
But thou at length hast made me
   sage,
If I am sage in aught.

Little I know from other men,
Too little they from me,
But thou hast pointed well the
   pen
That writes these lines to
   thee.

Thanks for expelling Fear and
   Hope,
One vile, the other vain;
One's scourge, the other's
   telescope,
I shall not see again:

Rather what lies before my
   feet
My notice shall engage—
He who hath braved Youth's
   dizzy heat
Dreads not the frost of Age.

Walter Savage Landor

Youth

WHAT SHALL HE TELL THAT SON?

A father sees a son nearing manhood.
What shall he tell that son?
"Life is hard; be steel; be a rock."
And this might stand him for the
    storms
    and serve him for humdrum and
      monotony
    and guide him amid sudden
      betrayals
    and tighten him for slack moments.
"Life is soft loam; be gentle; go easy."
And this too might serve him.
Brutes have been gentled where lashes
    failed.
The growth of a frail flower in a
    path up
    has sometimes shattered and
      split a rock.
A tough will counts. So does desire.
So does a rich soft wanting.
Without rich wanting nothing arrives.
Tell him too much money has killed
    men
    and left them dead years before
      burial:
    and quest of lucre beyond a few
      easy needs
    has twisted good enough men
    sometimes into dry thwarted worms.
Tell him time as a stuff can be wasted.
Tell him to be a fool every so often
    and to have no shame over having
      been a fool
    yet learning something out of
      every folly
    hoping to repeat none of the
      cheap follies
    thus arriving at intimate
      understanding
    of a world numbering many fools.
Tell him to be alone often and get
    at himself,
    and above all tell himself no lies
      about himself

whatever the white lies and
    protective fronts
    he may use amongst other people.
Tell him solitude is creative if he is
    strong
    and the final decisions are made
      in silent rooms.
Tell him to be different from other
    people
    if it comes natural and easy being
      different.
Let him have lazy days seeking his
    deeper motives.
Let him seek deep for where he is a
    born natural.
    then he may understand
      Shakespeare
    and the Wright brothers,
      Pasteur, Pavlov,
    Michael Faraday and free
      imaginations
    bringing changes into a world
      resenting change.
He will be lonely enough
to have time for the work
he knows as his own.
Carl Sandburg

Rejoice, O young man, in thy youth; and let
thy heart cheer thee in the days of thy youth.
Ecclesiastes 11:9,
King James Version

MY LOST YOUTH

Often I think of the beautiful
   town
That is seated by the sea;
Often in thought go up and
   down
The pleasant streets of that
   dear old town,
And my youth comes back to me,
And a verse of a Lapland song
Is haunting my memory still:
"A boy's will is the wind's
   will,
And the thoughts of youth are
   long, long thoughts."

Strange to me now are the forms
   I meet
When I visit the dear old town;
But the native air is pure and
   sweet,
And the trees that o'ershadow
   each well-known street,
As they balance up and down,
Are singing the beautiful song,
Are sighing and whispering
   still:
"A boy's will is the wind's
   will,
And the thoughts of youth are
   long, long thoughts."

And Deering's Woods are fresh
   and fair,
And with joy that is almost
   pain
My heart goes back to wander
   there,
And among the dreams of the
   days that were
I find my lost youth again.
And the strange and beautiful
   song,
The groves are repeating it still:
"A boy's will is the wind's will.
And the thoughts of youth are
   long, long thoughts."
        Henry Wadsworth Longfellow

PORTRAIT OF A GIRL
WITH A COMIC BOOK

Thirteen's no age at all.
Thirteen is nothing.
It is not wit, or powder on
   the face,
Or Wednesday matinees, or
   misses' clothing,
Or intellect, or grace.
Twelve has its tribal customs.
But thirteen
is neither boys in battered
   cars nor dolls,
Not Sara Crewe or movie
   magazine,
Or pennants on the walls.

Thirteen keeps diaries and
   tropical fish
(A month, at most); scorns
   jumpropes in the spring;
Could not, would fortune grant
   it, name its wish;
Wants nothing, everything;
Has secrets from itself, friends
   it despises;
Admits none of the terrors that
   it feels;
Owns a half a hundred masks but
   no disguises;
And walks upon its heels.

Thirteen's anomalous—not that,
   not this:
Not folded bud, or wave that
   laps a shore,
Or moth proverbial from the
   chrysalis.
Is the one age defeats the meta-
   phor.
Is not a town, like childhood,
   strongly walled
But easily surrounded; is no city
Nor, quitted once, can it be quite
   recalled—
Not even with pity.
        Phyllis McGinley

189

MAUD MULLER

Maud Muller on a summer's day,
Raked the meadow sweet with hay.

Beneath her torn hat glowed
  the wealth
Of simple beauty and rustic health.

Singing, she wrought, and her
  merry glee
The mock-bird echoed from his
  tree.

But when she glanced to the
  far-off town,
White from its hill-slope looking down,

The sweet song died, and a
  vague unrest
And a nameless longing filled
  her breast,—

A wish that she hardly dared
  to own,
For something better than she
  had known.

The Judge rode slowly down the
  lane,
Smoothing his horse's
  chestnut mane.

He drew his bridle in the
  shade
Of the apple-trees to greet the
  maid,

And asked a draught from the
  spring that flowed
Through the meadow across the
  road.

She stooped where the cool
  spring bubbled up,
And filled for him her
  small tin cup,

And blushed as she gave it,
  looking down
On her feet so bare, and her
  tattered gown.

"Thanks!" said the Judge; "a
  sweeter draught
From a fairer hand was never
  quaffed."

He spoke of the grass and
  flowers and trees,
Of the singing birds and humming bees;

Then talked of the haying and
  wondered whether
The cloud in the west would
  bring foul weather.

And Maud forgot her brier-torn
  gown,
And her graceful ankles bare
  and brown;

And listened, while a pleased
  surprise
Looked from her long-lashed
  hazel eyes.

At last, like one who for delay
Seeks a vain excuse, he rode
  away.

Maud Muller looked and sighed:
  "Ah, me!
That I the Judge's bride might be!

"He would dress me up in silks
  so fine,
And praise and toast me at
  his wine.

"My father should wear a
  broadcloth coat;
My brother should sail a
  painted boat.

"I'd dress my mother so grand
and gay,
And the baby should have a new
toy each day.

"And I'd feed the hungry and
clothe the poor,
And all should bless me who
left our door."

The Judge looked back as he
climbed the hill,
And saw Maud Muller standing
still.

"A form more fair, a face more
sweet,
Ne'er hath it been my lot to
meet.

"And her modest answer and
graceful air
Show her wise and good as she
is fair.

"Would she were mine, and I
to-day,
Like her, a harvester of hay;

"No doubtful balance of rights
and wrongs,
Nor weary lawyers with endless
tongues,

"But low of cattle and song of
birds,
And health and quiet and loving
words."

But he thought of his sisters,
proud and cold,
And his mother, vain of her
rank and gold,

So, closing his heart, the Judge
rode on,
And Maud was left in the field
alone.

But the lawyers smiled that
afternoon,
When he hummed in court an old
love-tune;

And the young girl mused beside
the well
Till the rain on the unraked
clover fell.

He wedded a wife of richest
dower,
Who lived for fashion, as he
for power.

Yet oft, in his marble hearth's
bright glow,
He watched a picture come and
go;

And sweet Maud Muller's hazel
eyes
Looked out in their innocent
surprise.

Oft, when the wine in his
glass was red,
He longed for the wayside well
instead;

And closed his eyes on his
garnished rooms
To dream of meadows and clover-
blooms.

And the proud man sighed, with
a secret pain,
"Ah, that I were free again!

"Free as when I rode that day,
Where the barefoot maiden
raked her hay."

She wedded a man unlearned and
poor,
And many children played around
her door.

But care and sorrow, and
childbirth pain,
Left their traces on heart and brain.

And oft, when the summer sun
shone hot
On the new-mown hay in the
meadow lot,

And she heard the little spring
brook fall
Over the roadside, through
the wall,

In the shade of the apple-tree
  again
She saw a rider draw his rein;

And, gazing down with timid
  grace,
She felt his pleased eyes
  read her face.

Sometimes her narrow kitchen
  walls
Stretched away into stately halls;

The weary wheel to a spinnet
  turned,
The tallow candle an astral
  burned,

And for him who sat by the chimney lug,
Doing and grumbling o'er
  pipe and mug,

A manly form at her side she saw,
And joy was duty and love was
  law.

Then she took up her burden of
  life again,
Saying only, "It might have
  been."

Alas for maiden, alas for
  Judge,
For rich repiner and house-
  hold drudge!

God pity them both! And pity
  us all,
Who vainly the dreams of
  youth recall.

For of all sad words of tongue
  or pen,
The saddest are these: "It
  might have been!"

Ah, well for us all some
  sweet hope lies
Deeply buried from human eyes;

And, in the hereafter, angels may
Roll the stone from its grave
  away!
        John Greenleaf Whittier

THE BUTTERFLY AND THE CATERPILLAR

A butterfly, one summer morn,
Sat on a spray of blossoming
  thorn
And, as he sipped and drank his
  share
Of honey from the flowered air,
Below, upon the garden wall,
A caterpillar chanced to crawl.
"Horrors!" the butterfly ex-
  claimed,
"This must be stopped! I am
  ashamed
That such as I should have to be
In the same world with such
  as he.
Preserve me from such hideous
  things!
Disgusting shape! Where are
  his wings!
Furry and gray! Eater of clay!
Won't someone take the worm
  away!"

The caterpillar crawled ahead,
But, as he munched a leaf,
  he said,
"Eight days ago, young butterfly,
You wormed about, the same as I;
Within a fortnight from today
Two wings will bear me far
  away,
To brighter blooms and lovelier
  lures,
With colors that outrival yours.
So, flutter-flit, be not so proud;
Each caterpillar is endowed
With power to make him by and
  by,
A blithe and brilliant butter-
  fly.
While you, who scorn the common
  clay,
You, in your livery so gay,
And all the gaudy moths and
  millers,
Are only dressed-up caterpillars."
        Joseph Lauren

Kindness

DAY WELL SPENT

If you sit down at set of sun
And count the acts that you have
    done,
And, counting, find
One self-denying deed, one word
That eased the heart of him who
    heard—
One glance most kind,
That fell like sunshine where it
    went—
Then you may count that day well
    spent.

George Eliot

Pride goeth before destruction, and an haughty spirit before a fall.

Proverbs 16:18,
King James Version

None of us liveth to himself, and no man dieth to himself.

Romans 14:7,
King James Version

CAUSE AND EFFECT

Once someone said something
    nice about me,
And, all undeserved though
    I knew it to be,
I treasured it there on
    my heart's deepest shelf,
Till one day I quite
    surprised even myself
By honestly making
    an effort to be
That nice thing that
    somebody said about me!

Helen Lowrie Marshall

Let every dawn of the morning be to you as the beginning of life. And let every setting of the sun be to you as its close. Then let everyone of these short lives leave its sure record of some kindly thing done for others; some good strength or knowledge gained for yourself.

John Ruskin

KINDNESS

A little word in kindness
    spoken,
A motion, or a tear,
Has often healed the heart
    that's broken
And made a friend sincere.

A word, a look, has crushed
    to earth
Full many a budding flower,
Which, had a smile but owned
    its birth,
Would bless life's darkest hour.

Then deem it not an idle thing
A pleasant word to speak;
The face you wear, the thought
    you bring,
A heart may heal or break.

John Greenleaf Whittier

To love life and men as God loves them—for the sake of their infinite possibilities, to wait like Him, to judge like Him without passing judgment, to obey the order when it is given and never look back—then He can use you—then, perhaps, He will use you. And if He doesn't use you—what matter. In His hand, every moment has its meaning, its greatness, its glory, its peace.

Dag Hammarskjöld

OH, HOW DIFFICULT IT IS TO BE YOUNG

Oh, how difficult it is to be
    young
And worried.
Like me.
I worry all the time.
What will it be like when
I am grown?
What will become of me?
Where will I live, and with
    whom?
Will I have a home?
Will I be loved?
Will I be rich?
Or must I work?
Will I travel and see the
    world?
Or spend my life in one room
    in a basket?
Who will have me and what will
    THEY be like?
Or must I roam the alleyways
    for fish heads
And shiver through the nights
    of sleet and rain
Behind some hoarding?
What will life be like?
I who know nothing
But one long worry
Find it very difficult to be
    young.

(From *Honorable Cat*)
Paul Gallico

We are here to help each other, to try to make each other happy.

Saying of the Polar Eskimos

THE TASK

I would not enter on my list
    of friends,
(Though grac'd with polish'd
    manners and fine sense
Yet wanting sensibility) the
    man
Who needlessly sets foot upon
    a worm.

William Cowper

LITTLE LOST PUP

He was lost!—not a shade of
    doubt of that;
For he never barked at a
    slinking cat,
But stood in the square
    where the wind blew raw
With a drooping ear and a
    trembling paw
And a mournful look in his
    pleading eye
And a plaintive sniff at the
    passer-by
That begged as plain as a
    tongue could sue,
"O Mister! please may I
    follow you?"
A lorn wee waif of a tawny brown
Adrift in the roar of a heed-
    less town.
Oh, the saddest of sights in
    the world of sin
Is a little lost pup with his
    tail tucked in!

Now he shares my board and he
    owns my bed.
And he faintly shouts when
    he hears my tread;
Then, if things go wrong,
    as they sometimes do,
And the world is cold and
    I'm feeling blue,
He asserts his right to
    assuage my woes
With a warm, red tongue and
    a nice, cold nose
And a silky head on my arm
    or knee
And a paw as soft as a paw can be.
When we rove the woods for a
    league about.
He's all full of pranks as a
    school let out;
For he romps and frisks
    like a three months' colt,
And he runs me down like a
    thunderbolt.
Oh, the blithest of sights
    in the world so fair
Is a gay little pup with
    his tail in the air!

Arthur Guiterman

IF I CAN

If I can stop one heart from
    breaking,
I shall not live in vain;
If I can ease one life the
    aching,
Or cool one pain,
Or help one fainting robin
Unto his nest again,
I shall not live in vain.
Emily Dickinson

Die when I may, I want it said of me by those
who knew me best, that I always plucked a
thistle and planted a flower where I thought a
flower would grow.

Abraham Lincoln

MERCY

The quality of mercy is not
    strained,
It droppeth as the gentle rain
    from heaven
Upon the place beneath: it is
    twice blest;
It blesseth him that gives,
    and him that takes:
'Tis mightiest in the mightiest:
    it becomes
The throned monarch better than
    his crown:
His scepter shows the force of
    temporal power,
The attribute to awe and
    majesty,
Wherein doth sit the dread and
    fear of kings;
It is an attribute to God him-
    self;
And earthly power doth then show
    likest God's
When mercy seasons justice.
William Shakespeare

Down in their hearts, wise men know this truth:
the only way to help yourself is to help others.
Elbert Hubbard

Kind hearts are the gardens
Kind thoughts are the roots,
Kind words are the flowers,
Kind deeds are the fruits.

Take care of the gardens,
And keep them from the weeds.
Fill, fill them with flowers,
Kind words and kind deeds.
Henry Wadsworth Longfellow

Kindness is a language which the deaf man can
hear and the blind man read.

Mark Twain

I will not willingly offend,
Nor be easily offended;
What's amiss I'll strive to
    mend,
And endure what can't be mended.
Isaac Watts

Oh, it is excellent
To have a giant's strength;
    but it is tyrannous
To use it like a giant.
William Shakespeare

Kind words are the music of the world. They
have a power which seems to be beyond natural
causes, as though they were some angel's song
which had lost its way and come to earth.
Frederick William Faber

THE ARROW AND THE SONG

I shot an arrow into the air,
It fell to earth, I knew not
  where;
For, so swiftly it flew, the
  sight
Could not follow it in its
  flight.

I breathed a song into the air,
It fell to earth, I knew not
  where;
For who has sight so keen and
  strong,
That it can follow the flight
  of song?

Long, long afterward, in an
  oak
I found the arrow, still un-
  broke;
And the song, from beginning
  to end,
I found again in the heart of
  a friend.
    Henry Wadsworth Longfellow

I expect to pass through life but once. If therefore, there be any good thing I can do to any
fellowbeing, let me do it now, and not defer
or neglect it, as I shall not pass this way again.
    William Penn

Be not forgetful to entertain strangers; for
thereby some have entertained angels unawares.
    Hebrews 13:2,
    King James Version

Great Spirit, help me never to judge another
until I have walked two weeks in his moccasins.
    Sioux Indian Prayer

Therefore all things whatsoever ye would that
men should do to you, do ye even so to them.
    Matthew 7:12,
    King James Version

A kind heart is a fountain of gladness making
everything in its vicinity freshen into smiles.
    Washington Irving

In men whom men condemn as ill
I find so much of goodness still,
In men whom men pronounce divine
I find so much of sin and blot,
I do not dare to draw a line,
Between the two, where God has
  not.

    Joaquin Miller

The greater a man is, the greater the courtesy.
    Alfred, Lord Tennyson

Wisdom

AS A MAN THINKETH

Man is; and as he thinks, so he is. A perception and realization of these two facts alone—of man's being and thinking—lead into a vast avenue of knowledge which cannot stop short of the highest wisdom and perfection. One of the reasons why men do not become wise is that they occupy themselves with interminable speculations about a soul separate from themselves—that is, from their own mind—and so blind themselves to their actual nature and being. The supposition of a separate soul veils the eyes of man so that he does not see himself, does not know his mentality, is unaware of the nature of his thoughts without which he would have no conscious life.

Man's life is actual; his thoughts are actual; his life is actual. To occupy ourselves with the investigation of things that are, is the way of wisdom. Man considered as above, beyond, and separate from mind and thought, is speculative and not actual, and to occupy ourselves with the study of things that are not, is the way of folly.

Man cannot be separated from his mind; his life cannot be separated from his thoughts. Mind, thought, and life are as inseparable as light, radiance, and color, and are no more in need of another factor to elucidate them than are light, radiance, and color. The facts are all-sufficient, and contain within themselves the groundwork of all knowledge concerning them.

Man as mind is subject to change. He is not something "made" and finally completed, but has within him the capacity for progress. By the universal law of evolution he has become what he is, and is becoming that which he will be. His being is modified by every thought he thinks. Every experience affects his character. Every effort he makes changes his mentality. Herein is the secret of man's degradation, and also of his power and salvation if he but utilize this law of change in the right choice of thought.

To live is to think and act, and to think and act is to change. While man is ignorant of the nature of thought, he continues to change for better or worse; but, being acquainted with the nature of thought, he intelligently accelerates and directs the process of change, and only for the better. . . .

James Allen

Wisdom is before him that hath understanding.
Proverbs 17:24,
King James Version

Wisdom is ofttimes nearer when we stoop than when we soar.

William Wordsworth

As we acquire more knowledge, things do not become more comprehensible but more mysterious.

Albert Schweitzer

A man should never be ashamed to say he has been in the wrong, which is but saying in other words that he is wiser today than he was yesterday.

Alexander Pope

Patriotism

INCIDENT OF THE FRENCH CAMP

You know, we French stormed
   Ratisbon;
A mile or so away,
On a little mound, Napoleon
Stood on our storming-day;
With neck out-thrust, you fancy
   how,
Legs wide, arms locked behind,
As if to balance the prone brow
Oppressive with its mind.

Just as perhaps he mused, "My
   plans
That soar, to earth may fall,
Let once my army-leader Lannes
Waver at yonder wall"—
Out 'twixt the battery smokes
   there flew
A rider, bound on bound
Full-galloping; nor bridle drew
Until he reached the mound.

Then off there flung in smiling
   joy,
And held himself erect
By just his horse's mane, a boy;
You hardly could suspect—
(So tight he kept his lips com-
   pressed,
Scarce any blood came through)
You looked twice ere you saw
   his breast
Was all but shot in two.

"Well," cried he, "Emperor, by
   God's grace
We've got you Ratisbon!
The Marshal's in the market-place,
And you'll be there anon
To see your flag-bird flap his
   vans
Where I, to heart's desire,
Perched him!" The chief's eye
   flashed; his plans
Soared up again like fire.

The chief's eye flashed; but
   presently
Softened itself, as sheathes
A film the mother-eagle's eye
When her bruised eaglet breathes;
"You're wounded!" "Nay," the
   soldier's pride
Touched to the quick, he said:
"I'm killed, Sire!" And, his
   chief beside,
Smiling the boy fell dead.
           Robert Browning

I do not agree with a word that you say, but I
will defend to the death your right to say it.
           Voltaire

FOUR THINGS

Four things in any land must
   dwell,
If it endures and prospers
   well:
One is manhood true and good;
One is noble womanhood;
One is child life, clean
   and bright;
And one an altar kept alight.
           Author Unknown

God grant that not only the love of liberty, but
a thorough knowledge of the rights of man may
pervade all nations of the earth, so that a philosopher may set his foot anywhere on its surface, and say, "This is my country."
           Benjamin Franklin

THE ATHENIAN OATH

We will never bring disgrace to this, our nation, by any act of dishonesty or cowardice, nor ever desert our suffering comrades in the ranks. We will fight for the ideals of the nation both alone and with others. We will revere and respect our nation's laws, and do our best to incite a like respect and reverence in those above us who are prone to annul and set them at naught. We will strive unceasingly to quicken the public's sense of civic duty. Thus in all these ways we will transmit this nation not only not less but greater, better, and more beautiful than it was transmitted to us.

MY NATIVE LAND

Breathes there a man with
   soul so dead,
Who never to himself hath
   said,
This is my own, my native
   land?
Whose heart hath ne'er within
   him burn'd
As home his footsteps he hath
   turn'd
From wandering on a foreign
   strand?

Sir Walter Scott

A NATION'S STRENGTH

What makes a nation's pillars
   high
And its foundations strong?
What makes it mighty to defy
The foes that round it throng?

It is not gold. Its kingdoms
   grand
Go down in battle shock;
Its shafts are laid on sinking
   sand,
Not on abiding rock.

Is it the sword? Ask the red
   dust
Of empires passed away;
The blood has turned their
   stones to rust,
Their glory to decay.

And is it pride? Ah, that
   bright crown
Has seemed to nations sweet;
But God has struck its luster
   down
In ashes at His feet.

Not gold but only men can
   make
A people great and strong;
Men who for truth and honor's
   sake
Stand fast and suffer long.

Brave men who work while
   others sleep,
Who dare while others fly—
They build a nation's pillars
   deep
And lift them to the sky.

Ralph Waldo Emerson

Show me that age and country where the rights and liberties of the people were placed on the sole chance of their rulers being good men, without a consequent loss of liberty. I say that the loss of that dearest privilege has ever followed with absolute certainty, every such mad attempt.

Patrick Henry

Originality and initiative are what I ask for my country.

Robert Frost

Truth

Men differ about that which is unreal, not that which is real; they fight over error, and not over Truth.

James Allen

A BOY AND FALSE ALARMS

A shepherd's boy kept his sheep upon a common, and in sport and wantonness had gotten a roguish trick of crying, A wolf! a wolf! when there was no such matter, and fooling the country people with false alarms. He had been at this sport so many times in jest, that they would not believe him at last when he was in earnest; and so the wolves broke in upon the flock, and worried the sheep without resistance.

Aesop

Ye shall know the truth, and the truth shall make you free.

John 8:32,
King James Version

I was angry with my friend; I told my wrath, my wrath did end.

Author Unknown

LADY CLARE

It was the time when lilies blow,
And clouds are highest up in
    the air,
Lord Ronald brought a lily-
    white doe
To give his cousin, Lady Clare.

I trow they did not part in
    scorn:
Lovers long-betrothed were
    they:
They two will wed the morrow
    morn,—
God's blessing on the day!

"He does not love me for my
    birth,
Nor for my lands so broad and
    fair;
He loves me for my own true
    worth,
And that is well," said Lady Clare.

In there came old Alice
    the nurse,
Said, "Who was this that
    went from thee?"
"It was my cousin," said
    Lady Clare,
"Tomorrow he weds with me."

"O God be thanked!" said Alice
    the nurse,
"That all comes round so just
    and fair:
Lord Ronald is heir of all your
    lands,
And you are not the Lady Clare."

"Are ye out of mind, my nurse,
    my nurse,"
said Lady Clare, "that ye speak
    so wild?"
"As God's above," said Alice the nurse,
"I speak the truth: you are my child.

"The old earl's daughter died at
    my breast;
I speak the truth, as I live by
    bread!
I buried her like my own sweet
    child,
And put my child in her stead."

"Falsely, falsely have ye done,
O mother," she said, "if this
  be true,
To keep the best man under
  the sun
So many years from his due,"

"Nay now, my child," said
  Alice the nurse,
"But keep the secret for your
  life,
And all you have will be Lord
  Ronald's,
When you are man and wife."

"If I'm a beggar born," she
  said,
"I will speak out, for I dare
  not lie.
Pull off, pull off, the brooch
  of gold,
And fling the diamond necklace
  by."

"Nay, now, my child," said
  Alice the nurse,
"The man will cleave unto
  his right."
"And he shall have it," the
  lady replied,
"Though I should die to-night."

"Yet give one kiss to your
  mother dear,
Alas, my child, I sinned for
  thee."
"O mother, mother, mother,"
  she said,
"So strange it seems to me.

"Yet here's a kiss for my mother
  dear,
My mother dear, if this be so,
And lay your hand upon my
  head,
And bless me, mother, ere I
  go."

She clad herself in a russet
  gown,
She was no longer Lady Clare:
She went by dale, and she went
  by down,
with a single rose in her hair.

The lily white doe Lord Ronald
  had brought
Leaped up from where she lay,
Dropped her head in the maiden's
  hand,
And followed her all the way.

Down stepped Lord Ronald from
  his tower:
"O Lady Clare, you shame your
  worth!
Why come you dressed like a
  village maid,
That are the flower of the
  earth?"

"If I come dressed like a vil-
  lage maid,
I am but as my fortunes are:
I am a beggar born," she said,
"And not the Lady Clare."

"Play me no tricks," said Lord
  Ronald,
"For I am yours in word and
  in deed;
Play me no tricks," said Lord
  Ronald,
"Your riddle is hard to read."

O, and proudly stood she up!
Her heart within her did
  not fail;
She looked into Lord Ronald's
  eyes,
And told him all her nurse's
  tale.

He laughed a laugh of merry
  scorn:
He turned and kissed her where
  she stood:
"If you are not the heiress born,
And I," said he, "the next in
  blood—

"If you are not the heiress
  born,
And I," said he, "the lawful
  heir,
We two will wed to-morrow morn,
And you shall still be Lady Clare."
        Alfred, Lord Tennyson

TRUTH

Truth strikes us from behind, and in the dark,
as well as from before and in broad daylight.

Henry David Thoreau

Woe unto them that call evil good, and good
evil; that put darkness for light, and light for
darkness; that put bitter for sweet, and sweet
for bitter!

*Isaiah 5:20,
King James Version*

THE PIED PIPER OF HAMELIN

Hamelin Town's in Brunswick,
By famous Hanover city;
The river Weser, deep and wide,
Washes its wall on the
    southern side;
A pleasanter spot you never
    spied;
But, when begins my ditty,
Almost five hundred years ago,
To see the townsfolk suffer so
From vermin was a pity.

Rats!
They fought the dogs, and kill'd
    the cats,
And bit the babies in the
    cradles,
And ate the cheeses out of the
    vats,
And lick'd the soup from the
    cook's own ladles,
Split open the kegs of salted
    sprats,
Made nests inside men's Sunday
    hats,
And even spoil'd the women's
    chats,
By drowning their speaking
With shrieking and squeaking
In fifty different sharps and
    flats.

At last the people in a body
To the Town Hall came flocking:
" 'Tis clear," cried they, "our
    Mayor's a noddy;
And as for our Corporation—
    shocking
To think we buy gowns lined with
    ermine
For dolts that can't or won't
    determine
What's best to rid us of our
    vermin!
You hope, because you're old and
    obese,
To find the furry civic robe
    ease?
Rouse up, sirs! Give your brains
    a racking
To find the remedy we're
    lacking,
Or, sure as fate, we'll send
    you packing!"
At this the Mayor and
    Corporation
Quaked with mighty consternation.

An hour they sate in counsel,
At length the mayor broke
    silence:
"For a guilder I'd my ermine
    gown sell;
I wish I were a mile hence!
It's easy to bid one rack one's
    brain—
I'm sure my poor head aches
    again,
I've scratch'd it so, and all
    in vain.
Oh for a trap, a trap, a trap!"
Just as he said this, what
    should hap
At the chamber-door but a gentle
    tap? . . .

"Come in!" the Mayor cried,
    looking bigger:
And in did come the strangest
    figure!
His queer long coat from heel
    to head
Was half of yellow and half of
    red;

And he himself was tall and thin,
With sharp blue eyes, each like
  a pin,
And light loose hair, yet
  swarthy skin,
No tuft on cheek nor beard on
  chin,
But lips where smiles went out
  and in—
There was no guessing his kith
  and kin! . . .

He advanced to the council-
  table:
And, "Please your honors," said
  he, "I'm able,
By means of a secret charm, to
  draw
All creatures living beneath the sun,
That creep, or swim, or fly,
  or run,
After me so as you never saw!
And I chiefly use my charm
On creatures that do people harm,
The mole, and toad, the newt, and
  viper;
And people call me the Pied Piper."
(And here they noticed round
  his neck
A scarf of red and yellow stripe,
To match with his coat of the
  selfsame check;
And at the scarf's end hung a pipe;
And his fingers, they noticed,
  were ever straying
As if impatient to be playing
Upon this pipe, as low it
  dangled
Over his vesture, so old-fangled.)
"Yet," said he, "poor piper as I am,
In Tartary I freed the Cham,
Last June, from his huge swarm of
  gnats;
I eased in Asia the Nizam
Of a monstrous brood of vampyre
  bats;
And, as for what your brain be-
  wilders—
If I can rid your town of rats,

Will you give me a thousand
  guilders?"
"One? fifty thousand!" was the
  exclamation
Of the astonish'd Mayor and Corporation.

Into the street the Piper stept,
Smiling first a little smile,
As if he knew what magic slept
In his quiet pipe the while;
Then, like a musical adept,
To blow the pipe his lips he
  wrinkled,
And green and blue his sharp eyes
  twinkled,
Like a candle-flame where salt
  is sprinkled;
And ere three shrill notes the
  pipe had utter'd,
You heard as if an army mutter'd;
And the muttering grew to a
  grumbling;
And the grumbling grew to a mighty
  rumbling;
And out of the houses the rats
  came tumbling.
Great rats, small rats, lean
  rats, brawny rats,
Brown rats, black rats, gray
  rats, tawny rats,
Grave old plodders, gay young
  friskers,
Fathers, mothers, uncles, cousins,
Cocking tails, and pricking
  whiskers,
Families by tens and dozens
Brothers, sisters, husbands, wives—
Follow'd the Piper for their
  lives.
From street to street he piped
  advancing,
And step for step they follow'd
  dancing,
Until they came to the river
  Weser,
Wherein all plunged and
  perish'd. . . .

You should have heard the
  Hamelin people
Ringing the bells till they
  rocked the steeple;
"Go," cried the Mayor, "get long
  poles!
Poke out the nests and block up
  the holes!
Consult with carpenters and builders,
And leave in our town not even
  a trace
Of the rats!"—when suddenly
  up the face
Of the Piper perk'd in the
  market-place,
With a, "First, if you please,
  my thousand guilders!"

A thousand guilders! The
  Mayor look'd blue;
So did the Corporation too. . . .
To pay this sum to a wandering
  fellow
With a gypsy coat of red and yellow!
"Beside," quoth the Mayor, with
  a knowing wink,
"Our business was done at the
  river's brink;
We saw them with our eyes the
  vermin sink,
And what's dead can't come
  to life, I think.
So, friend, we're not the
  folks to shrink
From the duty of giving you
  something for drink,
And a matter of money to put in
  your poke;
But, as for the guilders, that
  we spoke
Of them, as you very well know,
  was in joke.
Beside, our losses have made
  us thrifty;
A thousand guilders! Come,
  take fifty!"

The Piper's face fell and he cried,
"No trifling! I can't wait! beside,
I've promised to visit by dinner-
  time
Bagdad, and accept the prime

Of the Head Cook's pottage,
  all he's rich in,
For having left, in the
  Caliph's kitchen,
Of a nest of scorpions no
  survivor . . . .
And folks who put me in a passion
May find me pipe to another
  fashion."

"How?" cried the Mayor, "d'ye
  think I'll brook
Being worse treated than a Cook?. . .
You threaten us, fellow?
  Do your worst,
Blow your pipe there till you
  burst!"

Once more he stept into the
  street;
And to his lips again
Laid his long pipe of smooth
  straight cane;
And ere he blew three notes
  such sweet
Soft notes as yet musician's
  cunning
Never gave the enraptured air.
There was a rustling that
  seemed like a bustling
Of merry crowds justling at
  pitching and hustling,
Small feet were pattering,
  wooden shoes clattering,
Little hands clapping, and
  little tongues chattering,
And, like fowls in a farm-
  yard when barley is scattering,
Out came the children running.
All the little boys and girls,
With rosy cheeks and flaxen
  curls,
And sparkling eyes and teeth
  like pearls,
Tripping and skipping, ran
  merrily after
The wonderful music with
  shouting and laughter.

The Mayor was dumb, and the
  Council stood
As if they were changed into
  blocks of wood,
Unable to move a step, or cry
To the children merrily skip-
  ping by—
And could only follow with the
  eye
That joyous crowd at the Piper's
  back.
But how the Mayor was on the
  rack,
And the wretched Council's
  bosoms beat,
As the Piper turn'd from the
  High Street
To where the Weser roll'd its
  waters
Right in the way of their sons
  and daughters!
However, he turned from south
  to west,
And to Koppelberg Hill his
  steps address'd,
And after him the children press'd;
Great was the joy in every
  breast.
"He never can cross that
  mighty top!
He's forced to let the piping drop,
And we shall see our children
  stop!"
When, lo, as they reach'd the
  mountain's side,
A wondrous portal open'd wide,
As if a cavern was suddenly
  hollow'd;
And the Piper advanced and the
  children follow'd
And when all were into the
  very last,
The door in the mountain-side
  shut fast.

Did I say all? No! one was
  lame,
And could not dance the whole of
  the way,
And in after years, if you would
  blame
His sadness, he was used to say,

"It's dull in our town since my
  playmates left!
I can't forget that I'm bereft
Of all the pleasant sights
  they see,
Which the Piper also promised
  me,
For he led us, he said, to a
  joyous land,
Joining the town and just at
  hand,
Where waters gush'd and fruit
  trees grew,
And flowers put forth a fairer
  hue,
And everything was strange and
  new;
The sparrows were brighter than
  peacocks here,
And the dogs outran our fallow
  deer,
And honey-bees had lost their
  stings,
And horses were born with
  eagles' wings;
And just as I became assured
My lame foot would be speedily
  cured,
The music stopp'd, and I stood
  still,
And found myself outside the
  Hill,
Left alone against my will,
To go now limping as before,
And never hear of that country
  more! . . ."

Robert Browning

To make your children capable of honesty is the
beginning of education.

John Ruskin

God is truth and light his shadow.

Plato

If you shut up truth and bury it under the
ground, it will but grow, and gather to itself
such explosive power that the day it bursts
through it will blow up everything in its way.

Émile Zola

Church

THE LITTLE CHURCH

The little church of Long Ago,
  where as a boy I sat
With mother in the family pew,
  and fumbled with my hat—
How I would like to see it now
  the way I saw it then,
The straight-backed pews, the
  pulpit high, the women and
  the men
Dressed stiffly in their Sunday
  clothes and solemnly devout,
Who closed their eyes when
  prayers were said and never
  looked about—
That little church of Long Ago,
  it wasn't grand to see,
But even as a little boy it
  meant a lot to me.
The choir loft where father sang
  comes back to me again;
I hear his tenor voice once more
  the way I heard it when
The deacons used to pass the
  plate, and once again I see
The people fumbling for their
  coins, as glad as they could be
To drop their quarters on the
  plate, and I'm a boy once more
With my two pennies in my fist
  that mother gave before
We left the house, and once
  again I'm reaching out to try
To drop them on the plate
  before the deacon passes by.

It seems to me I'm sitting in
  that high-backed pew, the
  while
The minister is preaching in
  that good old-fashioned style;
And though I couldn't understand
  it all somehow I know
The Bible was the text book in
  that church of Long Ago;

He didn't preach on politics,
  but used the word of God,
And even now I seem to see the
  people gravely nod,
As though agreeing thoroughly
  with all he had to say,
And then I see them thanking
  him before they go away.

The little church of Long Ago
  was not a structure huge,
It had no hired singers or no
  other subterfuge
To get the people to attend,
  'twas just a simple place
Where every Sunday we were told
  about God's saving grace;
No men of wealth were gathered
  there to help it with a gift;
The only worldly thing it had—
  a mortgage hard to lift.
And somehow, dreaming here to-
  day, I wish that I could know
The joy of once more sitting
  in that church of Long Ago.
                Edgar Guest

THE VILLAGE PREACHER

There, where a few torn shrubs
  the place disclose,
The village preacher's modest
  mansion rose.
A man he was to all the
  country dear,
And passing rich with forty
  pounds a year;
Remote from towns he ran his
  godly race,

Nor e'er had changed, nor
  wished to change, his place;
Unpractised he to fawn, or
  seek for power,
By doctrines fashioned to the
  varying hour;
Far other aims his heart
  had learned to prize,
More skilled to raise the
  wretched than to rise.
His house was known to all the
  vagrant train;
He chid their wanderings, but
  relieved their pain:
The long-remember'd beggar
  was his guest,
Whose beard descending swept
  his aged breast;
The ruined spendthrift, now
  no longer proud,
Claimed kindred there, and
  had his claims allowed;
The broken soldier, kindly
  bade to stay,
Sat by his fire, and talked
  the night away,
Wept o'er his wounds, or,
  tales of sorrow done,
Shouldered his crutch and
  showed how fields were won.
Pleased with his guests, the
  good man learned to glow,
And quite forgot their vices
  in their woe;
Careless their merits or
  their faults to scan,
His pity gave ere charity
  began.

Thus to relieve the wretched
  was his pride,
And e'en his failings leaned
  to virtue's side;
But in his duty prompt at
  every call,
He watched and wept, he prayed
  and felt, for all;
And, as a bird each fond
  endearment tries
To tempt its new-fledged offspring to the skies,

He tried each art, reproved
  each dull delay,
Allured to brighter worlds,
  and led the way.

Beside the bed where parting
  life was laid,
And sorrow, guilt, and pain,
  by turns dismayed,
The reverend champion stood.
  At his control
Despair and anguish fled the
  struggling soul;
Comfort came down the trembling
  wretch to raise,
And his last faltering accents
  whispered praise.

At church, with meek and un-
  affected grace,
His looks adorned the venerable place;
Truth from his lips prevailed
  with double sway,
And fools, who came to scoff,
  remained to pray.
The service past, around the
  pious man,
With steady zeal, each honest
  rustic ran;
E'en children followed with
  endearing wile,
And plucked his gown, to
  share the good man's smile.
His ready smile a parent's
  warmth expressed;
Their welfare pleased him, and
  their cares distressed:
To them his heart, his love,
  his griefs were given,
But all his serious thoughts
  had rest in heaven.
As some tall cliff that lifts
  its awful form,
Swells from the vale, and mid-
  way leaves the storm,
Though round its breast the
  rolling clouds are spread,
Eternal sunshine settles on
  its head.

Oliver Goldsmith

HOW TO GET THE MOST OUT OF THE BIBLE

1. Come to the Word expectantly.
2. Come surrendering to the truths here revealed.
3. Come expecting to use the truths here revealed.
4. Come unhurriedly.
5. Come with a proper emphasis.
6. Come to it even if nothing apparently comes from your coming.

E. Stanley Jones

WE LOVE THE VENERABLE HOUSE

We love the venerable house
Our fathers built to God;
In heaven are kept their
grateful vows,
Their dust endears the sod.

Here holy thoughts a light
have shed
From many a radiant face,
And prayers of humble virtue
spread
The perfume of the place.

And anxious hearts have pondered here
The mystery of life,
And prayed th' Eternal Light to
clear
Their doubts and aid their
strife.

They live with God, their
homes are dust;
Yet here their children pray,
And in this fleeting life-time
trust
To find the narrow way.

Ralph Waldo Emerson

I never weary of great churches. It is my favorite kind of mountain scenery. Mankind was never so happily inspired as when it made a cathedral.

Robert Louis Stevenson

How lovely is your Temple, O Lord of the armies of heaven.

I long, yes, faint with longing to be able to enter your courtyard and come near to the Living God. Even the sparrows and swallows are welcome to come and nest among your altars and there have their young, O Lord of heaven's armies, my King and my God! How happy are those who can live in your Temple, singing your praises.

Happy are those who are strong in the Lord, who want above all else to follow your steps. When they walk through the Valley of Weeping it will become a place of springs where pools of blessing and refreshment collect after rains! They will grow constantly in strength and each of them is invited to meet with the Lord in Zion. . . .

A single day spent in your Temple is better than a thousand anywhere else! I would rather be a doorman of the Temple of my God than live in palaces of wickedness. For Jehovah God is our Light and our Protector. He gives us grace and glory. No good thing will he withhold from those who walk along his paths.

O Lord of the armies of heaven, blessed are those who trust in you.

Psalm 84,
The Living Bible

GUESTS OF GOD

You enter this church not as a stranger but as a guest of God. He is your heavenly Father. Come, then, with joy in your hearts and thanks on your lips, offering Him your love and service. Be grateful to the strong and loyal men and women and children who in the name of God builded this place of worship, and to all who have beautified it and hallowed it with their prayers and praises. May all who love this house of faith find the inspiration of their labor and rejoice in the power and love of God, that His blessing may rest on you both on your going out and on your coming in.

Twelfth Century English Church

Courage

In whatever arena of life one may meet the challenge of courage, whatever may be the sacrifices he faces if he follows his conscience—the loss of his friends, his fortune, his contentment, even the esteem of his fellow men—each man must decide for himself the course he will follow. The stories of past courage can define that ingredient—they can teach, they can offer hope, they can provide inspiration. But they cannot supply courage itself. For this each man must look into his own soul.

John F. Kennedy

Fortune favors the bold.
Virgil

Cowards die many times before
  their deaths;
The valiant never taste of death
  but once.

William Shakespeare

Courage is resistance to fear, mastery of fear—not absence of fear.

Mark Twain

Never look down to test the ground before taking your next step: only he who keeps his eye fixed on the far horizon will find his right road.

Dag Hammarskjöld

FRIDAY'S ESCAPE

I was surprised one morning early with seeing no less than five canoes all on shore together on my side of the island; and the people who belonged to them all landed, and out of my sight. The number of them broke all my measures; for seeing so many and knowing that they always came four, or six, or sometimes more, in a boat, I could not tell what to think of it, or how to take my measures, to attack twenty or thirty men singlehanded; so I lay still in my castle, perplexed and discomforted. However, I put myself into all the same postures for an attack that I had formerly provided, and was ready for action if anything had presented; having waited a good while, listening to hear if they made any noise, at length being very impatient, I set my guns at the foot of my ladder and clambered up to the top of the hill by my two stages as usual, standing so, however, that my head did not appear above the hill, so that they could not perceive me by any means; here I observed, by the help of my perspective glass, that they were no less than thirty in number, that they had a fire kindled, that they had had meat dressed. How they had cooked it, that I knew not, or what it was; but they were all dancing in I know not how many barbarous gestures and figures, their own way, round the fire.

While I was thus looking on them, I perceived by my perspective two miserable wretches dragged from the boats, where, it seems, they were laid by, and were now brought out for slaughter. I perceived one of them immediately fell, being knocked down, I suppose, with a club or wooden sword, for that was their way, and two or three others were at work immediately, cutting him open for their cookery, while the other victim was left standing by himself, till they should be ready for him. In that very moment, this poor wretch, seeing himself a

little at liberty, Nature inspired him with hopes of life, and he started away from them, and ran with incredible swiftness along the sands directly towards me, I mean towards that part of the coast where my habitation was.

I was dreadfully frighted (that I must acknowledge) when I perceived him to run my way; and especially when, as I thought, I saw him pursued by the whole body; and now I expected that part of my dream was coming to pass, and that he would certainly take shelter in my grove; but I could not depend by any means upon my dream for the rest of it, viz., that the other savages would not pursue him thither, and find him there. However, I kept my station, and my spirits began to recover when I found that there was not above three men that followed him; and still more was I encouraged when I found that he outstripped them exceedingly in running and gained ground of them; so that if he could but hold it for half an hour, I saw easily he would fairly get away from them all.

There was between them and my castle the creek which I mentioned often at the first part of my story, when I landed my cargoes out of the ship; and this I saw plainly he must necessarily swim over, or the poor wretch would be taken there. But when the savage escaping came thither, he made nothing of it, though the tide was then up; but plunging in, swam through it about thirty strokes or thereabouts, landed, and ran on with exceeding strength and swiftness; when the three persons came to the creek, I found that two of them could swim, but the third could not, and that standing on the other side, he looked at the other, but went no farther; and soon after went softly back again, which, as it happened, was very well for him in the main.

I observed that the two who swam were yet more than twice as long swimming over the creek as the fellow that fled them. It came now very warmly upon my thoughts, and indeed irresistibly, that now was my time to get me a servant, and perhaps a companion, or assis-

tant; and that I was called plainly by Providence to save this poor creature's life; I immediately ran down the ladder with all possible expedition, fetched my two guns, for they were both but at the foot of the ladders, as I observed above; and getting up again, with the same haste, to the top of the hill, I crossed towards the sea; and having a very short cut, and all down hill, clapped myself in the way between the pursuers and the pursued, hallooing aloud to him that fled, who, looking back, was at first perhaps as much frighted at me as at them; but I beckoned with my hand to him to come back, and in the meantime I slowly advanced towards the two that knocked him down with the stock of my piece; I was loath to fire, because I would not have the rest hear; though at that distance, it would not have been easily heard; and being out of sight of the smoke too, they would not have easily known what to make of it. Having knocked this fellow down, the other who pursued him stopped, as if he had been frighted; and I advanced apace towards him; but as I came nearer, I perceived presently he had a bow and arrow, and was fitting it to shoot at me; so I was then necessitated to shoot at him first; which I did, and killed him at the first shot. The poor savage who fled, but had stopped though he saw both his enemies fallen and killed, as he thought, yet was so frighted with the fire and noise of my piece, that he stood stock still and neither came forward or went backward, though he seemed rather inclined to fly still than to come on; I hallooed again to him, and made signs to come forward, which he easily understood, and came a little way, then stopped again, and then a little farther, and stopped again; and I could then perceive that he stood trembling, as if he had been taken prisoner, and had just been to be killed, as his two enemies were; I beckoned him again to come to me, and gave him all the signs of encouragement that I could think of; and he came nearer and nearer, kneeling down every ten or twelve steps in token of acknowledgement for my saving his life.

. . . I carried him, not to my castle, but quite away to my cave, on the farther part of the island; so I did not let my dream come to pass in that part, viz., that he came into my grove for shelter.

Here I gave him bread and a bunch of raisins to eat, and a draught of water, which I found he was indeed in great distress for, by his running, and having refreshed him, I made signs for him to go lie down and sleep, pointing to a place where I had laid a great parcel of rice straw, and a blanket upon it, which I used to sleep upon myself sometimes; so the poor creature lay down and went to sleep.

(From *Robinson Crusoe*)
Daniel DeFoe

Soldiers are dreamers; when the guns begin they think of firelit homes, clean beds, and wives.

Siegfried Sassoon

Successful living requires courage. Perhaps courage is a basic life quality which God gives us, since it is of spirit. Moments may come when courage alone shall stand between us and disaster. In the long pull across the years there will be times when we shall need dogged courage to keep us going when the going is hard. And what is the source of such rugged courage? Surely that sense of God's presence when we hear Him say, "I am with you always."

Norman Vincent Peale

Sorrow

PILGRIM

This is a road
  One walks alone;
Narrow the track
  And overgrown.

Dark is the way
  And hard to find,
When the last village
  Drops behind.

Never a footfall
  Light to show
Fellow traveller—
  Yet I know

Someone before
  Has trudged his load
In the same footsteps—
  This is a road.
     Anne Morrow Lindbergh

ALCHEMY

I lift my heart as spring lifts
  up
A yellow daisy to the rain;
My heart will be a lovely cup
Altho' it holds but pain.

For I shall learn from flower
  and leaf
That color every drop they
  hold,
To change the lifeless wine of
  grief
To living gold.
     Sara Teasdale

There will be no song on our lips if there be
no anguish in our hearts.
     Karl Barth

I sit and look out upon all
  the sorrows of the world,
and upon all oppression and
  shame;
I hear secret convulsive sobs
  from young men,
at anguish with themselves,
remorseful after deeds done,
I see in low life the mother
  misused by her children,
dying, neglected, gaunt, desperate,
I see the wife misused by her
  husband—
I see the treacherous seducer
  of young women,
I mark the ranklings of jeal-
  ousy and unrequited love
attempted to be hid, I see these
  sights on the earth,
I see the workings of battle,
  pestilence, tyranny—
I see martyrs and prisoners,
I observe a famine at sea,
I observe the sailors
casting lots who shall be kill'd
to preserve the lives of the
  rest,
I observe the slights and deg-
  radations
cast by arrogant persons upon
laborers, the poor, and upon
  Negroes, and the like;
All these—all the meanness and
  agony without end I sitting look out upon,
See, hear, and am silent.
     (From *Leaves of Grass*)
     Walt Whitman

Shadow owes its birth to light.

     John Gay

DOVER BEACH

The sea is calm to-night,
The tide is full, the moon
  lies fair
Upon the straits—on the
  French coast the light
Gleams and is gone; the cliffs
  of England stand,
Glimmering and vast, out in
  the tranquil bay.
Come to the window, sweet is
  the night air!
Only, from the long line of
  spray
Where the sea meets the moon-
  blanch'd land,
Listen! you hear the grating
  roar
Of pebbles which the waves
  draw back, and fling,
At their return, up the high
  strand,
Begin, and cease, and then
  again begin,
With tremulous cadence slow,
  and bring
The eternal note of sadness
  in.

Sophocles long ago
Heard it on the Aegean, and
  it brought
Into his mind the turbid ebb
  and flow
Of human misery; we
Find also in the sound a thought,
Hearing it by this distant
  northern sea.

The Sea of Faith
Was once, too, at the fill,
  and round earth's shore
Lay like the folds of a bright
  girdle furl'd
But now I only hear
Its melancholy, long, with-
  drawing roar,
Retreating, to the breath
Of the night wind, down the
  vast edges drear
And naked shingles of the
  world.

Ah, love, let us be true
To one another! for the
  world, which seems
To lie before us like a land
  of dreams,
So various, so beautiful, so
  new,
Hath really neither joy, nor
  love, nor light,
Nor certitude, nor
  peace, nor help for pain;
And we are here as on a
  darkling plain
Swept with confused alarms of
  struggle and flight,
Where ignorant armies clash by
  night.

        Matthew Arnold

Heavy the sorrow that bows
  the head
When love is alive and hope is
  dead.

        W. S. Gilbert

THIS I KNOW

Grief has its rhythm—first the
  wild,
Swift tide of dark despair;
The time of bleak aloneness,
When even God's not there.

And then the slow receding
Till quiet calms the sea,
And bare, washed sand
  is everywhere
Where castles used to be.

The gentle lapping of the waves
Upon the shore—and then
The pearl-lined shells of
  memories
To help us smile again.

        Helen Lowrie Marshall

LORD LOVEL

Lord Lovel he stood at his
  castle gate,
A-combing his milk-white
  steed;
When along came Lady Nancy Bell,
A-wishing her lover good speed,
  speed, speed,
A-wishing her lover good speed.

"Oh where are you going, Lord
  Lovel?" she said,
"Oh where are you going?" said
  she.
"I'm going, my dear Lady Nancy
  Bell,
Strange countries for to see,
  see, see,
Strange countries for to see."

"When will you be back, Lord
  Lovel?" she said;
"When will you be back?" said
  she.
"In a year or two or three at
  the most
I'll return to my Lady Nancee—
  cee, cee,
I'll return to my Lady Nancee."

He'd not been gone but a year
  and a day,
Strange countries for to see,
When laughing thoughts came
  into his mind
Lady Nancy Bell he would see.

He rode and he rode on his milk-
  white steed,
Till he reached fair London
  town;
And there he heard St. Varney's
  bell
And the people all around.

"Is any one dead?" Lord
  Lovel he said;
"Is any one dead?" said he.
"A lady is dead," the people
  all said,
"And they call her Lady Nancy."

He ordered the grave to be
  opened forthwith,
The shroud to be folded down;

And then he kissed her clay
  cold lips
Till the tears came trickling
  down.

Lady Nancy she died as it might
  be today,
Lord Lovel he died tomorrow.
Lady Nancy she died of pure,
  pure grief,
Lord Lovel he died of sorrow.

Lady Nancy was laid in St.
  Clement's churchyard,
Lord Lovel was buried close
  by her;
And out of her bosom there
  grew a red rose,
And out of his backbone a briar.

They grew and they grew on
  the old church tower,
Till they couldn't grow up
  any higher;
And there they tied in a true
  lover's knot,
For all true lovers to admire.
Anonymous

Most of the shadows of life are caused by standing in our own sunshine.
Ralph Waldo Emerson

Come unto me, all ye that labour and are heavy laden, and I will give you rest.
  Take my yoke upon you, and learn of me; for I am meek and lowly in heart: and ye shall find rest unto your souls.
  For my yoke is easy, and my burden is light.
Matthew 11:28–30,
King James Version

WAIT FOR THE LORD

The Lord is my light and my
    salvation;
whom shall I fear?
The Lord is the stronghold of
    my life;
of whom shall I be afraid?

When evildoers assail me,
uttering slanders against me,
my adversaries and foes,
they shall stumble and fall.

Though a host encamp against
    me,
my heart shall not fear;
though war arise against me,
yet I will be confident.

One thing have I asked of the
    Lord,
that will I seek after;
that I may dwell in the house
    of the Lord
all the days of my life,
to behold the beauty of the Lord,
and to inquire in his temple.

For He will hide me in his
    shelter
in the day of trouble;
he will conceal me under the
    cover of his tent,
he will set me high upon a rock....

I believe that I shall see the
    goodness of the Lord
in the land of the living!
Wait for the Lord;
be strong, and let your heart
    take courage;
yea, wait for the Lord!
            Psalm 27:1–5,13–14
        Revised Standard Version

Man's extremity is God's opportunity.
                  John Flavel

Sometimes life has a way of putting us on our
backs in order to force us to look up.
                  Charles L. Allen

GETHSEMANE

All those who journey, soon
    or late,
Must pass within the garden's
    gate;
Must kneel alone in darkness
    there,
And battle with some fierce
    despair.
God pity those who cannot say:
"Not mine but thine"; who only
    pray:
"Let this cup pass," and cannot
    see
The purpose in Gethsemane.
           Ella Wheeler Wilcox

Sweet are the uses of
    adversity;
Which, like the toad, ugly and
    venomous,
Wears yet a precious jewel in
    his hand.
           William Shakespeare

Afflictions are but the shadow of God's wings.
                George Macdonald

Only in Winter can you tell which trees are
truly green. Only when the winds of adversity
blow can you tell whether an individual or a
country has courage and steadfastness.
                John F. Kennedy

AN OLD WOMAN OF THE ROADS

O, to have a little house!
To own the hearth and stool
    and all!
The heaped-up sods upon the
    fire,
The pile of turf against the
    wall!

To have a clock with weights
    and chains
And pendulum swinging up and
    down!
A dresser filled with shining
    delph,
Speckled and white and blue
    and brown!

I could be busy all the day
Clearing and sweeping hearth
    and floor,
And fixing on their shelf
    again
My white and blue and speckled
    store!

I could be quiet there at night
Beside the fire and by myself,
Sure of a bed and loath to
    leave
The ticking clock and the
    shining delph!

Och! but I'm weary of mist and
    dark,
And roads where there's never
    a house or bush,
And tired I am of bog and road
And the crying wind and the
    lonesome hush!

And I am praying to God on
    high,
And I am praying Him night
    and day,
For a little house—a house of
    my own—
Out of the wind's and the rain's
    way.

        Padraic Colum

NO SCAR?

Hast thou no scar?
No hidden scar on foot, or side,
    or hand?
I hear thee sung as mighty
    in the land,
I hear them hail thy bright
    ascendant star,
Hast thou no scar?

Hast thou no wound?
Yet I was wounded by the
    archers, spent,
Leaned Me against a tree to
    die; and rent
By ravening beasts that com-
    passed Me, I swooned:
Hast thou no wound?

No wound? No scar?
Yet, as the Master shall the
    servant be,
And pierced are the feet that
    follow Me;
But thine are whole: can he
    have followed far
Who has not wound or scar?
        Amy Carmichael

In thee is rest which forgetteth all toil.
        St. Augustine

LOST, TWO GOLDEN HOURS

Lost, yesterday, somewhere between Sunrise
and Sunset, two golden hours, each set with
sixty diamond minutes. No reward is offered
for they are gone forever.
        Horace Mann

Comfort

WHEN TROUBLES ASSAIL YOU, GOD WILL NOT FAIL YOU

When life seems empty
And there's no place to go,
When your heart is troubled
And your spirits are low,
When friends seem few
And nobody cares
There is always God
To hear your prayers-
And whatever you're facing
Will seem much less
When you go to God
And confide and confess,
For the burden that seems
Too heavy to bear
God lifts away
On the wings of prayer—
And seen through God's eyes
Earthly troubles diminish
And we're given new strength
To face and to finish
Life's daily tasks
As they come along
If we pray for strength
To keep us strong—
So go to Our Father
When troubles assail you
For His grace is sufficient
And He'll never fail you.

Helen Steiner Rice

Walk on a rainbow trail;
walk on a trail of song,
and all about you will be
beauty. There is a way out
of every dark mist, over a
rainbow trail.

Navajo Song

God tempers the wind to the shorn lamb.

Lawrence Sterne

TO ONE IN SORROW

Let me come in where you are
   weeping, friend,
And let me take your hand.
I, who have known a sorrow
   such as yours,
Can understand.
Let me come in—I would be
   very still
Beside you in your grief;
I would not bid you cease your
   weeping, friend,
Tears bring relief.
Let me come in—I would only
   breathe a prayer,
And hold your hand,
For I have known a sorrow
   such as yours,
And understand.

Grace Noll Crowell

I will love thee, O Lord, my strength. The Lord
is my rock, and my fortress, and my deliverer;
my God, my strength, in whom I will trust; my
buckler, and the horn of my salvation, and my
high tower. I will call upon the Lord, who is
worthy to be praised: so shall I be saved from
mine enemies.

The sorrows of death compassed me, and the
floods of ungodly men made me afraid.

The sorrows of hell compassed me about: the
snares of death prevented me.

In my distress I called upon the Lord, and
cried unto my God: he heard my voice out of
his temple, and my cry came before him, even
into his ears.

*Psalm 18:1–6,
King James Version*

THE RAGGED PRINCE

In the ancient city of London, on a certain autumn day in the second quarter of the sixteenth century, a boy was born to a poor family of the name of Canty, who did not want him. On the same day another English child was born to a rich family of the name of Tudor, who did want him. All England wanted him too. England had so longed for him, and hoped for him, and prayed God for him that now that he was really come, the people went nearly mad for joy. Mere acquaintances hugged and kissed each other and cried. Everybody took a holiday, and high and low, rich and poor, feasted and danced and sang, and got very mellow; and kept this up for days and nights together. By day London was a sight to see, with gay banners waving from every balcony and housetop and splendid pageants marching along. By night it was again a sight to see, with its great bonfires at every corner and its troops of revelers making merry around them. There was no talk in all of England but of the new baby, Edward Tudor, Prince of Wales, who lay lapped in silks and satins, unconscious of all this fuss, and not knowing what great lords and ladies were tending him and watching over him—not caring either. But there was no talk about the other baby, Tom Canty, lapped in his poor rags, except among the family paupers whom he had just come to trouble with his presence. . . .

. . . Tom got up hungry, and sauntered hungry away, but with his thoughts busy with the shadowy splendors of his night's dreams. He wandered here and there in the city, hardly noticing where he was going or what was happening around him. People jostled him, and some gave him rough speech; but it was all lost on the musing boy.

. . . Tom discovered Charing Village presently and rested himself at the beautiful cross built there by a bereaved king of earlier days; then idled down a quiet, lovely road past the great cardinal's stately palace, toward a far more mighty and majestic palace beyond—Westminster. Tom stared in glad wonder at the vast pile of masonry, the wide-spreading wings, the frowning bastions and turrets, the huge stone gateway, with its gilded bars and its magnifi-

cent array of colossal granite lions, and other signs and symbols of English royalty. Was the desire of his soul to be satisfied at last? Here indeed was a king's palace. Might he not hope to see a prince now, a prince of flesh and blood, if heaven were willing?

At each side of the gilded gate stood a living statue, that is to say, an erect and stately and motionless man-at-arms clad from head to heel in shining steel armor. At a respectful distance were many country folk and people from the city waiting for any chance glimpse of royalty that might offer. Splendid carriages with splendid people in them and splendid servants outside were arriving and departing by several other noble gateways that pierced the royal enclosure.

Poor little Tom, in his rags, approached and was moving slowly and timidly past the sentinels, with a beating heart and a rising hope, when all at once he caught sight through the golden bars of a spectacle that almost made him shout for joy. Within was a comely boy, tanned and brown with sturdy outdoor sports and exercises, whose clothing was all of lovely silks and satins, shining with jewels—at his hip a little jeweled sword and dagger, dainty buskins on his feet, with red heels, and on his head a jaunty crimson cap with drooping plumes fastened with a great sparkling gem. Several gorgeous gentlemen stood near—his servants, without a doubt. Oh! He was a prince—a prince, a living prince, a real prince—without the shadow of a question; and the prayer of the pauper-boy's heart was answered at last.

Tom's breath came quick and short with excitement, and his eyes grew big with wonder and delight. Everything gave way in his mind instantly to one desire: that was to get close to the prince and have a good, devouring look at him. Before he knew what he was about, he had his face against the gate bars. The next instant one of the soldiers snatched him rudely away and sent him spinning among the gaping crowd of country gawks and London idlers.

The soldier said, "Mind thy manners, thou young beggar!"

The crowd jeered and laughed, but the young prince sprang to the gate with his flushed face and his eyes flashing with indignation and cried out, "How darst thou use a poor lad like that! How darst thou use the king my father's meanest subject so! Open the gates and let him in!"

You should have seen that fickle crowd snatch off their hats then. You should have heard them cheer and shout, "Long Live the Prince of Wales!"

The soldiers presented arms with their halberds, opened the gates, and presented again as the little Prince of Poverty passed in, in his fluttering rags, to join hands with the Prince of Limitless Plenty.

Edward Tudor said, "Thou lookest tired and hungry: thou'st been treated ill. Come with me."

Half a dozen attendants sprang forward to—I don't know what; interfere, no doubt. But they were waved aside with a right royal gesture, and they stopped stock-still where they were, like so many statues. Edward took Tom to a rich apartment in the palace, which he called his cabinet. By his command a repast was brought such as Tom had never encountered before except in books. The prince, with princely delicacy and breeding, sent away the servants so that his humble guest might not be embarrassed by their critical presence; then he sat nearby and asked questions while Tom ate.

"What is thy name, lad?"

"Tom Canty, an' it please thee, sir."

"'Tis an odd one. Where dost live?"

"In the city, please thee, sir. Offal Court, out of Pudding Lane."

"Offal Court! Truly 'tis another odd one. Hast parents?"

"Parents have I, sir, and a grandam likewise that is but indifferently precious to me—God forgive me if it be offense to say it—also twin sisters, Nan and Bet."

"Then is thy grandam not over kind to thee, I take it."

"Neither to any other is she, so please your Worship. She hath a wicked heart and worketh evil all her days."

"Doth she mistreat thee?"

"There be times that she stayeth her hand, being asleep or overcome with drink; but when she hath her judgment clear again, she maketh it up to me with goodly beatings."

A fierce look came into the little prince's eyes, and he cried out, "What! Beatings?"

"Oh, indeed, yes, please you, sir."

"*Beatings!* And thou so frail and little. Hark ye; before the night come she shall hie her to the Tower. The king my father—"

"In sooth, you forget, sir, her low degree. The Tower is for the great alone."

"True, indeed. I had not thought of that. I will consider of her punishment. Is thy father kind to thee?"

"Not more than Gammer Canty, sir."

"Fathers be alike, mayhap. Mine hath not a doll's temper. He smiteth with a heavy hand, yet spareth me; he spareth me not always with his tongue, though, sooth to say. How doth thy mother use thee?"

"She is good, sir, and giveth me neither sorrow nor pain of any sort. And Nan and Bet are like her in this."

"How old be these?"

"Fifteen, an' it please you, sir."

"The lady Elizabeth, my sister, is fourteen, and the lady Jane Grey, my cousin, is of mine own age, and comely and gracious withal; but my sister the lady Mary, with her gloomy mien and—Look you, do thy sisters forbid their servants to smile, lest the sin destroy their souls?"

"They? Oh, dost think, sir, that *they* have servants?"

The little prince contemplated the little pauper gravely a moment, then said, "And prithee, why not? Who helpeth them undress at night? Who attireth them when they rise?"

"None, sir. Wouldst have them take off their garment and sleep without—like beasts?"

"Their garment! Have they but one?"

"Ah, good your Worship, what would they do with more? Truly they have not two bodies each."

"It is a quaint and marvelous thought! Thy pardon, I had not meant to laugh. But thy good Nan and thy Bet shall have raiment and lackeys enow, and that soon too; my cofferer shall look to it. No, thank me not; 'tis nothing. Thou speakest well; thou hast an easy grace in it. Art learned?"

"I know not if I am or not, sir. The good priest that is called Father Andrew taught me, of his kindness, from his books."

"Knowst thou the Latin?"

"But scantly, sir, I doubt."

"Learn it, lad; 'tis hard only at first. The Greek is harder; but neither these nor any tongues else, I think, are hard to the lady Elizabeth and my cousin. Thou shouldst hear those damsels at it! But tell me of thy Offal Court. Hast thou a pleasant life there?"

"In truth, yes, so please you, sir, save when one is hungry. There be Punch-and-Judy shows, and monkeys—oh, such antic creatures, and so bravely dressed!—and there be plays wherein they that play do shout and fight till all are slain, and 'tis main hard to get the farthing, please your Worship."

"Tell me more."

"We lads of Offal Court do strive against each other with the cudgel, like to the fashion of the 'prentices, sometimes."

The prince's eyes flashed. Said he, "Marry, that would not I mislike. Tell me more."

"We strive in races, sir, to see who of us shall be fleetest."

"That I would like also. Speak on."

"In summer, sir, we wade and swim in the canals and in the river, and each doth duck his neighbor, and spatter him with water, and dive and shout and tumble and—"

"'Twould be worth my father's kingdom but to enjoy it once! Prithee go on."

"We dance and sing about the Maypole in Cheapside; we play in the sand, each covering his neighbor up; and times we make mud pastry —oh, the lovely mud, it hath not its like for delightfulness in all the world!—we do fairly wallow in the mud, sir, saving your Worship's presence."

"Oh, prithee say no more; 'tis glorious! If that I could but clothe me in raiment like to thine, and strip my feet, and revel in the mud once, just once, with none to rebuke or forbid, meseemeth I could forgo the crown!"

"And if that I could clothe me once, sweet sir, as thou art clad, just once—"

"Oho, wouldst like it? Then so shall it be. Doff thy rags and don these splendors, lad! It is a brief happiness, but will be not less keen for

that. We will have it while we may, and change again before any come to molest."

A few minutes later the little Prince of Wales was garlanded with Tom's fluttering odds and ends, and the little Prince of Pauperdom was tricked out in the gaudy plumage of royalty. The two went and stood side by side before a great mirror, and lo, a miracle: There did not seem to have been any change made! They stared at each other, then at the glass, then at each other again. At last the puzzled princeling said, "What dost thou make of this?"

"Ah, good your Worship, require me not to answer. It is not meet that one of my degree should utter the thing."

"Then will I utter it. Thou hast the same hair, the same eyes, the same voice and manner, the same form and stature, the same face and countenance that I bear. Fared we forth naked, there is none could say which was you, and which the Prince of Wales. And now that I am clothed as thou wert clothed, it seemeth I should be able the more nearly to feel as thou didst when the brute soldier—Hark ye, is not this a bruise upon your hand?"

"Yes; but it is a slight thing, and your Worship knoweth that the poor man-at-arms—"

"Peace! It was a shameful thing and a cruel!" cried the little prince, stamping his bare foot. "If the king—Stir not a step till I come again! It is a command!"

In a moment he had snatched up and put away an article of national importance that lay upon a table, and was out the door and flying through the palace grounds in his bannered rags, with a hot face and glowing eyes. As soon as he reached the great gate, he seized the bars and tried to shake them, shouting, "Open! Unbar the gates!"

The soldier that had maltreated Tom obeyed promptly and as the prince burst through the portal, half smothered with royal wrath, the soldier fetched him a sounding box on the ear that sent him whirling to the roadway and said, "Take that, thou beggar's spawn, for what thou got'st me from his Highness!"

The crowd roared with laughter. The prince picked himself out of the mud and made fiercely at the sentry, shouting, "I am the Prince of Wales, my person is sacred; and thou shalt hang for laying thy hand upon me!"

The soldier brought his halberd to a present arms and said mockingly, "I salute your gracious Highness." Then angrily, "Be off, thou crazy rubbish!"

Here the jeering crowd closed around the poor little prince and hustled him far down the road, hooting him and shouting, "Way for his Highness! Way for the Prince of Wales!"

From *The Prince and The Pauper*
Mark Twain

If God be for us, who can be against us?

Romans 8:31,
King James Version

Earth has no sorrow that Heaven cannot heal.

Thomas Moore

OUR BURDEN BEARER

The little sharp vexations
And the briars that cut the
    feet,
Why not take all to the
    Helper
Who has never failed us yet?

Tell Him about the heartache,
And tell Him the longings too,
Tell Him the baffled purpose
When we scarce know what to
    do.
Then, leaving all our weakness
With the One divinely strong,
Forget that we bore the burden
And carry away the song.

Phillips Brooks

Comfort ye, comfort ye my people, saith your God. . . . Every valley shall be exalted, and every mountain and hill shall be made low: and the crooked shall be made straight, and the rough places plain: and the glory of the Lord shall be revealed, and all flesh shall see it together: for the mouth of the Lord hath spoken it.

Isaiah 40:1,4–5,
King James Version

NOW AND THEN

There were hours when life was
    bitter
With the anguish of defeat,
When strange it seemed that
    anything
Had ever tasted sweet.

And we scarce knew how to bear
    it,
But One came o'er the wave,
And the peace He gave us with
    a word
Then made us strong and brave.

There are hours when work is
    pressing,
Just little homely work
That must be done, that we must
    do,
That it were shame to shirk,
And in those hours full often,
To crown the petty cares,
Has fallen upon the house
    a gleam
Of God's Heaven unawares.

So, for our hallowed hours
We find them, where our Lord
Has called us into service meet
For blessing and reward;
They are sometimes in the
    closet,
They are often in the mart,
And the Lord can make them any-
    where,
His "desert place apart."

Margaret Sangster

SOMETIMES A LIGHT SURPRISES

Sometimes a light surprises
The Christian while he sings;
It is the Lord who rises
With healing in his wings.

God moves in a mysterious way
His wonders to perform;
He plants his footsteps on the
    sea
And rides upon the storm.
William Cowper

THIS VAST TREASURE OF CONTENT

Bring unto the sorrowing,
    All release from pain;
Let the lips of Laughter
    Overflow again.
And with all the needy,
    O divide, I pray,
This vast treasure of content
    That is mine today!
James Whitcomb Riley

I SHALL BE GLAD

If I can put new hope within
    the heart
Of one who has lost hope,
If I can help a brother up
Some difficult long slope
That seems too steep for tired
    feet to go,
If I can help him climb
Into the light upon the hill's
    far crest,
I shall begrudge no time
Or strength that I can spend,
    for well I know
How great may be his need.
If I can help through any
    darkened hour,
I shall be glad indeed.

For I recall how often I have
    been
Distressed, distraught,
    dismayed,
And hands have reached to help,
    and voices called
That kept me unafraid.
If I can share this help that
    I have had,
God knows I shall be glad.
Grace Noll Crowell

THE BEST REMEDY

The best remedy for those who are afraid, lonely or unhappy is to go outside, somewhere where they can be quite alone with the heavens, nature, and God. Because only then does one feel that all is as it should be and that God wishes to see people happy, amidst the simple beauty of nature. As long as this exists, and it certainly always will, I know that then there will always be comfort for every sorrow, whatever the circumstances may be.
Anne Frank

O! Many a shaft at random
    sent,
Finds mark the archer little
    meant,
And many a word, at random
    spoken,
May soothe or wound a heart
    that's broken.
Sir Walter Scott

WHAT GOD HATH PROMISED

God hath not promised
Skies always blue,
Flower-strewn pathways
All our lives through;
God hath not promised
Sun without rain,
Joy without sorrow
Peace without pain.

But God hath promised
Strength for the day,
Rest for the labor,
Light for the way,
Grace for the trials,
Help from above,
Unfailing sympathy,
Undying love.
Annie Johnson Flint

NO CROSS, NO CROWN

No pain, no palm;
No thorns, no throne;
No gall, no glory;
No cross, no crown.
William Penn

PRAYER

O Holy Spirit, descend plentifully into my heart. Enlighten the dark corners of this neglected dwelling and scatter there Thy cheerful beams.

St. Augustine

I am an old man and I have known a great many troubles, but most of them have never happened.
Mark Twain

THOU ART NEAR

O love Divine, that stooped
to share
Our deepest pang, our bitter-
est tear,
On Thee we cast each earth-born
care,
We smile at pain while Thou art
near.

Though long the weary way we
tread,
And sorrow crown each lingering
year
No path we shun, no darkness
dread,
Our heart still whispering
"Thou art near."
Oliver Wendell Holmes

Let us be of good cheer, remembering that the misfortunes hardest to bear are those which never come.

Amy Lowell

Worry never robs tomorrow of its sorrow; it only saps today of its strength.

A. J. Cronin

THE LORD IS MY SHEPHERD

Because the Lord is my Shepherd, I have everything I need!

He lets me rest in the meadow grass and leads me beside the quiet streams. He restores my failing health. He helps me do what honors him the most.

Even when walking through the dark valley of death I will not be afraid, for you are close beside me, guarding, guiding all the way.

You provide delicious food for me in the presence of my enemies. You have welcomed me as your guest; blessings overflow!

Your goodness and unfailing kindness shall be with me all of my life, and afterwards I will live with you forever in your home.

Psalm 23,
The Living Bible

GOD MAKES A PATH

God makes a path, provides a
  guide,
And feeds a wilderness;
His glorious name, while
  breath remains,
O that I may confess.

Lost many a time, I have no
  guide,
No house but a hollow tree!
In stormy winter night no
  fire,
No food, no company;

In Him I found a house, a
  bed,
A table, company;
No cup so bitter but's made
  sweet,
Where God shall sweetening be.
Roger Williams

BETROTHAL

Then Evangeline lighted the
  brazen lamp on the table,
Filled, till it overflowed
  the pewter tankard with
  home-brewed
Nut-brown ale, that was famed
  for its strength in the
  village of Grand-Pré;
While from his pocket the
  notary drew his papers and
  inkhorn,
Wrote with a steady hand the
  date and the age of the
  parties,
Naming the dower of the bride
  in flocks of sheep and in
  cattle.
Orderly all things proceeded,
  and duly and well were completed,
And the great seal of the law
  was set like a sun on the
  margin.
Then from his leathern pouch
  the farmer threw on the table
Three times the old man's fee
  in solid pieces of silver;
And the notary rising, and
  blessing the bride and the
  bridegroom,
Lifted aloft the tankard of
  ale and drank to their
  welfare.
Wiping the foam from his lip,
  he solemnly bowed and departed,
While in silence the others sat
  and mused by the fireside,
Till Evangeline brought the
  draught-board out of its
  corner.
Soon was the game begun. In
  friendly contention the old
  men
Laughed at each lucky hit, or
  unsuccessful manoeuvre,
Laughed when a man was crowned,
  or a breach was made in the
  king-row.
Meanwhile apart, in the twilight
  gloom of a window's embrasure,

Sat the lovers, and whispered
together, beholding the moon
rise
Over the pallid sea, and the
silvery mists of the
meadows.

Thus was the evening passed.
Anon the bell from the belfry
Rang out the hour of nine, the
village curfew, and straight-
way
Rose the guests and departed;
and silence reigned in the
household.
Many a farewell word and sweet
good-night on the doorstep
Lingered long in Evangeline's
heart, and filled it with
gladness.
Carefully then were covered the
embers that glowed on the
hearth-stone,
And on the oaken stairs re-
sounded the tread of the
farmer.
Soon with a soundless step
the foot of Evangeline followed.
Up to the staircase moved a luminous space in the darkness,
Lighted less by the lamp than
the shining face of the
maiden.
Silent she passed the hall, and
entered the door of her chamber.
Simple that chamber was, with
its curtains of white, and
its clothes-press
Ample and high, on whose
spacious shelves were carefully folded
Linen and woollen stuffs, by the
hand of Evangeline woven.
This was the precious dower
she would bring to her husband in marriage,
Better than flocks and herds,
being proofs of her skill
as a housewife.

Soon she extinguished her lamp,
for the mellow and radiant
moonlight
Streamed through the windows,
and lighted the room, till
the heart of the maiden
Swelled and obeyed its power,
like the tremulous tides of
the ocean.
Ah! she was fair, exceeding
fair to behold, as she stood
with
Naked snow-white feet on the
gleaming floor of her chamber!
Little she dreamed that below,
among the trees of the orchard,
Waited her lover and watched for
the gleam of her lamp and her
shadow.
Yet were her thoughts of him,
and at times a feeling of
sadness
Passed o'er her soul, as the
sailing shade of clouds in
the moonlight
Flitted across the floor and
darkened the room for a
moment.
And, as she gazed from the window, she saw serenely the
moon pass
Forth from the folds of a
cloud, and one star follow
her footsteps,
As out of Abraham's tent
young Ishmael wandered with
Hagar! . . .

*The lovers are
parted by the
vengeance of war,
and for years
Evangeline wanders
through many lands
seeking Gabriel.
Finally, old, ex-
hausted, and with-
out hope, she gives
up the search.*

. . . In that delightful land
   which is washed by the Delaware
   waters,
Guarding in sylvan shades the
   name of Penn the apostle,
Stands on the banks of its
   beautiful stream the city
   he founded.
There all the air is balm,
   and the peach is the emblem
   of beauty,
And the streets still re-echo
   the names of the trees of
   the forest,
As if they fain would ap-
   pease the Dryads whose haunts
   they molested.
There from the troubled sea
   had Evangeline landed, an
   exile,
Finding among the children
   of Penn a home and a country.

. . . So, when the fruitless
   search, the disappointed en-
   deavor,
Ended, to recommence no more
   upon earth, uncomplaining,
Thither, as leaves to the
   light, were turned her
   thoughts and her footsteps.
As from the mountain's top the
   rainy mists of the morning
Roll away, and afar we behold
   the landscape below us,
Sun-illumined, with shining
   rivers and cities and ham-
   lets,
So fell the mists from her mind,
   and she saw the world far
   below her,
Dark no longer, but all il-
   luminated with love; and
   the pathway
Which she had climbed so far,
   lying smooth and fair in
   the distance.

Gabriel was not forgotten.
   Within her heart was his
   image,
Clothed in the beauty of love
   and youth, as last she beheld
   him,
Only more beautiful made by
   his death-like silence and
   absence.
Into her thoughts of him time
   entered not, for it was not.
Over him years had no power;
   he was not changed, but
   transfigured;
He had become to her heart
   as one who is dead, and not
   absent;
Patience and abnegation of self,
   and devotion to others,
This was the lesson a life of
   trial and sorrow had taught
   her.
So was her love diffused, but,
   like to some odorous spices,
Suffered no waste, nor loss,
   though filling the air with
   aroma.
Other hope had she none, nor
   wish in life, but to follow
Meekly, with reverent steps,
   the sacred feet of her
   Saviour.

Thus many years she lived as a
   Sister of Mercy; frequenting
Lonely and wretched roofs in
   the crowded lanes of the city,
Where distress and want conceal-
   ed themselves from the sunlight,
Where disease and sorrow in
   garrets languished neglected.
Night after night, when the
   world was asleep, as the
   watchman repeated
Loud, through the gusty streets,
   that all was well in the city,
High at some lonely window he
   saw the light of her taper.

Day after day, in the gray of
the dawn, as slow through
the suburbs
Plodded the German farmer, with
flowers and fruits for the
market,
Met he that meek, pale face, returning home from its watchings.

Then it came to pass that a
pestilence fell on the city,
Presaged by wondrous signs, and
mostly by flocks of wild
pigeons,
Darkening the sun in their
flight, with naught in their
craws but an acorn.
And, as the tides of the sea
arise in the month of Sep-
tember,
Flooding some silver stream,
till it spreads to a lake
in the meadow
So death flooded life, and,
o'erflowing its natural
margin,
Spread to a brakish lake, the
silver stream of existence.
Wealth had no power to bribe,
nor beauty to charm, the op-
pressor;
But all perished alike beneath
the scourge of his anger;—
Only, alas! the poor, who had
neither friends nor
attendants,
Crept away to die in the alms-
house, home of the homeless.
Then in the suburbs it stood,
in the midst of meadows and
woodlands;—
Now the city surrounds it; but
still, with its gateway and
wicket
Meek, in the midst of splendor,
its humble walls seemed to
echo
Softly the words of the Lord:
"The poor ye always have
with you."

Thither, by night and by day,
came the Sister of Mercy.
The dying
Looked up into her face, and
thought, indeed, to behold
there
Gleams of celestial light en-
circle her forehead with
splendor,
Such as the artist paints o'er
the brows of saints and
apostles,
Or such as hangs by night o'er
a city seen at a distance.
Unto their eyes it seemed the
lamps of the city celestial,
Into whose shining gates erelong
their spirits would enter.

Thus, on a Sabbath morn, through
the streets, deserted and silent,
Wending her quiet way, she entered the door of the alms-
house.
Sweet on the summer air was
the odor of flowers in the
garden;
And she paused on her way to
gather the fairest among
them,
That the dying once more might
rejoice in their fragrance
and beauty.
Then, as she mounted the stairs
to the corridors, cooled
by the east-wind,
Distant and soft on her ear
fell the chimes from the
belfry of Christ Church,
While, intermingled with these,
across the meadows were
wafted
Sounds of psalms, that were
sung by the Swedes in their
church at Wicaco.
Soft as descending wings fell
the calm of the hour on her
spirit:
Something within her said, "At
length thy trials are ended";

And with light in her looks,
  she entered the chambers of
  sickness.
Noiselessly moved about the
  assiduous, careful at-
  tendants,
Moistening the feverish lip,
  and the aching brow, and
  in silence
Closing the sightless eyes of
  the dead, and concealing
  their faces,
Where on their pallets they
  lay, like drifts of snow
  by the roadside.
Many a languid head, upraised
  as Evangeline entered,
Turned on its pillow of pain
  to gaze while she passed, for
  her presence
Fell on their hearts like a
  ray of sun on the walls of
  a prison.
And, as she looked around, she
  saw how Death, the consoler,
Laying his hand upon many a
  heart, had healed it forever.
Many familiar forms had dis-
  appeared in the night time;
Vacant their places were, or
  filled already by strangers.

Suddenly, as if arrested by
  fear or a feeling of wonder,
Still she stood, with her
  colorless lips apart, while
  a shudder
Ran through her frame, and,
  forgotten, the flowerets
  dropped from her fingers,
And from her eyes and cheeks
  the light and bloom of the
  morning.
Then there escaped from her lips
  a cry of such terrible
  anguish,
That the dying heard it, and
  started up from their pillows.

On the pallet before her was
  stretched the form of an
  old man.
Long, and thin, and gray were
  the locks that shaded his
  temples;
But as he lay in the morning
  light, his face for a moment
Seemed to assume once more the
  forms of its earlier manhood;
So are wont to be changed the
  faces of those who are dying.
Hot and red on his lips still
  burned the flush of the
  fever,
As if life, like the Hebrew,
  with blood had besprinkled
  its portals,
That the Angel of Death might
  see the sign, and pass over.
Motionless, senseless, dying,
  he lay, and his spirit exhausted
Seemed to be sinking down
  through the infinite depths
  in the darkness,
Darkness of slumber and death,
  forever sinking and sinking.
Then through those realms of
  shade, in multiplied rever-
  berations,
Heard he that cry in pain, and
  through the hush that suc-
  ceeded
Whispered a gentle voice, in
  accents tender and saint-
  like,
"Gabriel! O my beloved!"
  and died away into silence.

Then he beheld, in a dream,
  once more the home of his
  childhood;
Green Acadian meadows, with
  sylvan rivers among them,
Village, and mountain, and
  woodlands; and, walking
  under their shadow,
As in the days of her youth,
  Evangeline rose in his
  vision.

Tears came into his eyes;
  and as slowly he lifted his
  eyelids,
Vanished the vision away, but
  Evangeline knelt by his
  bedside.
Vainly he strove to whisper her
  name, for the accents un-
  uttered
Died on his lips, and their
  motion revealed what his
  tongue would have spoken.
Vainly he strove to rise; and
  Evangeline, kneeling beside
  him,
Kissed his dying lips, and
  laid his head on her bosom.
Sweet was the light of his eyes;
  but suddenly sank into darkness,

As when a lamp is blown out
  by a gust of wind at a casement.

All was ended now, the hope,
  and the fear, and the sorrow,
All the aching of the heart,
  the restless, unsatisfied
  longing,
All the dull, deep pain, and
  constant anguish of patience!
And, as she pressed once more
  the lifeless head to her
  bosom,
Meekly she bowed her own, and
  murmured, "Father, I thank
  thee!"

(From *Evangeline*)
Henry Wadsworth Longfellow

My
Personal Favorites
Scrapbook

INDEX OF AUTHORS AND OTHER SOURCES

INDEX OF TITLES AND FIRST LINES

INDEX OF SUBJECTS